MW01061864

FRIENDLY FIRE

FRIENDLY FIRE

How Israel Became Its Own Worst Enemy and the Hope for Its Future

AMI AYALON
with Anthony David

FOREWORD BY DENNIS ROSS

TRUTH TO POWER
an imprint of
STEERFORTH PRESS
LEBANON, NEW HAMPSHIRE

Copyright © 2020 by Amichay Ayalon
Foreword Copyright © 2020 by Dennis Ross

All Rights Reserved

For information about permission to reproduce
selections from this book, write to:
Steerforth Press L. L. C., 31 Hanover Street, Suite 1
Lebanon, New Hampshire 03766

Cataloging-in-Publication Data is available from the Library of Congress

Printed in the United States of America

ISBN 978-1-58642-297-4

1 3 5 7 9 10 8 6 4 2

I now believe that all journeys are ridiculous:
the only journey from which you don't always come
back empty-handed is the journey inside yourself.

— Amos Oz, *A Tale of Love and Darkness*

CONTENTS

FOREWORD

Ami Ayalon is a remarkable man. I met him when he was the head of the Shin Bet and I was the lead American negotiator on the Arab-Israeli conflict in the 1990s. I spent a great deal of time shuttling between Israelis and Palestinians, and between the US and the Middle East. On every visit — and during every shuttle — I made a point of going to see Ami at his headquarters. I wanted to compare what I was seeing in my dealings with Yasser Arafat and all of his negotiators and get a feel for how Shin Bet saw Palestinian reality.

I say Shin Bet because Ami would bring in his deputies and his key Palestinian watchers — those who were the operators and dealt daily with the Palestinians on the ground and those who were analysts of the Palestinians and their society. While I was, of course, speaking to Palestinians apart from those with whom I was negotiating, I also came to value what I would hear at the Shin Bet headquarters. In this organization, which is a cross between our FBI and CIA and largely responsible for Israeli internal security and prevention of terror, I quickly discovered there was not a "Shin Bet" view of the Palestinians; there were different views and vantage points.

Ami made sure I heard them all. At this time when there were negotiations and acts of Palestinian terror, he would respond to my questions and observations, and then I would see many of those who worked for him take different positions and offer different explanations for Palestinian behaviors. Some were highly skeptical of Arafat, his underlings, and their purposes. Others were far more sympathetic to the pressures they were under and the searing effect that Israeli actions — settlement construction, checkpoints, arrests, and closures — had on them.

I saw that Ami was not only personally honest but that he was also intellectually honest. He wanted to hear all points of view, including from those who would challenge what he thought — and he did not mind them doing this in front of me.

It is no surprise to me, therefore, that he would write a memoir in which he is introspective and honest with himself. Like others who will read his story, I learned much about his background and his personal evolution. Ami grew up as a kibbutznik in an environment of communal living, egalitarianism, back-breaking work, simple pleasures, and ideological debates. Life was hard and constantly threatening. Living below the Golan Heights, the Syrians constantly shelled the kibbutz and fired on those working the fields. "Settlement and security" were the guiding principles, especially with the rejection of Israel's existence by its neighbors and their employment of terror against this fledging new state. Israel's borders were defined by presence and readiness to fight for them and not recognition by its Arab neighbors or even what the international community was prepared to do on Israel's behalf —which at the time was very little.

Growing up in such an environment, convinced of the Jewish right to reclaim the land of their biblical patrimony, and of ongoing threats to the state's existence, Ami chooses the most dangerous and demanding of all military paths. He will be a commando in Flotilla 13 — the Israeli equivalent of our navy SEALs. The training is brutal, the missions into enemy territory from the sea extremely dangerous; he would be grievously wounded and yet return to conduct and lead operations. He would be connected with Flotilla 13 for twenty-two years, coming to lead it and later becoming the head of the Israeli navy.

His was a world of kill or be killed. His recruits and friends like Haim Sturman would die — the third generation of his family (like his grandfather and father) to be killed in warfare with the Arabs. While Ami would carry out or participate in missions that killed very senior Palestinian terrorist operatives — as well as those who gave them the orders such as the cofounder of Fatah, Abu Jihad — he had a code that guided him to kill only the target and avoid killing others. His code would lead him to resist orders from those like General Raful Eitan, then head of the Israeli Defense Forces, who seemed to think that "collateral damage" would send a message not only that no Palestinian operative was beyond Israel's reach but also that the price on Palestinian civilians would be high for acts of terror against Israelis.

But Ami's code did not lead him to question this seemingly zero-sum world — a world in which perpetual killing of terrorists seemed to be the only answer. He does have a revelatory moment when, in the 1980s, as deputy commander of the navy and regularly speaking to Palestinian fishermen, he goes into a refugee camp in Gaza, his jeep is stoned, and he sees a teenager staring at him with a look of sheer hatred. He somehow relates this stare to his own feeling as a teenager when he faced daily threats on the kibbutz and longed for freedom and an end to that oppressive environment — *Was that not*, he asks himself, *what this Palestinian boy was also feeling, and was he, in his military jeep, not the symbol of oppression?*

The real change in his worldview, however, takes place only when he becomes head of the Shin Bet. He is brought in to head the Shin Bet as a complete outsider after the assassination of Yitzhak Rabin — and early on confronts a wave of suicide bombings in Israel. He comes to realize that killing terrorists or arresting them before they can strike is absolutely necessary — but not sufficient to stop terrorism. He seeks to understand what drives those who carry out suicide bombings and discovers that often the Israeli killings of their relatives or humiliations of members of their families by Israeli soldiers or settlers have contributed. He also sees that hopelessness, despair, and victimization create a climate that serves to promote the recruitment of new terrorists and suicide bombers by Hamas and Islamic Jihad — two radical Islamist groups that reject Israel's existence.

While Ami will wage a relentless fight against them and their operatives, he also sees that only if Arafat and the Palestinian Authority fight and discredit them can terrorism be defeated. From his vantage point, he believes that Rabin, Netanyahu, and

Barak made mistakes with Arafat: Rabin because he should have given an ultimatum that the peace process would stop if Arafat did not do more to fight terror, and Netanyahu and Barak because they failed to understand that if Arafat could not show that the occupation would end, his ability to fight Hamas would be undercut. He and his men could not and would not look like they were collaborating with Israel to perpetuate its occupation — and, in Ami's eyes, the notion of always demanding of the Palestinians but rarely delivering to them actually damaged Israeli security.

In my dealings with Ami during this time, I saw him act on these beliefs and speak truth to power. I saw it with Netanyahu and Barak, and I saw it with Arafat. After a bombing in Jerusalem, I asked then Prime Minister Netanyahu if I could organize a meeting with Arafat and his heads of the security organizations in Gaza with both Amnon Shahak (the head of the Israeli Defense Forces) and Ami — and have them discuss in my presence what needed to be done. Bibi and Arafat agreed, and in the meeting I watched Ami be brutally direct with Arafat on what the Palestinian Authority was not doing and the specific steps that must be taken. Arafat let his commanders answer Ami. Most said the Israelis asked Palestinians to take difficult steps when there was no political progress and little hope of it, to which Ami responded by saying that his role was security not politics, but without security there would be no political progress.

He pulled no punches. He would not mislead Arafat or those around him, but he also learned in the process. And, when he ended his tenure in Shin Bet, he sought to educate the Israeli public on Israeli responsibilities to do their part to end terror by acting to make peace more likely. This led him to work with Sari Nusseibeh on principles for peace that could gain grassroots support among Israelis and Palestinians.

The principles, reduced to one page, are largely consistent with the much more detailed Clinton parameters — parameters that we presented earlier, in December 2000, as a bridging proposal to end the conflict. I know from several of the Palestinian negotiators who received the parameters in the White House on

December 22, 2000, that they wanted to accept them, but Arafat did not. One of the former Palestinian negotiators a year ago asked me wistfully, "Can you imagine where we would be today if Arafat had accepted the Clinton parameters?"

The parameters were based on the premise that both sides had needs and no peace was possible without addressing the needs of each side. Peace requires both sides to adjust to reality and to give up their mythologies. Peace does not require either side to surrender their narratives, but it does require them to accept that the other side also has a story that defines its history and identity.

Ami came to understand that. He developed empathy for Palestinians but never lost it for his fellow Israelis, including those who believed he was naive about Palestinian perfidy and who were deeply critical of his efforts to promote peace with the Palestinians after he left the Shin Bet.

The reader will see how, in preparing this book, Ami reaches out to his critics to listen to them and to see if it is possible to build understanding. He speaks to Pinchas Wallerstein, a leader of the settler movement, and makes clear that he believes Israeli settlers have much in common with his parents and the kibbutzim, who also saw themselves as liberating the land of Israel. He feels deeply for the settlers who are forced to leave Gaza as a result of Ariel Sharon's decision to withdraw and believes that Israelis must welcome them given the trauma they experience in being forced to evacuate their homes, their synagogues, and their cemeteries.

But Ami is not just about promoting peace as a good in and of itself. He is not about trying to do the Palestinians a favor. He is driven by his commitment to Israel and by what he sees as the need to preserve its Zionist ideals of building and preserving a Jewish and democratic state. He sees the drift that is leading Israel to become one state for two people — which will either preserve it as a democracy but not a Jewish state or a Jewish state that is not a democracy. Either way it will lose its character and identity.

He is right about the path Israel is on and its consequences. I may be more willing than he to lay responsibility on Palestinian leadership — first Arafat and now Mahmoud Abbas — for failing to build the institutions of statehood and for rejecting peace proposals in 2000 (the Clinton parameters), 2008 (Ehud Olmert's offer), and 2014 (Obama's principles). But he is surely right that Israeli leaders after Rabin did much to weaken their Palestinian counterparts and rarely took their needs into account.

Regrettably, with the Trump peace plan, largely shaped by Prime Minister Netanyahu, Israeli needs (practically and psychologically) are met while Palestinian needs (politically and symbolically) are largely ignored. The state offered to Palestinians in the Trump plan does not look like one — and as a result, Palestinians are already giving up on two states and increasingly embracing the principle of one state with a mantra that will resonate internationally: one state, one person, one vote.

Ami wrote this book, this memoir, to try in his words to "reimagine" Israel and its past in the hope that it could yet shape a different future. He wants Israelis to learn the lessons he has; he wants them to see that Palestinians are also a people with an identity and with needs. He wants his fellow Israelis to accept that while the Jewish people have the right to self-determination in a land of their history, it is not an exclusive, absolute right. That is why he believes in two states for two peoples — Israel as the nation-state of the Jewish people and Palestine as the nation-state of the Palestinian people.

There are both Israelis and Palestinians who reject that vision. I don't know how soon Ami's vision can become a reality — or even whether it will become a reality. But his is a vision, and a book, written by an Israeli patriot who fought with unspeakable courage as a warrior and now continues his fight for the state that he loves.

Dennis Ross
Bethesda, Maryland
May 2020

CHRONOLOGY

1938 — Parents immigrate from Transylvania to Palestine

1947 — UN Partition Plan for Palestine

May 1948 — Israeli Declaration of Independence

May 1948 – March 1949 — Israel's War of Independence

1948 — *Nakba*, Palestinian exodus from Israel

1963 — Joins Flotilla 13

June 1967 — Six-Day War

June 1968–August 1970 — War of Attrition

July 1969 — Green Island raid

October 1973 — Yom Kippur War

December 1987–September 1993 — First Intifada

November 1988 — Palestinian Declaration of Independence

1992–1996 — Commander of the Israeli navy

September 1993 — Signing of Oslo Peace Accord

November 1995 — Yitzhak Rabin assassination

1995–1996 — Shimon Peres's prime ministership

1996–2000 — Director of Shin Bet

1996–1999 — Benjamin Netanyahu's first prime ministership

1999–2001 — Ehud Barak's prime ministership

2000 — Retirement from Shin Bet

September 2000–February 2005 — Second Intifada

March 2002 — Arab Peace Initiative

2002–2007 — People's Voice campaign

2006–2008 — Politics, member of Knesset and minister of the government

2012 — *The Gatekeepers*

PROLOGUE

HOPE IS A SECURITY ASSET

Until I turned off my cell phone around midnight, it had been buzzing nonstop with friends and complete strangers calling to give me a piece of their mind. The prime-time interview I had given earlier that evening on the Channel Two news program had scandalized many of the one million viewers. "What the fuck were you thinking?" one particularly indignant fellow asked.

Who could blame them? It was late October 2000, and Israelis were reeling from a resurgence of terror attacks. The day before, a mob in Ramallah had murdered two Israeli reservists with metal bars and knives. Had I been a peacenik who denied our right to defend ourselves, with lethal force when necessary, people wouldn't have minded what I said because they wouldn't have listened. But for the former director of the Shin Bet, or "Shabak" — the Israeli mash-up of the FBI and the Secret Service — to express the slightest empathy for our enemies was like spitting on the country I had served since I was an eighteen-year-old sea commando.

Instead of calling for Palestinian heads on pikes, I had come out with the unalloyed truth: PLO leader Yasser Arafat, the man Israelis loved to blame for all the mayhem, couldn't have stopped the bloodletting even if he'd wanted to. His people would have lynched him had he tried. My experiences in and out of the Shabak interrogation room — along with the friends I've buried and enemies I've killed — shattered my lifelong preconceptions about Palestinians. If we wanted to end terrorism, we couldn't continue regarding them as eternal enemies, and we needed to stop dehumanizing them as animals on the prowl. They are people who desire, and deserve, the same national rights we have. The people who lynched our two soldiers had lost hope that the Israeli government would ever end the occupation and allow the Palestinians to be free. "And we've given them little reason to trust us," I concluded.

I've always been a strange bird, an outsider to the society I served, and I lost no sleep over people's recriminations that night. The following morning at around six, I set out with my wife, Biba, on an early walk with our two dogs from our home in Kerem Maharal, a moshav, or cooperative community, on the southern slopes of Mount Carmel. After passing through the high white security fence the government erected around our home during my years at the Shabak to prevent a potential assassin from getting a clear shot at me, we headed down a dirt path to tend our olive grove. If you look around our moshav — and for years I was too blinkered to do so — you'll find traces of the past at every turn. The newer part of our house was built in the early 1950s to shelter Holocaust survivors from Czechoslovakia; the much older part, made of quarried stone, once belonged to an Arab family who built it when Kerem Maharal was still the prosperous Arab village of Ijzim, the second largest in the Haifa District, home to doctors and teachers and to the farmers who tended the fields that now belong to us. Whoever owned our house fled when Israeli forces took the town during the 1948 war.

On the right side of the dirt path is another Arab-built house with trees growing from cracks in the walls, and at the end of the path, just past the stables, is an old farm building with a lock still hanging from a broken front door. I can imagine someone showing the rusty key to his grandchildren in the West Bank, Jordan, or Lebanon while retelling the story of their loss of Palestine — what they call the *Nakba*. The Catastrophe.

History is everywhere in a country where you can't dig a hole without turning up some trace from eight strata of time. Canaanites, Israelites from the First and Second Temple periods, Persians, Greeks, Byzantines, Arabs, and Ottomans all established settlements in our area, and a Roman road leads up from our valley to a hilltop, from which you can see the Mediterranean several miles away.

But I didn't have the luxury of contemplating ancient history that morning. In the fields, just as we began pruning branches, my cell phone buzzed with a call from a man whose name I recognized, Aryeh Rutenberg. I didn't need a secret police file on him to know that he was a big shot in Israel's media and advertising world, a man adept at branding banks, yogurt, rock stars — and politicians: He was one of the pundits who helped the Labor Party's Ehud Barak beat Prime Minister Benjamin Netanyahu and his Likud Party in the elections a couple of years earlier.

Without explaining why, he asked to see me in person, so I invited him to my cramped office in Tel Aviv, where I worked as chairman of a drip irrigation company, the job I took after retiring from the Shabak.

Two days later I greeted Rutenberg with a firm handshake.

"Thanks for taking the time to meet me, Mr. Ayalon."

"Please, call me Ami."

I asked what I could do for him, though I assumed he was there to do in person what people had been doing for two days straight, denounce me as a turncoat.

"Ami, that interview the other night . . ." he began, just as I had expected. He went on to explain that he had been taking out the trash when his wife, ill with terminal cancer, called out, "Aryeh, come, come! You're not going to believe this!" Seeing a former director of the Shabak on TV was shocking enough. From the Shin Bet's beginning in the 1940s until 1996, when with great reluctance I took over the agency in the wake of Yitzhak Rabin's murder, the identity of the organization's director was a closely held state secret. He remained a shadowy figure working behind a curtain of anonymity and intrigue, the agency's motto being "Defender That Shall Not Be Seen." My predecessor was known simply as "K," like the protagonist in Kafka's *The Castle*, or "M" in the James Bond movies. Now the newly retired "Defender" not only was on TV but was also spouting heresies.

Aryeh, a rational-minded conservative in the world of Israeli politics, said his jaw dropped when he heard what I had to say. He then lectured me on what I and every Israeli knew: As Prime

Minister Barak had declared, Arafat and the Palestinians paid lip service to peace but really wanted to drive the Jews into the sea. They were no partners. Behind Arafat's mask was an incorrigible enemy. What I had to say was, in his opinion, "bullshit."

I repeated to Aryeh what I had said on TV, that this "no partner" business was claptrap. I had said the same to Prime Minister Barak when, following the failed summit organized by President Clinton at Camp David, he had asked for my help as the former Shin Bet director to sell his "no partner" mantra to the international press.

"Does Arafat deep down really want peace with us?" I asked Aryeh rhetorically. "Go ask a psychiatrist what's deep down inside him. But I can tell you this: Barak never even tried to find a partner in him."

During our short conversation I didn't have time to take him through my personal history and all of the changes I'd gone through over the years. Growing up on a kibbutz I had been taught that not only were we Jews a people fighting for our survival, demanding rights like everyone else and resolved to fight for them, but we were also revolutionaries whose Zionism gave us the right to expand our settlements to all areas of the Land of Israel. I entered military service at the age of eighteen prepared to defend a three-thousand-year-old connection that nothing, not the Romans, not the Arab conquest, not the Crusades, and not the Holocaust, had severed.

In Flotilla 13, the Israeli version of the Navy SEALs, where I served for nearly twenty years, Palestinian militants were mere targets I took out without flinching. The essence of my ethos as a fighter was an unswerving fidelity to facts as I saw them: My men and I had to kill the enemy because the Arabs would never willingly accept our claims. Killing for survival and defense of our rights as Jews to the Land of Israel would be our fate probably until the end of time.

As commander of the Israeli navy for four years, my views remained the same.

During my time in the Shabak, however, this way of seeing the world gave way to a new set of facts. In the sea commandos and later in the navy I had learned that our five senses are frequently incapable of detecting what is below the surface. To do this we need a different set of sensors: in the case of submarine warfare, for instance, sonar. But fighting terrorism as director of the Shin Bet required developing sensors that took me beyond my customary us-versus-them thinking. Whatever you call it — empathy, understanding, pulling my head out of the sand — to address the root causes of terrorism, I had to first try to actually understand the terrorists, as well as their families, neighbors, and friends. I had to reckon with Palestinians' stories — their psychology, their feelings of humiliation, their rage.

Seeing Palestinians as people changed me. I saw them no longer as abstract targets but instead as people with dreams mostly thwarted because of Israelis' determination to actualize our own dreams. Learning to view Palestinians as human beings with rights alerted me to a basic flaw in our approach to security: Our absence of empathy corrupted our ability to assess dangers and opportunities. Fear made us overreact.

My work in combating Islamist terror was still so highly classified that I couldn't give Aryeh details about working with Arafat and his top security people, men who at one time I would have shot without blinking. What I said, instead, was the simple truth: Palestinians had been my partners, and they could be Israel's partners in the future. Of that I hadn't the slightest doubt. Politicians, journalists, and people sitting in front of the TV after dinner could perhaps be forgiven for neatly dividing up the world into groups of friends or foes; those of us on the front line could not. I told Aryeh that I could prove with almost mathematical precision that when Israel carries out antiterrorist operations in a political context of hopelessness, the Palestinian public supports violence, because they have nothing to lose.

Aryeh wasn't buying it. "I'll believe you when I hear Palestinian leaders publicly affirm Israel's right to exist as a state," he said. "If they do, I'll gladly help you convince the Israeli public that we have partners for peace."

"I'll do it," I shot back. I told him I'd make it my business to seek Palestinian leaders willing to do exactly that.

My pledge to Aryeh, coupled with the Holy Land's rapid descent into a terrorist bloodbath, led me to travel to London the next year, 2001, for a panel discussion among prominent Israelis and Palestinians of the ongoing mutual slaughter I had worked in vain for years to prevent.[1]

With the blessing of Prime Minister Tony Blair, the British Foreign Office served as official host to a meeting organized by the London School of Economics professor Mary Kaldor. We met on a drizzly day in the Foreign and Commonwealth Office building in Whitehall. Ascending the stone steps off King Charles Street, I admired the allegorical statues representing the gods of art, law, and commerce. *Funny*, I thought while closing my umbrella, *the sculptor left out Ares, the god of war*. Inside the imposing stone structure, constructed for administering the world's greatest empire, I continued up the grand marble staircase and then down a corridor to a room lined with polished oak panels. During World War II code breakers had done their work inside this chamber, as good a place as any to try to decipher where the explosion of violence in Israel and the Palestinian territories was taking us.

Among the Palestinians invited to the talks, I recognized three. One was the pollster Khalil Shikaki. I knew his family well. His brother was assassinated for his role as a founder of the terror group Islamic Jihad. At the Shabak, I studied Khalil's scientifically conducted polls, because they explained the thinking of ordinary Palestinians in a way that no blindfolded prisoner in a dungeon ever could.

Another participant familiar to me was the philosopher Sari Nusseibeh, the president of Al Quds University in East Jerusalem and Arafat's top man in Jerusalem.

Finally there was Dr. Eyad Sarraj, a Palestinian psychiatrist, another man whose work I had studied during my days at the Shin Bet. I'd come to regard him as a useful sensor for detecting and interpreting the psychological undercurrents of the terrorist mind. Born in Beersheba in 1944, a year before I came into the world, Sarraj fled with his family to Gaza in 1948. In 2001 he was the head of the Palestinian Independent Commission for Citizens' Rights, a watchdog organization in Gaza. And as a psychiatrist he worked with children suffering from the post-traumatic stress of having parents or family members arrested, maimed, or killed — by us. Children beaten by our soldiers, I read in his extensive publications on the subject, all too often grow up to commit acts of terrorist violence. Or as W. H. Auden famously observed in a poem marking the outbreak of World War II:

I and the public know
what all schoolchildren learn
those to whom evil is done
do evil in return.

Sarraj's curriculum vitae also includes time in a Gaza prison because he wrote publicly against Arafat's dictatorial regime.

The first session was surprisingly absent of rancor. The soft carpeted magnificence of the commonwealth building exerted a calming effect. During the break I headed to a table piled high with refreshments. Just as I was stirring creamer into bad English coffee, I noticed out of the corner of my eye — I was trained to pick up on such things — Dr. Sarraj peering at me through steel-rimmed glasses. I turned to meet his gaze, and he said, "Hi, Ami, how are you?"

I appreciated hearing him call me by my first name.

We stood for a moment assessing each other. His bearing, in a stylish blue suit, was almost aristocratic. Though it wasn't yet noon, he wore a five-o'clock shadow, and a bright white T-shirt peeked out from behind the unbuttoned top button of his dress shirt, which was a shade of blue that matched his suit. I was wearing a dress shirt and jacket my wife, Biba, had packed for me, a departure from the antibourgeois aesthetic of my socialist kibbutz upbringing.

When I took his hand and gripped it firmly, the tenderness in his twinkling brown eyes surprised me. I can only imagine what he was thinking at that moment. In the popular Palestinian imagination, the head of the Shabak is a vicious bone-breaker and ruthless executioner.

"So good to finally meet you," I said.

"Likewise, though I won't conceal my disappointment with you," he said with a half smile, like a man laying a snare.

"And why is that?" I took another sip of bad coffee.

"Why, for not congratulating us. That's not very sporting of you." His English sounded like he learned it from the BBC World Service or *Masterpiece Theatre*. Dr. Sarraj poured himself a cup of coffee, blew on it a bit, and slurped it black. With his other hand he shook out a neatly folded handkerchief to wipe off the sweat that had formed on his forehead since I'd approached.

"I would be happy to congratulate you, my friend, just tell me for what."

"Why, for defeating you!"

"You defeating us?" I stammered back, incredulous. By that stage in what was now being called the Second Intifada, the proportion of Palestinians to Israelis killed was in the range of one hundred to one. We were mowing them down by the dozens.

"Indeed, at long last we are on the side of victory," he continued, with the same pleasant countenance, the sweat still gleaming on his forehead. "What do you military men call it? Oh yes, we have achieved a balance of power. In the end Hamas's suicide bombings have canceled out your F-16s. For such a feat, we are savoring our victory."

Nothing inflames me more than praising terrorism. I jabbed my finger at his chest. "Dr. Sarraj, let me remind you that we've killed hundreds of your people in just the last few weeks." I thought simple facts could wipe the cheerful look off his face. "What's worse, you're about to lose the crumbs of liberation you have. You've fought for decades to win your freedom, and for what? Martyrs and graveyards? You call that *victory*?"

Moving two or three steps backward, almost as if he expected me to splash coffee in his face, he grabbed a Danish and took a quick bite. "Yes, that's precisely what I'm saying."

His next remark offended my professional pride: "After all this time, you still don't understand us, do you?" His liquid brown eyes widened. "We've lived in terror since 1967. That both our peoples now live in fear is a victory for us."

My thoughts turned to a recent Hamas attack. Twenty-two-year-old Saeed Hotari, a pious Muslim and karate aficionado, left the West Bank town of Qalqilya disguised as an Orthodox Jew in a kaftan. No one paid him any mind when he boarded a bus to Tel Aviv. His target was the Dolphinarium, a beachside discotheque popular with Russian Jewish teenagers. The young girls standing in line outside the club dismissed Saeed as a religious nut pounding on his chest like an angry Moses and rambling on in bad Hebrew that "something's going to happen." No one suspected that behind his costume was a suicide vest tightly packed with hundreds of ball bearings as lethal as bullets.

The ensuing explosion killed fourteen Israeli teenagers. After the massacre, Saeed's neighbors in Qalqilya arranged flowers in his honor in the shapes of a heart and of a suicide vest. Children vowed to follow him to the martyrs' paradise.

"In our mutual experience of collective trauma," he said, adjusting his spectacles, "we are at long last equals."

That maddening smile returned to his face gradually, the way you squeeze a trigger. I pride myself on my quick comebacks, but words failed me. All I managed to do was spit out, "Go to hell, Doctor!"

I had stuck out my neck on Israeli television by insisting the Palestinian people are not our enemies, and here comes this man I'd long respected seemingly justifying the kind of mass murder I'd spent my lifetime fighting. *Fuck you!* was what I really wanted to say.

"As you wish, Ami." With a gentlemanly nod of his head, he swallowed the rest of his pastry and returned to his table.

My heart rate slowly returned to normal as I walked back to my table to prepare for the next panel discussion. From my seat I noticed the doctor watching me, his expression unchanged, lips pressed tightly together, as though he had slipped something in my coffee and was expecting me to crumble to the carpet.

My stomach in knots, I scratched at the scar tissue on my neck, a reminder of my own history of armed conflict. What the devil did he mean by *victory*? In pure military terms our dominance was overwhelming. With one word from the minister of defense, our fighter pilots could pulverize Gaza.

The more I thought about it, however, the more I had to acknowledge that we Israelis had never felt more defeated. How could we call ourselves winners if we were afraid to board a bus or sit in a bar? I can't say how long I remained lost in thought, but in that interlude, all my assumptions of war crumbled. In classical war theory, massive force is supposed to compel the enemy leadership to submit to the victor's will. Here the opposite was happening. The more we employed our vast military superiority to pound the Palestinian population, the more Hamas grew in strength. It was a variation on the old dilemma of winning every battle and losing the war. We Israelis had become like the ancient Egyptians facing our own biblical ancestors in the Book of Exodus: "The more they afflicted them, the more they multiplied and the more they spread abroad." The irony did not escape me. In fact, it overwhelmed me.

Something the wheelchair-bound founder of Hamas, Sheikh Ahmed Yassin, told his followers in his high-pitched whisper before we assassinated him suddenly clicked: "The Jews are stupid. They think with their atom bombs they can defeat Islam; no, faith and patience will lead to victory." Those of us in Israel's massive and sophisticated security apparatus — the IDF, the Mossad, and the Shin Bet — thought we were always one step ahead of our Islamist enemies. But they'd been watching us even more closely, and we hadn't even noticed. Hamas terror masters didn't expect to defeat us militarily. Through fear, they wanted us to overreach, to employ tanks and hundred-million-dollar fighter planes. They wanted to bankrupt our treasuries and our democratic ideals. Most of all, they wanted to show us that they would never surrender, and for us, in turn, to demonstrate to the Palestinian population, and to people around the world, that Israelis could never be their partners — and we'd fallen for it.

Now I understood the peace-loving, violence-hating doctor's point. The Islamists were winning because most Israelis were out for Palestinian blood. They were winning because each time a bereaved Palestinian mother wept on CNN she undermined what we needed most: confidence that we could win the war on terror without betraying our values. They were winning because everyone, from the prime minister down to the cabdriver and the advertising executive, repeated like a mantra, "No partner." This ideological us-versus-them approach, I suddenly realized, was the most lethal threat to Israeli security, and to our survival as a democratic Jewish state, because it left the Palestinians with nothing to lose.

Our most pressing security question was, therefore, no longer a military one. It was how best to foster hope among Palestinians. Our security was contingent upon millions of Palestinians, in their ramshackle cities and squalid camps, believing they could soon be free from our domination. Hope, Palestinian hope, was essential to Israel's security. Only when the Palestinians believe that the political process will lead to an end to the occupation and discrimination, and to the establishment of their own state alongside Israel, will they stop supporting terror. My mind returning to the pledge I had given Aryeh, I said to myself, *I need to find a partner. Right here. Right now.*

I returned to the panel table and proposed to Professor Kaldor that we scrap the planned discussion and instead probe the meaning of victory in the modern Middle East. Shedding all pretenses, we began shouting over one another as if we were haggling in a bazaar. Partway through the rowdy debate, I quietly sketched on a napkin several points that, if agreed to by all parties, I thought could give Israelis sustainable security and deliver hope to the Palestinians.

When there was an opening, I held up the napkin and read my list of points. I then asked who among my fellow Israelis or

Palestinians would be willing to publicly support a document based on the principles I had just outlined. An awkward silence ensued, and most of my fellow panelists averted their eyes, with one exception. The philosopher Sari Nusseibeh raised his hand.

Sari and I would eventually launch a grassroots peace movement based on the notes I'd written on the napkin. By 2004 more than 450,000 Israelis and Palestinians had signed off on our plan to end the occupation and establish a Palestinian state in the ancient biblical lands we Jews call Judea and Samaria.

The genesis of this book came five years later, after an Israeli publisher asked me to write my memoirs. I wanted to tell the truth, to write frankly about my personal involvement combating terrorism — battles fought, men killed, friends buried, and attacks thwarted — and to update war theory by exploring and extolling the importance of hope.

But years then passed without my writing a word. In retrospect, it was for the best. Until 2013, the same year Dr. Sarraj died of cancer, I had not gained an understanding of two elemental things: myself and my country.

In 2013 a book of philosophy shattered my lifelong views of myself and of my country: *A Political Theory for the Jewish People* by Tel Aviv University law professor Chaim Gans. Gans translated for me the story of my life into a meaningful theoretical framework. As individuals, we Israelis, citizens of the Start-Up Nation, are optimists with can-do attitudes. But our body politic — our voting habits, military tactics, and sense of our place in the world — are dominated by fear. From his book's opening pages, Gans forced me to turn my tools of interrogation inward. At long last I began to understand myself — and to understand the country I had served all of my life. The source of Israeli pessimism is not Palestinian hostility. It came from us — or, more precisely, from the fatally flawed Zionist stories we tell ourselves about the past.

Reading Gans's book set me on a painful inner journey, a harsh cross-examination of the previous decades of my past, and a clear-eyed consideration of my own core beliefs and my country's identity. At the same time, his book awakened me to the need to change the Zionist narrative I was raised on and to look for an alternative one, a way of viewing the past that could restore our faith in the future and quite possibly save Israel as a Jewish and democratic state.

I make no claim to superior intelligence or morality. I'm not a historian or scholar, nor am I plagued by guilt for the people I've killed. I don't believe in utopias. No matter what we do, terrorism, like violent crime, will continue to plague our society and other Western-style democracies. To quote a 2007 book by the British general Rupert Smith, *The Utility of Force*, "War no longer exists. Confrontation, conflict, and combat undoubtedly exist all around the world." War today is "war amongst the people." To win this kind of war, our missiles do more harm than good because they wreak so much collateral damage that entire populations rush into the arms of our enemies. To kill terrorist leaders without addressing the despair of their supporters is a fool's errand and produces more frustration, more despair, and more terrorism. The more we "win" such a misbegotten war — the more we debase civil society and democratic norms — the more we turn our society into an Orwellian dystopia in which truth and lies are indistinguishable. I am also not trying to place the blame on others in Israeli society, such as West Bank settlers who proclaim the Jews' God-given right to Greater Israel. If Israel becomes an Orwellian dystopia, it won't be thanks to a handful of armed theologians dragging us into the dark past. The secular majority will lead us there, motivated by fear and propelled by silence.

Through this book, I hope to show that democracies can only win their ongoing struggle against terror by taking up the humanistic values upon which our societies are based as both our sword and our shield. Crude nationalism, a resort to lies and propaganda, fearmongering, and what I've come to call the "incremental tyranny" that increasingly plagues modern democracies will not defeat terror. Only the liberal values of pluralism and equality can, and hopefully will.

FRIENDLY FIRE

1

HALUZIM – "LIBERATING" THE LAND OF ISRAEL

Shortly after Sari and I launched the People's Voice, former US senator George Mitchell, best known for his role in the Good Friday Agreement ending decades of civil conflict in Northern Ireland, moderated a discussion between Sari and me on the leafy campus of Macalester College in St. Paul, Minnesota. To fill the hall, the good people at Macalester oversold our talk as a "Mideast Peace Summit."

Senator Mitchell kicked off the evening by inviting Sari to the dais to share a few words about himself and his family's legacy in Jerusalem, an unbroken line of scholars, judges, merchants, and imams stretching back to the days of Omar the Great in the seventh century. Sari shared some sublime facts — for instance, to this day his Muslim family has one of the few sets of keys to the Church of the Holy Sepulchre, the most sacred site in Christendom — and stories of loss, such as his father losing a leg to sniper fire during Israel's 1948 War of Independence.

When Senator Mitchell signaled that it was my turn to stand and speak, I felt myself caught in a dilemma. The Jewish people, of course, have a glorious history. But my parents' generation of Zionists, in order to build a state, erased the past two thousand years of exile. They chose a state-building narrative that leapt from the Bar Kokhba revolt in 132 CE to Herzl, and from the Maccabean battles against the Greeks to the heroes of Tel Hai in 1920. In school Israeli Jews are taught to identify with the prophets and warriors of the Bible as well as with the military heroes, guerrilla fighters, and revolutionaries of antiquity. With ancient history anchored in our minds, we almost never talked about Jewish life in the Diaspora. I was raised believing that European Jews emerged from exile to reclaim our ancient identities, which had been frozen in time, like a woolly mammoth in the Siberian tundra. We saw ourselves as Hebrews, not Jews; we spoke Hebrew, not Yiddish. Arabs who had once lived on our land were ignored, and our bulldozers made sure there wasn't much to see.

My parents were not from the Holy Land but rather from Transylvania, in central Romania, and they never spoke of their childhoods. At Kibbutz Ma'agan, on the south shore of the Sea of Galilee, the lowest freshwater lake on earth, history's biggest crime, the Holocaust, was rarely mentioned. I was ten before I learned that Father, or Abba, lost his younger brother, his sister, and her husband in the Holocaust. His parents and older brother survived and were still alive, but I never met them. In the Land of Israel my parents changed their last name from Hirsch to Ayalon and disregarded their family trees. Abba became our kibbutz's spokesman, business manager, overseer of the banana plantation, and chief ideologue — a man of unbending ideological purity and frenetic energy, always talking about the future we would build with our hands. He buried the past for the sake of the future.

The amiable atmosphere in the room at Macalester College melted away for me as I awkwardly approached the dais. Raising my empty palms, I said to the gathering of people, "I have no past. I suppose I've never given it much thought because I'm the product of a rebellion against the past." To actualize our dreams of redeeming the Land of Israel, we needed plows, workers, cement mixers, and soldiers, not tears and historians of the Diaspora. What's the point in memorializing what you keenly wish to forget?

Even after I put my painful realization into words, however, its meaning did not sink in. I would not understand its import and take it to heart for another decade, when I read and thought about Professor Gans's *Political Theory of the Jewish People*. For the event at Macalester, Sari and I had agreed to avoid discussions of the past and to focus our initiative on building a better future, so for the rest of the evening we emphasized the work of our peace organization, People's Voice.

When my mother died two years later in 2005, I lost the chance to ask her about her life in Europe. Only at that point did a creeping suspicion begin to grow in my consciousness that we Israelis were haunted by a past we doggedly pretended didn't matter. Following my mother's funeral, determined not to lose my father's stories, too, I gave Abba a thick spiral notebook, the kind kids use in school. I asked him to write his stories, for my sake and for the sake of my children and grandchildren. I wanted to better understand my parents. Abba took the notebook but made no promises.

It wasn't until a couple of years later when I visited him, still living at Kibbutz Ma'agan, that I learned he'd taken my request seriously. He was waiting for me on the porch of the two-room bungalow he'd shared with my mother for half a century, one of the identical concrete shacks erected by the thousands in the early years of the State of Israel. His woolen blazer and V-neck sweater betrayed his Central European roots, as did his slight Hungarian accent.

The conversation, most remarkable for what we didn't say, was typical.

"*Ma-shlomcha?*" I asked. "Is your heart still giving you trouble?"

"They say it might rain this week," he responded, turning his attention to a few dark clouds to the east, as if willpower alone could conjure up a storm from the Mediterranean.

"So I've heard."

He lit a cigarette — he got hooked on smoking because our kibbutz used to hand out cheap packs — and indicated with a gesture that he'd like to inspect the receding shoreline. We walked past the long-closed communal dining hall and shuttered House of Culture, the kibbutzniks having succumbed to such middle-class luxuries as private TVs. Cranes and pelicans sunned themselves in the warm waters of the blue-green lake.

Upon reaching the shore, I looked north to the stony canyons of the Golan Heights, a patina of green over the otherwise rust-colored cliffs. By this point, I was keenly aware of something that I never knew as a child: Before the War of Independence, the Arab village of al-Samra stretched along the coastal land where our kibbutz's plantations now grew bananas and mangoes. Abba never told me how our forces drove out the Arabs. We were only taught that they attacked us, and we conquered their territories fair and square with weapons and plows. The millions of our people murdered in the Holocaust, and the bitterness of the battles in the Jordan Valley, left no room to regret what we did during the war or to think about the fate of Arab refugees who now lived in squalid camps across the Jordanian border. Besides, the Land of Israel was our birthright. Everyone knew the villainous Romans drove us out and, after two thousand years, we at long last returned determined never to leave again.

When we returned to his shack that day, I noticed the blue notebook open on his kitchen table, his Hebrew scrawl filling the pages. I said nothing at the time.

After he died in 2008, I discovered the notebook among his few belongings. In it I found stories that I'd never heard him tell, beginning with the European past I assumed he had exorcised from his memory. For the first time, I learned the bare-bone facts of his life. My grandparents, Jacob and Hannah Hirsch, lived in Sovata, a village not far from Cluj. Jacob, a flour mill owner and a man of traditional religious views, reserved a room in his large stone house for the village's ten Jewish families to gather during the High Holidays.

Though he had no rabbinical training, the members of the community looked up to my grandfather as their leader. The gentiles, evenly divided between Hungarians and Romanians, had a live-and-let-live attitude toward their Jewish neighbors.

My father was born in 1918, a period of geopolitical upheaval; Transylvania, once a part of the Austro-Hungarian Empire, now belonged to Romania. Romanians, like the citizens of other new nation-states in the region, set out to reinvent the past. For instance, in Cluj, a largely ethnically Hungarian city, the Romanians erected a statue across from the cathedral that was an exact replica of the Capitoline Wolf, which depicts a scene from the legendary founding of Rome, with the twins Romulus and Remus suckling the she-wolf. The Romanian government wanted to project the idea that the creation of their state was akin to the Latin-speaking soldiers in the Roman province of Dacia, after two thousand years, rising from the dead to restore an ancient heritage.

Even though anti-Semitism never took root as deeply in Romania as it did in other parts of Central Europe, Jews remained outsiders in the newly formed state. Most Jews didn't speak Romanian, nor did they identify with ancient Roman soldiers or that other Romanian folk hero, the psychopathic tyrant Vlad the Impaler, the model for Bram Stoker's Count Dracula.

From the age of three Abba studied at the cheder in the local synagogue, but his passion was sports. An athlete with strong, quick movements, he never had trouble with anti-Semites. *If only all the Jews were like you!* the gentiles liked to say after a spirited game of soccer. Yet he still longed for a national identity of his own. One day he went with some friends to see a propaganda film featuring the noble socialist farmers of Kibbutz Ein Harod. Abba was hooked, though it would take him a couple of years to muster the courage to tell his father, "I'm becoming a Zionist," which in those days was tantamount to leaving his religion.

Abba's brand of Zionism, however, could not have been further from that of the gentlemen in top hats in London. The Romanian youth groups who roamed the countryside building bonfires and crooning patriotic songs were Abba's inspiration, not religion. He and his young friends were obsessed with "revolutionary constructivism," the process through which the Zionist sheds the bourgeois, capitalist egotism of his upbringing, the petty concerns and fancies of Exile, and pours his creative efforts into building a utopian society more just, more equal, and most of all rooted in the native Motherland — what Zionists call the *Moledet*.

Abba eventually left the village and moved to Cluj for high school. Together with his friend Jonah, whom he met in Cluj and was the son of a factory owner, Abba joined the local chapter of the Zionist movement, as well as the Haluz club, which got its name from Moses's command to the Israelites: "We will pass over armed — *haluzim* — into the land of Canaan, that the possession of our inheritance on this side of the Jordan may be ours."

His parents' remonstrations were futile. In 1937, as Nazi Germany grew more powerful, he dropped out of school. For Abba, this was no time to prepare for a bourgeois way of life. It was a time to liberate the Land of Israel.

Meanwhile Arab nationalists declared war on Jewish immigration and threatened the British authorities, who administered "Mandatory Palestine," with all-out rebellion if Zionist colonization didn't stop. Anwar Nusseibeh, the Cambridge-educated judge and father of my future peace partner Sari, partook in the nonviolent part of this uprising. Others, most notably the Islamic revivalist preacher from Syria, Izz ad-Din al-Qassam, a graduate of the Al-Azhar Mosque in Cairo, opted for the jihadist method of laying bombs and ambushing kibbutzim. Hamas's Qassam Brigades are a tribute to his memory.

In 1939, just as my father and his group were planning to leave Europe for Palestine, the English introduced the White Paper, sharply curtailing immigration and banning new land sales to Jews. David Ben-Gurion, the Zionist leader in Palestine, responded with "the war of (illegal) immigration," because he believed Zionism would succeed and the Jewish people would win control over their future through demographics and land. As part of this effort, Abba was assigned to one of the first ships bound for Palestine. But before embarking, he returned to his parents' stone house in the village, where his father shook his hand and his mother, crying, hugged him before pressing into his hand the ring her father had given her on the day of her wedding. It had been in the family for generations, she said, and he should take it with him so he'd always remember her. Father looped the ring on a chain around his neck and was off.

In July 1939, at a port on the Black Sea, Abba boarded the *Colorado*, a small freighter, which transferred him to the *Atarato*, a steamer anchored offshore. The passage in the overcrowded *Atarato*, with its rancid food, stale air, and clogged toilets, was made more unnerving by the fact that from the moment the steamer entered Palestine's territorial waters, the passengers were outlaws in the eyes of the British.

As the *Atarato* approached the northern coastal town of Nahariya near the Lebanese border, Abba and the others boarded smaller boats that transported them furtively to land, where they dispersed before British soldiers could round them up. Whereas middle-class Jews from Poland and Germany built hotels and opened shops in Tel Aviv and Haifa, most illegal immigrants like Abba disappeared into the growing network of Jewish settlements. After a few days of work on a kibbutz, Abba got enough of a tan to look local and left for Haifa with counterfeit papers. From there it was by train to the Sea of Galilee and the Hatzer Kinneret, a settlement from the early years of the twentieth century built as an agricultural school for settlers who continued on to kibbutzim. There he was joined by his friend from Cluj, Jonah Rosen. They picked up kibbutzim ideals from books and long arguments into the night. They forswore private property; even the clothes on their backs belonged to the collective. Photos from those days show Abba with his teenage friends bare-chested, smiles stretched across their faces. Women, too, stood with them, their tanned arms strong from working the fields.

In the notebook Abba described visiting Jonah's house in Cluj shortly before the two of them left for Palestine. It was there that he first set eyes on my mother, Jonah's thirteen-year-old sister, Varda Magdalena. Mother had told me about this first meeting as well. She said she fell in love with Abba right there and then, but that it took him a few years to come around. In early 1938, Jonah implored his father in Cluj to send Varda to Palestine, as he saw no future for young Jews in their corner of Europe. Their father agreed, on the condition that Jonah follow her. He didn't want Varda wandering around Palestine alone like a vagabond. Since she came to study, her immigration was legal, and she brought a large wooden crate containing her dowry: a hand-painted bone china tea set, embroidered tablecloths, and silverware. Varda ended up at an agricultural high school on the outskirts of Jerusalem, run by Rahel Yanait Ben-Zvi, wife of the future Israeli president Yitzhak Ben-Zvi.

I recall as a child hearing Mother, or Imma, speak highly of the school and especially of Rahel Ben-Zvi and her hybrid of socialism and nationalism, the way she instilled in her pupils what she described as the "wonderful feeling of being born again in our homeland." With Varda's childhood infatuation with Yitzhak as strong as ever, the very day she finished school she happily joined Jonah on the kibbutz, just as her father had instructed. My father eventually reciprocated her love, though his notebooks reveal few juicy details, and the two of them moved into a double tent and got married kibbutz-style: a gathering of friends, some wine, and no rabbi. Their matrimonial home was a cramped room illuminated by kerosene lamps.

Unlike Abba, who relished every day of his life on the kibbutz, Imma never fully adapted to the frontier life of Hatzer Kinneret. At seven hundred feet below sea level, summers were a hellish inferno. This scorched landscape of scorpions and malarial mosquitoes was no Land of Milk and Honey. Nor did she enjoy the endless debates about radical socialism. Father gave up every possession he had, including his mother's ring, and never looked back — not to Europe, his family, or middle-class comfort. Mother, on the other hand, deposited her dowry box with bourgeois relatives in Haifa for safekeeping, because otherwise Abba would have sold it to buy seeds or pruning shears for the kibbutz.

I inherited my name from a Jewish boy named Ami from a nearby kibbutz, who was shot dead by Arab horse thieves who wanted the pony he was riding. Ami, short for Amichai, literally "my people are alive," was a popular name after the Holocaust. I was still in Varda Magdalena's womb when her mother, my grandmother, died of typhus in the Auschwitz barracks on the day before the Red Army liberated the death camp.

Just after my birth, Ben-Gurion dispatched my father on a three-year mission to Hungary to lead a smuggling operation bringing some of the hundreds of thousands of Jewish refugees and Holocaust survivors into Palestine. He replaced Jonah, who was the operation's original leader but had been caught and taken to a Russian prison on suspicion of being an English spy. This was when Abba changed his name from Hirsch to Ayalon; he was a Hebrew, he spoke Hebrew, he had a Hebrew name.

I began life in the communal nursery where infants slept on plywood planks because, in kibbutz theory, that was how you raised a generation of hardy pioneers. It was only after my cousin Ruthi, Uncle Jonah's daughter, nearly froze to death that we got mattresses.

Though I was only three and my memory is fuzzy, I remember the day when a smiling man strode into the sunlit children's dormitory, took me by the hand, and led me to the shore of the Sea of Galilee. "I am your father," he said, gripping my shoulders. I never knew just how perilous Abba's return journey had been until I read his notebook. Upon disembarking, he drove from the coastal port through the Jezreel Valley in an armored car because Arab snipers were targeting Jews.

Abba had returned to Palestine immediately after the British left and war broke out. The Syrian army occupied the former British police station at Samakh, an Arab town of three thousand on the shore of the Sea of Galilee and threatened all of our settlements in the Jordan Valley. David Ben-Gurion sent us children to Haifa, where we'd be out of harm's way. Mother came with me, and for several more months I did not see the father with whom I had just been reunited. When the British left Palestine in April 1948, Abba joined the battles that broke out between our forces and the Jordanian army over the Gesher police station on the Jordan River. Syrian armored units reached nearby Kibbutz Degania, where members of the kibbutz stopped their advance. The story I heard as a child had the Arab townspeople fleeing Samakh when the Syrians lost the battle, but unbiased historians today tell me that Israeli forces expelled anyone who did not leave on their own. The Syrian advance ended with the Battle of Degania, when their forces withdrew to the Golan Heights. When the fighting died down around Samakh, a ghost town for the taking by this point, the Israel Defense Forces (IDF), the new name for the Haganah, set up camp in the old British base.

After the war, Abba and his comrades left Hatzer Kinneret

behind and pushed to establish a kibbutz on newly conquered land. With both the British and much of the Arab population gone, there was ample real estate and several options available. They chose a former British base on the Sea of Galilee, in part for its proximity to a precious resource — water — but primarily to secure the contested border between the new State of Israel and Syria.

My father, Yitzhak, and his best friend, Jonah, could finally realize the dreams they first imagined in their *haluz* camp in Romania of restoring our ancient patrimony to Jewish control. Building a state for the Jewish people meant armed farmers planting a kibbutz on the front line. None of them would have dreamed of limiting settlement to within a demarcation line they considered arbitrary. They looked for any opportunity to expand the borders of the State of Israel.

They called the kibbutz *Ma'agan*, or "harbor." Our dining hall was a former military building, and until the pioneers erected concrete huts, the soldiers' barracks were our homes. Because of the danger of infiltrators from Syria and Jordan, men occupied the watchtower and patrolled the barbed-wire fence surrounding our new kibbutz around the clock.

Abba's notebook doesn't say much about the years following the War of Independence. I had been old enough, though, to remember how each time Abba and his comrades tilled the fields in the no-man's-land between us and the Syrian positions, the Syrian army fired mortar shells at them.[2]

We buried our dead and moved the school to a bomb shelter, but we never paused from efforts to "liberate" more land. Sitting in our makeshift underground classroom, I had no idea that the former inhabitants of Samakh lived in tent camps across enemy lines. While our teachers taught us only ancient history — Joshua, the Maccabees, and other Hebrew heroes — children across the border studied a recent event: the *Nakba*, the Catastrophe, the story of their own exile.

2

MEIR SHALEV AND THE FANTA MAN

My father was neither a poet nor a man of great introspection. In writing down his family's stories, he generally reduced them to events on a time line. Rarely did he mention how anyone felt. Hopes, dreams, fears — all were absent from his narrative. Did my grandfather feel betrayed when my father left Romania? Jews had been living in Transylvania for centuries. How did my grandfather feel about Zionism, and about Abba venturing off as an illegal immigrant? How nervous was Abba traveling around Palestine on counterfeit papers like an outlaw?

The emotion I most sought to understand was his fierce, almost instinctual, love for the Land of Israel. Since the notebook lacked insight to this central, driving passion, I decided to turn to novelist Meir Shalev for help. Shalev writes about Galilee and the generation of pioneers who gave up everything — their native tongues, their families in Europe, even their names — to settle there. Critics often compare his works to those by William Faulkner, whose books plumb the psyches of people from his native Mississippi. More than any other Israeli novelist, Shalev tells the story of the pioneering settlements built by our parents' generation: their stubbornness in the face of seemingly impossible obstacles, their ideological quarrels, their dreams, and their manias.

Early on the morning of the day that I was scheduled to meet Shalev, in July 2017, I first had work to do with my wife, Biba. Israel was in the middle of another heat wave, and we needed to make sure the water from our drip irrigation system was reaching the roots of our olive trees. We also had to help clear some thirsty weeds.

At seven the phone started ringing; it had to be a journalist. Israeli journalists, as in most democracies, routinely call on "experts" to weigh in on whatever crisis is driving the news. Days before there had been a terrorist attack on the Temple Mount, a thirty-acre plateau that is the holiest spot on earth for Jews and number three for Muslims, who call it *Haram esh-Sharif*, the Noble Sanctuary. Sentiments in Jerusalem had reached the boiling point, and journalists had been chasing me for days seeking my commentary.

The religious, political, and cultural sensitivity of the Temple Mount, home to the iconic Dome of the Rock shrine and numerous other structures of significance, is a subject I've studied professionally. In the late 1990s I warned my government, as well as the CIA director and top American diplomats, that Israeli actions in the Temple Mount could lead to an explosion — a new intifada. Ever since that nightmarish prediction grimly came true, I've kept an eye on the site. A couple of years ago thousands of members of the Islamist group Hizb ut-Tahrir gathered in the courtyards of Al Aqsa Mosque on the Temple Mount to participate in an appeal to "the Islamic nation and the Muslim armies in order to establish the caliphate and move armies to liberate Al Aqsa Mosque and the rest of Palestine from Jewish occupation." Hizb ut-Tahrir's founder, Taqiuddin al-Nabhani, was born in Kerem Maharal when it was still the Arab community of Ijzim and fled with his family in 1948.[3]

Breathing exhaust fumes for two hours on the perpetually jammed Haifa–Tel Aviv highway to discuss the insanity of government policies in a radio or TV studio did not interest me. Besides, a talk show was not the right forum to reveal to Israelis the fault lines imperiling our country's survival. Doing the topic justice would require a complex and nuanced discussion, and talk shows do not handle complexity and nuance well. So I had been saying no to all requests.

The person calling me to appear that morning was from one of Israel's most popular radio programs. The hosts, one right-wing and the other left, entertained a million listeners on their way to work by arguing, shouting, laughing, and interrupting each other and their guests.

"Find someone else," I snapped, but the producer was persistent, as if the future of the Jewish people in the Land of Israel depended on my sage advice. He said I could take the call from home, or in my case from under the shade of a gnarled five-hundred-year-old olive tree. I gave in.

"Sure," I said.

As I swatted away horseflies, I listened to the hosts present some background to their listeners. On July 14 three Israeli Arabs inspired by the Hizb ut-Tahrir movement smuggled Carl Gustaf submachine guns and a pistol onto the Temple Mount and murdered two Druze policemen, members of a small ethnic group of Arabic speakers from the Golan Heights whose religion split from mainstream Islam centuries ago; most serve in the Israeli armed forces. One of the victims, Sergeant Kamil Shinan, was the son of an old friend of mine.[4]

Our government responded by placing metal detectors at the entrance of the mosque area, and Palestinians, along with much of the Muslim world, were up in arms. Riots broke out following Friday prayers, during which our forces killed three Palestinians and wounded many more. Later that same evening a Palestinian terrorist from a West Bank village, to avenge the "Jewish takeover of the *Haram esh-Sharif*," slipped into the Jewish settlement of Halamish and stabbed to death three family members on a Friday evening while they celebrated the birth of a grandson.

The radio hosts, after a few minutes of talking over each other, wanted my assessment of the government's decision to set up the metal detectors. There were many things I could have said. From my years as director of the Shin Bet, I knew better than most how volatile Jerusalem's sacred sites could be. If an apocalypse was going to engulf our region, it would start somewhere inside the hallowed walls of Jerusalem's Old City.

"Look," I said, "metal detectors aren't the real issue. The Vatican uses them to protect the Sistine Chapel, and Israelis pass through them every time we go to the movies."

"So why are the Arabs rioting?" asked the right-wing host, who spit out the word *Arabs* with a sneer.

"For one, we didn't consult anyone before installing the metal detectors, not the Jordanians and not the Palestinians. Our unilateral decision making makes it easy for the Islamists to spin legitimate security concerns into a plot to take over their holy site." I went on to express the opinion that what was happening in Jerusalem that day was even more dangerous than the various eruptions of rioting and terror we saw in the 1990s. Back then our conflict was over borders — where to draw the final frontier between the states of Israel and Palestine. With no viable peace process, the situation had become more toxic.

My grim assessment set off a heated debate between the two interviewers. The right-winger, as if reading a script, preached the standard line in Israel today, that the conflict is religious and therefore intractable. How can we negotiate with people who reject our God-given right to this land? Palestinians are "terrorists," "security risks" who deserve what they get.

"You're wrong," I said, trying to tamp down the rancor in my voice. It's demagoguery to blame all Palestinians, who live under occupation after all, for murderous acts perpetrated by a minority. "We have Arab partners." I reminded him that the People's Voice movement I launched years earlier with Sari collected almost half a million signatures, approximately 275,000 Israeli and 200,000 Palestinian. "Polls tell us that most Palestinians still believe in a two-state solution — which is the only way to secure Israel as a Jewish democracy. It's imperative that we work together with Palestinians, or a religious war could destroy everything we've built." I'm sure the radio hosts were disappointed I wouldn't participate in their verbal brawl, especially given my background as a man of action. I wouldn't blame the producer if he never invited me back.

I finished my chores and headed back to the house. For the rest of the morning I ignored continued phone calls from journalists and prepared for my afternoon visit with Meir Shalev. Biba, who comes from a literary family, is always pushing me to read more fiction. As a child, I followed Jules Verne into unknown regions under the sea and Isaac Asimov into outer space, but after I joined the sea commandos in 1963 my reading was chiefly "professional," an error in judgment that might explain why it took me so long to understand the turmoil simmering under the surface of my own country.

Later that afternoon, after our standard summer lunch of gazpacho and cold beer, I hopped in my Toyota and set off for the Galilean village of Alonei Abba. On the radio I heard reports of more attacks and counterattacks in Jerusalem, which brought back memories of burning Egged buses and of interrogation sessions — hooded prisoners handcuffed to chairs — under my watch at the Shin Bet.

I switched stations and listened instead to classical music as I inched along in traffic through the Jezreel Valley. Through the window I admired booming Israel: a new gas-powered power plant off to the left, factories that feed coastal tech companies with components to the right. When I was a boy, Israel exported Jaffa oranges, and that was about it. Today we're the Start-Up Nation, a success story of which we Israelis should feel proud. If only our political leaders weren't digging a grave deep enough to bury our prodigious accomplishments.

I turned off the highway and drove for half an hour into the hills before reaching Alonei Abba. I knew about the village from Shalev's novel *Fontanelle*, one of the books Biba insisted I read before engaging its author. It was founded during the Ottoman days by German Templers — who originally called it Waldheim, forest home. The British kicked out the Germans during World War II, and members of the Zionist youth movement resettled the town and gave it a Hebrew name. Today many well-known Jewish artists and writers call the bucolic village home.

As I pulled up to his house and got out of the car, Shalev was waiting for me. With his round glasses, T-shirt, and cutoffs, he looked the picture of a bohemian novelist, a man of stories and imagination, an architect of counternarratives. Just the kind of person I needed to talk to.

I followed Shalev through a garden and into a bungalow that seemed modest for such a celebrated author. A simple wooden table stacked with loose papers — printouts of his latest novel, I assumed — dominated his living room. Shelves displaying his books, including translated editions in a variety of languages — German, Dutch, Korean, English, and French — lined the walls. I recognized *Esau*, *Four Meals*, *Alone in the Desert*, *A Pigeon and a Boy* — which Biba raves about — his last novel *Ginat Bar* (My Wild Garden), and his memoir *My Russian Grandmother and Her American Vacuum Cleaner*. The décor was appropriately Spartan for a man who in his writing identifies so strongly with moshav life.

We sat on small couches facing each other, with a coffee table between us. Though Meir and I had met a few times, we'd never had a proper conversation. I'd explained on the phone why I wanted to meet with him.

"So you're writing a memoir but it's not about you?" he asked, taking off his glasses. I noticed for the first time that his eyes were brown, the color of tilled soil.

I explained that it was about me only to the extent my life mirrors much of what has happened in Israel over the past seventy or so years. I didn't get into details of how some aspects of Chaim Gans's writing had dramatically shaped my thinking, or how, with the book I envisioned, I was a man on a mission. I wasn't there for therapy, to share with him the tragic flaw I had discovered in my own story. I was there to listen, and learn. "I want to reimagine a different Israel," I explained. But I needed the assistance of other people whose ideas and expertise could help get me to my destination. "I want to include your story inside mine, if that makes any sense to you."

He fixed me with a look of uncertainty, smiled, and changed the subject: "I'm a terrible host," he said warmly. "Can I offer you something strong to eat?"

"Strong to *eat*?"

"You'll see." He disappeared into the kitchen and reappeared a few moments later holding a tray with a thin-necked bottle of arak and a bowl of figs picked from a tree in his garden. He opened the arak, doused the figs, and demonstrated by popping one into his mouth. The ten or so alcohol-laced figs I gorged on, one after the other like popcorn, loosened my tongue, and I tried to explain why I felt the need to anchor my book with his perspective. Novelists and poets possess knowledge and skills I lack. They know that the same story can have different versions. Using their imaginations, they help us to see alternative interpretations of history. I told him I had come to realize that the history I was raised on is just one narrative of many that can be assembled from the same set of jigsaw puzzle pieces.

Meir's father, whose name was Yitzhak, just like my father's, had been a prominent Israeli poet. I told him that his uncle Mordechai had been my high school teacher. In our class Mordechai had read aloud one of his brother's poems celebrating the Jews' final triumph over the European crusaders. In the poem, the French crusader Raymond de Saint Gilles turns to Tancred, the Norman prince of the Galilee, and with resignation says:

It looks like we burned the whole community
In a single synagogue
And all that escaped
Were slaughtered
And now, see
Their flag is on the fortress
And ours has been lowered

I often come back to the poem because during the Holocaust family members on Biba's mother's side had been herded into a synagogue and, together with the entire Jewish community, burned to death. My commando unit, Flotilla 13, is based at the old Crusader fortress of Atlit.

"Your uncle Mordechai," I said, "always considered me one of his success stories." Not for my performance in the classroom, where I barely scraped by, but for my service as a commando in Flotilla 13. "His estimation of me changed, though, when I began promoting peace with Sari Nusseibeh. 'How could you do this,

Ami?' my former teacher castigated me once over the phone. 'You, who used to fight the Arabs, are now doing a waltz with them. It's worse than shameful.'"

"Doesn't surprise me," Shalev said. "My uncle was just like my father. Nationalistic to the bone."

His father, Yitzhak, from Jerusalem, was a member of Lehi, the paramilitary group also known as the Stern Gang, which fought to drive out the British. But he was an ideologue who fought with his pen, not a soldier. His mother was from the village of Nahalal, also the hometown of Moshe Dayan, and one of her relatives was a founder of the Mossad.

"And what about you?" I asked. "When and where were you born?"

"I was born in 1948."

"So I'm three years older than you."

"Here, old man, have another fig." Meir held out the bowl.

"What day?" I inquired.

"July 19."

"That was in the middle of the war, wasn't it?"

"During the second truce, actually. You could say I'm a peace child." He caustically chuckled because we both knew what happened during that very temporary cease-fire. That was around the time that Count Bernadotte, the Swedish diplomat who distinguished himself during the Holocaust by saving hundreds of Jews from Theresienstadt, came up with his idea of a partition, giving Jordan and Egypt the Negev and Israel the entire Galilee and the coast, with Jerusalem as an international city. People forced out of their homes, Arabs and Jews, would be given the option of returning to their towns and villages or receiving compensation. Both sides rejected his plan, and four members of Lehi, Yitzhak Shalev's terror outfit, murdered Bernadotte in an ambush.

As a boy Meir lived in Nahalal for a couple of years before his father took the family to Jerusalem. "But we kept visiting every chance I got."

"Which is the reason you've written so much about Nahalal?"

"As a kid I loved the passion of the place. I remember when I was thirteen, someone wanted to organize an evening around the American song 'Kisses Sweeter than Wine.' Remember it? 'When I was a young man never been kissed . . .' Anyway, two old angry men broke up the party because it was against the Hebrew revolution to do a sing-along in English."

Meir's abilities as a novelist were not the only reason I sought him out. His father and uncle had been adherents of "settlement and security" Zionism, the worldview I myself had long held and had been "cured" of by the Second Intifada. I explained all of this now to Meir, who leaned back in his chair, hands interlocked behind his head. He looked through the sliding glass doors at the Galilean landscape and told me about how his father turned the Bible into a nationalist text.

"When I was ten, Father took me to a high point in West Jerusalem so we could see over the barbed-wire-and-concrete barrier running through the city. He led me up a flight of stairs, to the rooftop of the Vatican-owned building, where he pointed to the Western Wall and the Dome of the Rock. 'One day,' he said gripping me by the shoulder, 'it'll all be ours again.' He turned to me and said with an earnestness that caused his voice to crack, 'You'll grow up, become a soldier, and liberate this for us.' Father hated the 1948 cease-fire lines because they cut us off from our biblical roots in Judea and Samaria. They castrated us."

"And you?"

"He taught me to love the Land of Israel," Meir said. "With the Bible in one hand and a map in the other, he took me to every biblical site in the country, and for that I am grateful. I have this country under my fingernails. I'll never leave Israel. Even when I take trips for my books, I can never stay away for more than a few days."

As for fulfilling his father's desire that he become a soldier, Meir said, "I was drafted in 1966 in one country. Two years later, I was released into a different country."

He served in the Golani reconnaissance unit, the elite unit of the Golani Brigades, and I smiled to myself as I pictured him in uniform.

"You remember what it was like before 1967!" he continued. "Israel was a humble place, a sort of Jewish Montenegro." Then came the Six-Day War. The Golani Brigades fought the Syrians in the Golan Heights, where some of the conflict's deadliest battles took place. The Arabs living there had already fled, abandoning their villages. "Six weeks or so later I ended up in Judea and Samaria. It was the first time I saw Palestinians. There were no checkpoints, and things were quiet, so I freely wandered into towns and cities. *My God*, I said to myself, *there are so many Arabs*, tens of thousands of people just as dazed as we were. What in the hell were we going to do with them? Make them citizens?"

He went on to relate a scene he witnessed that had haunted him ever since. "I saw this old man pushing a cart with Fanta bottles and a bucket of ice," he said. "He was trying to make some money by selling to soldiers. I wasn't paying any attention until, from the corner of one eye, I saw a reserve soldier, an officer maybe forty years old, march up to the Fanta man like he was some big security threat. 'What are you doing here?' he demanded." But the old man just stared back because he didn't understand Hebrew, Meir explained. "So what did this officer do? He kicked the cart over. Suddenly it struck me: That was what power could do to us. Turn us all into that officer kicking a man's cart over, just because he can."

One swift kick of an officer had thrust Meir across a chasm, and there was no way back for him. The exultation of victory, felt by nearly everyone else in Israel including myself and all my leftist kibbutz friends, had been snatched from him. Meir understood that our heroic army had handed us a poisoned chalice.

"When I went home for a few days of leave several weeks later," he went on, "my father was euphoric. His dreams had come true. The Land of Israel was now united — it was all ours. 'Father,' I said, 'we're going to choke on this.'"

"Did you ask him what he thought we should do about the Arabs? How we'd deal with the people in the conquered territories?"

"His solution was simple. We'd repeat what we had done in '48."

"Kick them out?"

"That's right. He began talking about 'transfer.' A weekend around my father's insanity and I was happy to get back to my unit."

"I'm sure I saw plenty of things like that officer and the Fanta man," I confessed to Shalev. "They just didn't register in my consciousness. In 1967, I went to the Wailing Wall, just before the IDF bulldozed the Arab neighborhood in front of it because General Dayan, like me and almost everyone else, considered it ours. In school we had read about it in Josephus.

"In Judea and Samaria all I saw were rocks and trees and empty land for us to settle. Somehow I never noticed the people living there. The only thing that kept me from becoming a settler was that I stayed in the military. Someone had to defend all that liberated land."

I found myself looking around at the room again, noticing new details. A white-brimmed hat hung from a hook on the wall. In his lap Meir's hands were thick and calloused, like a man who chops wood for exercise. Somewhere I had read that he hunts rats and vipers that come up from the valley with his bare hands.

With the sun setting outside, I slapped my knee, gesturing it was time to go. I thanked Meir for his time.

"Ami," he said with intensity, as if needing to get out a thought that had been rattling around in his brain. He set his hands down on the table the way a poker player lays down chips. "When I think about the future of our country, I see black. Pitch black. Sure, maybe we'll find a way out of the mess. We always seem to. But there is so much explosive material, like what just happened in Jerusalem a couple of days ago. Just imagine if some nut tosses a grenade into Al Aqsa."

Shalev's thin dark eyebrows rose and fell again as he made his point. "What I'm afraid of is magical thinking — the belief that God will swoop down and save us." He stared directly at me, his tone tinged with what sounded like resignation. "Do Bibi [Netanyahu] and our high-tech moguls have a long-term strategy for peace or for our survival here? I don't see it. The messianic religion of the settlers, that's what'll doom us. Ami, I've always believed in handing Judea and Samaria to the Palestinians. *Just take it!* is what we should say to them. But . . . is it too late? Please, tell the Arabs," he said as if I had a direct line to the masses, "tell them they can't get rid of us. We are here to stay."

Back in my Toyota, with Meir's dark portents on my mind, I drove past the shuttered Lutheran church. Maybe staring at it keeps Meir pondering life's tragedies. The Germans who constructed the stone building must have believed they'd be here until the end of time.

3

AUNT HAVA AND THE HOLOCAUST'S LONG SHADOW

The next morning before sunrise, as I stepped outside to retrieve my daily copy of *Haaretz*, I glanced as I often do at the Ottoman-era ruins across the street. The abandoned, dome-roofed khan once housed travelers and their camels. I looked down at the paper in my hands, and an article caught my eye. "*The bastard*," I muttered to myself. One of our messianic parliamentarians, capitalizing on the recent violence in Jerusalem, was demanding that we "re-establish Jewish sovereignty" over the Temple Mount.

I couldn't get Meir's Fanta man out of my head. I was trained to detect and neutralize threats. In 1967 the Fanta man was not a threat and so would have been, if not invisible to me, instantly forgotten. The fact that not only had Meir noticed the incident but also that it changed the course of his life, confirmed the wisdom of my decision to speak with a novelist at the outset of my memoir quest.

I remained a homebody over the days that followed, ignoring calls from journalists, battling weeds, and watching over our grandkids and their friends on a hot Saturday afternoon as they raced with beach towels around our swimming pool like superheroes in capes. All the while, the image I'd created in my mind's eye of the Fanta man continued to work on my psyche. Sitting on the poolside deck, sipping a cold beer while the kids splashed and laughed, I remembered a conversation I hadn't thought about in more than fifty years. In 1963, I joined the sea commandos, the most secretive unit in the IDF. Right before I left our kibbutz to report for duty, my uncle Jonah's wife, Hava, who lived in the concrete hut next door, said she had to tell me something. With uncanny clarity I recalled staring at Hava, with her neat bun and checkered apron, as she related the story of a German soldier who saved her life during the Holocaust. I responded to her overture by shrugging; I couldn't have cared less about her life in Europe.

The list of people I wanted to interview for this book couldn't have included Hava because she died in 2006, but I hadn't thought to seek out any Holocaust survivors at all, a telling omission. Now I couldn't stop thinking about how, as a kid, I had shrugged off Hava's personal account as I left the kibbutz to join the commandos, where I would train to kill or be killed. That afternoon, needing to know more about Hava and her life in Europe, I tracked down the telephone number of her son from her first marriage, Dani Keidar, an architect in a moshav on the north side of the Galilee, and he agreed to meet me a few days later at his office.

The drive to Tiberias would take me from Kerem Maharal through Emek Israel, our agricultural heartland, and down to the Sea of Galilee. It was another sweltering day, made even hotter by the precipitous drop in elevation; Tiberias is several hundred feet lower than Death Valley. The descent offered a panoramic view of the landscape of my youth. A few hotels were scattered below, but life is slow and change even slower in this part of Israel, very different from the tech-boom coast.

It's in this corner of Israel where one can visit Kinneret Cemetery, the final resting place of kibbutz Zionism's noble dead. Filled with carved limestone graves facing all directions and not, as prescribed by Judaism, solely toward Jerusalem, it's a Jewish cemetery devoid of religion. The plain gravestones lack traditional symbols of Judaism; poetry, philosophy, and socialism replaced thousands of years of futile longing.

This strict secularism is suitable for most of the cemetery's famous denizens, dreamers such as Moses Hess, author of *The Holy History of Mankind* and a collaborator of Karl Marx. Marx, some say, lifted from Hess the iconic line "religion is the opium of the masses." Hess's call for a Jewish socialist commonwealth in Palestine inspired Herzl to write *The Jewish State* and *Old New Land*, where the future democratic state of the Jews would grant Jews, Muslims,

Christians, and everyone else equal rights. Hess's neighbor in the Kinneret Cemetery is Nachman Syrkin, the visionary of a "Zionist Judaism" that "uproots religious Judaism" through an "ideology that can be elevated to the status of a religion."[5]

Our national poet Rachel Bluwstein is buried there, too. An iron chain tethers a book of her poetry to her grave's massive limestone slab, its pages torn and discolored from the hands of a thousand pilgrims. As a child I had memorized her lines:

I have not sung to you, my land
Nor have I glorified your name
Through deeds of heroism,
With the spoils of war:
Only a tree — have my hands planted
Along the quiet shores of the Jordan.

Dani's office is in a concrete building designed in the 1960s brutalist style. If the air-conditioning hadn't been going full-blast, we could have opened the windows and listened to the gentle splash of waves from the Sea of Galilee. Sitting across his desk from him, I told Dani, a man with the physique of a rugby player, about the memory that came back to me by the pool. When I called to set up the meeting, I'd said I hoped he could share something more about Hava's wartime experiences. He indicated a thick folder on the desk and explained that he had produced a written account of his mother's life in Europe. "Here's all I have," he said as he slid the folder toward me.

I opened the file to discover it contained images as well as his writing, and I pulled out a stack of photos. "I took those during a trip to Hungary and Romania in 2010," Dani explained. The pile included several of the family home and shoe factory in Budapest. He pointed to a picture of an older man in uniform. "That's Hava's father, who owned the shoe factory. She was thirteen when he was drafted into the Hungarian army. He died fighting for the Axis powers during their siege of Stalingrad." In Hungary, after Jews had become unwanted, they continued fighting and dying for their country.

"There was no time to mourn his death," Dani continued. A year later, in March 1943, the Nazis invaded Hungary and, almost immediately, Adolf Eichmann began organizing the transport of Jews to death camps. In April 1943, Hava wound up with her mother, her sister Lilli, and her brother Asher in a Jewish ghetto. A few months after that, in January 1944, Nazis with their Hungarian collaborators forced Hava, her mother, sister, brother, and cousin Judith onto a cattle car bound for Auschwitz-Birkenau. Josef Mengele, waiting for them with his clipboard, dispatched her and her cousin Judith to a work camp, while everyone else in the family was murdered in the gas chambers. I studied photos Dani had taken at Auschwitz in 2014.

After three months or so in the women's camp at Lager C, Hava and Judith were sent to Bergen-Belsen to work at an aircraft factory near Leipzig. They were there at the same time as Anne Frank. In January 1945, with the Red Army advancing on the German borders, the SS forced Hava and the other female prisoners, including Judith, on a sixteen-day death march to Theresienstadt. Dressed in bare rags, the half-starved women dragged themselves through the snow; prisoners who fell behind were shot. At one point Hava stumbled. Judith quickly helped her up, but Hava lost her shoes in the fall and wouldn't have lasted long with frozen feet. A regular army German soldier saved her from being shot by the SS. Instead of putting a bullet in her head as instructed by his commander, he told her to keep walking. He gave her a pair of shoes he'd pulled off a dead woman and draped his own wool coat over her emaciated shoulders.

They made it to Theresienstadt, where the Soviets liberated the camp. Hava and Judith, now free, were alone in the world. The only thing left for Hava in Budapest was her family's shoe factory, and what was a traumatized teenager going to do with that? It was in Budapest that she joined the effort that was run by Uncle Jonah to smuggle Jewish refugees into Palestine. She and Judith would eventually end up in Kibbutz Ma'agan.

Judging by the rolls of blueprints on his desk, Dani was a busy man, and I didn't want to hold up his workday. I thanked him for his time and left the office with an armful of photocopies of stories about Hava's life. From his office, I set off a short distance to the cemetery where my parents are buried next to Jonah, Hava, and Judith. The five of them began their lives in the Austro-Hungarian Empire and were now buried side-by-side beneath a row of identical headstones.

After placing a small stone on Hava's grave, I headed across the street to the kibbutz. The gates to the rusty chain-link fence, erected fifty years ago to keep out infiltrators from across the cease-fire lines, were wide open. As I entered, I heard a few roosters cackling. Not much has changed for the better on the kibbutz since I was a boy. I looked but failed to see many flourishes of contemporary Israeli life. No high-end German cars. No climbing walls for the kids.

To this day Ma'agan is my spiritual home, my symbol of the boyhood freedom to ramble, swim, and dream of a better world. Despite the constant shelling from Syrian guns, it was a place of optimism, best expressed by Hava, a woman who displayed no outward signs of trauma, no bitterness or fatalism because of her war experiences. She sought and found the best in everyone, including the German soldier who instead of shooting her in the head gave her shoes. She ran a school and taught generations of children in the Jordan Valley to believe in themselves, in the future, in peace.

After Abba died, I rarely returned to Ma'agan, and I don't know the people living in my parents' old unadorned concrete shack. As I blinked the sweat from my eyes, I marveled at how we had lived without air-conditioning. In socialist style my parents made do with plain pinewood furniture, only a few books because the kibbutz's expansive library had replaced the cult of the private bourgeois library of the Diaspora, and no décor — no oil paintings of European landscapes, no sofa in front of a TV, no kitchen like mine and Biba's with an espresso machine and dishwasher.

The wind kicked up as it does every afternoon in the summer. I peeled off my shirt and walked through a patch of dead grass to the shore for a dip. On my way to the beach I peered through the dust-laced windows of the woebegone House of Culture, now inhabited only by spiders and a family of feral cats. I smiled wistfully as I recalled the after-dinner gatherings when I was young, the plays and films and concerts, theater performances and folk dances, and all the debates, women and men filled to the brim with the belief that we were carrying the banner for humanity forward — idealists debating alternative brands of liberation: for women, for the working class, for the oppressed of the world.

Just before stripping off my trousers and plunging naked into the water, I paused in front of a monument to Peretz Goldstein, the Palmach commando who parachuted with Jonah into Yugoslavia in 1944. Though we didn't have God to worship, we had our heroes, and Abba, a kibbutz leader, had been determined to erect a shrine to what had been the most daring attempt by Jews in Palestine to save lives during the Holocaust.

If we knew nothing about the Holocaust, as kids we could recount every detail of Uncle Jonah's daredevilry. A man of action like Father, Jonah was a bon vivant enthralled by the thrill of danger and the adrenaline rush of adventure. He spent the last phase of World War II with the Special Operations Executive (SOE) set up by the British to conduct espionage, sabotage, and reconnaissance in occupied Europe. The poet Hannah Senesh, recruited by Jonah, also joined him and Goldstein.

They parachuted behind enemy lines in Yugoslavia, where they were joined by the partisans. On the evening before crossing the border into Hungary, Hannah read aloud a poem she had just composed. Goldstein was caught and sent to the death camps. Hannah, too, was caught, tortured, and executed by the Nazis in prison. Goldstein's and Hannah's arrest, torture, and murder turned the poem into one of the most famous songs during our War of Independence in 1948: "Blessed is the match consumed in kindling flame."[6]

I dove into the lake, tepid and oily with blooms of algae. As I swam to deeper, cooler waters, memories of my school days flooded back. The Syrian guns staring down at us children from the Golan ensured that we identified with the heroic characters in the Bible or Josephus — every morning our teachers read a passage to us over breakfast.[7] As for the past two thousand years of rabbinic Judaism, we had as little interest in its stories as we did in European shoe factory owners or flour mill bosses, or for that matter Moses Mendelssohn or Martin Buber, stick figures representing weakness, not strength. We identified with ancient militants and rebels such as the guerrilla fighters who stood up to the Romans. We admired power, preferring Samson the hero over Judah ha-Nasi, the man behind the Mishnah. Teachers kept us in our seats by regaling us with stories of Jewish military heroes, progenitors of the Palmach and the elite IDF commandos, and how we defeated enemies with our swords.

We, not God, were the central protagonists in our revolutionary saga of liberation. In *our* Passover Seder, the Hebrews led themselves out of captivity in ancient Egypt.[8] We were the *haluzim* who, shedding our own chains, entered the Land of Israel and kicked ass. And the wars of liberation continued, with every olive tree or sand dune we captured from the enemy.

My best friend on the kibbutz was Israel Guttman, whom we all called Srulik, a common nickname for Israel. As kids of seven or eight, the two of us, born three days apart, shared more than age and a common dormitory. Srulik was just like me; we loved nothing more than wrestling in the water, or playing war — one of us got to be the good guy, the noble Israeli, and the other the villainous Arab sneaking down from his position in the Golan.

Srulik's parents, sadly, moved him to the town of Kiryat Tiv'on in the early 1950s because of ideological squabbles on the kibbutz; our loquacious and quarrelsome socialist parents couldn't agree on the proper formula for universal brotherhood.[9] The Guttmans, nevertheless, visited our kibbutz every summer, and like Huck Finn and Tom Sawyer on the Mississippi, Srulik and I would resume roaming the empty wilderness just steps from the kibbutz. Each day we'd comb the shore and find new treasures: an Ottoman coin, an old beer bottle from an English soldier, the sun-bleached skull of a jackrabbit, a rusting bullet from the War of Independence.

As a boy, barefoot and splashing in the waters of the Galilee, I already dreamed of joining Flotilla 13, whose base was near Haifa at Atlit, the last outpost in the Holy Land to have been evacuated by the crusaders in 1291. I was possessed by stories of the most secretive unit in the entire Israel Defense Forces and was determined to join the group. My sidekick Srulik, less enamored of the sea, resolved to join an equally elite army combat unit.

I didn't see Srulik again for a couple of years because in 1959, the year I turned fourteen, Abba took Imma and me to Argentina on a mission, ostensibly for the kibbutz movement, though I suspected there was more to it. Two years later, just as I finally spoke enough Spanish to make a few friends in the neighborhood, the adventure ended abruptly when, one night, Abba woke me and said we had to pack our bags. From his notebooks I would eventually learn that he was involved in the cloak-and-dagger kidnapping of Adolf Eichmann. Once Eichmann was safely bundled up in the back of a plane bound for Israel, where he would face trial and eventually be hanged for his Nazi war crimes, the Argentine government considered us personae non gratae. On that terrifying night we escaped by boat across the river to Uruguay.

Imma used the trip back to Israel to introduce me to some of her European culture: She insisted on making a side trip to Florence to see Michelangelo's *David*. She even bought me a miniature version of the statue so I would never forget what beauty can look like.

Back in Israel my friendship with Srulik continued; he studied in Haifa at a military boarding school and spent his weekends at the kibbutz. In our last year in school, the two of us strapped on backpacks and walked from Ma'agan all the way to the Carmel Mountains, a grueling, arduous adventure meant to prepare us for the military.

The minute I turned eighteen, I signed up for Flotilla 13. Because I was an only child, joining any of the operational units, in particular Flotilla 13, required both parents' agreement. Abba, expecting no less from his son, had no objections. Had he not risked his own life smuggling refugees and fighting Iraqis during the siege at Kibbutz Gesher in the War of Independence? After all, establishing a kibbutz within range of trigger-happy Syrians was hardly a matter for the meek.

The problem was with Imma. She accepted, with grim fatalism, that I had to serve our country; where she drew the line was with the sea commandos. Had she not sacrificed enough already? She left the green Carpathian Mountains for a mosquito-infested swamp, gave up her jewelry to buy a tractor for our kibbutz, and worst of all accepted, against her very nature, that in our socialist system I slept in the children's dorm as if I belonged to the collective and not to her. Now, in 1963, she refused to permit that her only son would risk his life on daredevil missions not because he had to, but because he wanted to. "How can you even ask me to sign this?" she said, pushing the page back in my direction. Imma cared far more about family, children, theater, and music than she ever did about socialism. She sacrificed almost everything because she fell in love with an ideologue. She wasn't going to sacrifice her only son.

We stood in the concrete bungalow, sweat pouring from her furrowed brow in the pitiless heat. I took no pleasure in hurting her, but I'd been raised on glorious tales of the Maccabees and the Palmach, and seeking permission from my mother felt degrading. It was my life, and if I wanted to dive under a ship to attach a limpet mine, or penetrate enemy territory to photograph a communications tower, that was my affair, not hers.

After failing to bring her around, I resorted to an ultimatum I knew would work. "Imma," began the cruelest line ever to cross my lips, "if I'm on a mission, yes there's a chance I'll be killed. But if I can't join Flotilla 13 because of you, there is 100 percent certainty you will not see me again." With tears welling up in her eyes, she signed the form.

My final hurdle was the kibbutz itself. The members, too, demanded a right to approve my plan, and at the assembly in the House of Culture they voted no. Maybe Imma lobbied against me behind the scenes, I can't say. The kibbutz refused to give me permission to join what they deemed an example of the individualism they considered anathema: The New Man wasn't supposed to be a daredevil out for thrills. I should join a regular military unit like everyone else.

They gave me a chance to speak, and I presented more or less the same ultimatum I had given Imma. I looked at my parents and their comrades, people I admired because they had turned an inferno of desolation and malarial mosquitoes into a paradise. "I do not want to leave the kibbutz," I told them, "but your decision betrays everything the kibbutz has taught me about defending our hard-fought land from our enemies. What about the Syrians?" I said pointing in the general direction of their positions on the Golan. "Don't you risk your life every time you drive a tractor over the border? Why is your battle to expand our territory different from what I am determined to do, which is to defend it?" The only way they could raise their bananas was for others to protect them and, with luck, even conquer fresh land for settlement.

Jonah, sensing I really would walk away from the kibbutz and never return if they stuck to their guns, convinced people to reverse their ban. I was free.

4

THE SILENT ONES

Before returning to Kerem Maharal from the kibbutz, I stopped at a chain hamburger joint built on what had been the lands of Samakh. After I bit into my cheeseburger, I noticed another diner staring at me. He turned to his wife, who wore a hijab in the Druze tradition, and said something before standing up and striding toward my end of the restaurant. His dark hair, almost black, was in the style of a military buzz cut, and he walked with a soldier's steady cadence. "Mr. Ayalon," said the man, introducing himself as a former fellow officer, "can I have a moment of your time? I just want to say how much I wish you would return to politics. Israel needs a prime minister like you."

I gestured at the empty seat next to mine, but he said he preferred to stand. "Thank you," I responded, "but I'm really not cut out for politics." I explained as best I could that I lack the necessary moral flexibility, and he laughed with appreciation for my sarcasm. We ended up taking a group photo with his wife and son.

Traffic jams gave my thoughts ample time to wander on the drive home, and memories, sharp as razor wire, tore at me. Just beyond the dry hills I was moving past, my friend Haim Sturman lay buried in the cemetery at Kibbutz Ein Harod. Haim, with his sparkling dark eyes, puckish grin, and angular, stubbly jaw, embodied the Zionist ethos I grew up with. I had missed his funeral because I was in a hospital still recovering from the same battle that killed him. The ceremony was a national event because he was from the third generation of Sturmans to die for Israel and Jewish self-determination, a legacy of heroism of a sort that probably had not existed since the kingdoms of David and Solomon.

Haim's Ukrainian-born grandfather, also named Haim, set out with his comrades to drain the swampland between Mount Carmel and the Sea of Galilee and helped found Kibbutz Ein Harod, which Ari Shavit describes in *My Promised Land* as being "imprinted on every Israeli's psyche." He wrote that "in a sense it is our Source, our point of departure," because the kibbutzniks were aware "that what they were about to do might require violence. Their determination was to conquer the valley — come what may."

Haim Sr.'s peaceful idealism clashed with the reality on the ground. When Arabs began attacking Jewish communities during the great Arab revolt of the mid-1930s, he was among the earliest to join the Haganah defense organization and to champion the "Tower and Stockade" settlements, collective farms encircled by fences and protected by watchtowers that defended against raids. In 1938, while in a jeep reconnoitering land for a new kibbutz in the Beit She'an Valley, he hit a land mine and died. It had been planted by followers of Izz ad-Din al-Qassam, the Syrian Islamic revivalist preacher who deployed jihadist terror first against the French in Lebanon and then against Jews in Palestine. Haim Sr.'s son Moshe inherited his father's pistol, and when Arabs killed Moshe in a battle near Beit She'an in 1948, the gun was passed on to his three-year-old son, Haim.

I was Haim's commander and trainer in Flotilla 13, and we became close friends. The Navy SEALs have Hell Week; we had Hell Month, thirty days of physical and psychological torment designed to weed out all but the most determined. If you survived this crucible, then came three months of advanced infantry and weapons instruction, parachuting, maritime warfare, boat operations, explosives handling, and demolitions. Finally, we endured long months of diving in the open sea, by day and by night, to practice raids on ships and land-based targets.

To test our mettle, we'd wait for perfect storms, those cold fronts that howled down from the far north bringing blizzards to the Golan and driving rain to the coast. In the dead of night, we'd maneuver dinghies through ten-foot waves and plunge into the water off the coast of Atlit with sixty-pound packs on our backs. It wasn't the cold or the weight of our packs, however, that broke the most recruits; it was the radical isolation of swimming for hours through the deep waters of the bay so dark you could barely see the compass and depth gauge to navigate your way. We felt like blindfolded men pitched into a whirlpool. They called us the silent ones because deep underwater, divers can't hear a thing. This was survival of the fittest, and some of our modern-day Samsons lasted only half an hour.

Those who made it through faced still more training. We'd practice doing reconnaissance of enemy coastal defenses. Or we'd maneuver unwieldy, water-laden mini-subs through waves crashing against the rocky coast. We'd hit the beach after fighting currents trying to sweep us back out to sea. We'd scramble up and down cargo nets and across rope bridges, race up and down mountains, slither like vipers through minefields, and practice laying booby traps and explosive charges or scaling the sides of ships with silencers in hand.

To be frank, we were motivated neither by Zionist-socialist New Man ideology nor the post-Holocaust ethos of Never Again. It all came down to the thrill of adventure and danger, the intoxicating adrenaline of the fight — the desire to push our limits. Swimming faster, diving deeper, running farther, and shooting less out of careful deliberation than instinct and intuition constituted the formula for survival. In our line of work, if you hesitated, your target would drop you.

My sense of mission took on new dimensions after the 1967 war. Until then Israel's main enemies, the Syrians in the Golan, the Jordanians in the West Bank, and the Egyptians in Gaza and in the Sinai, were all across land borders. After 1967 the Red Sea facing Egypt became our most important border. Egypt instigated its War of Attrition, and we naval commandos were needed for special operations.

Egyptian raids were growing in number and deadliness, sparking a mounting mood of panic in Israel. Although I had signed up for Flotilla 13 for the sake of the challenge and the thrill of danger, the buildup to the Six-Day War had made me realize for the first time that our undertakings were a continuation of the wars our parents waged against the British blockade, against armed Arab insurgents, and against the Arab states that ganged up against us following the UN Partition Plan in 1947 and our Declaration of Independence in 1948. Our enemies still rejected our right to exist, and my comrades and I believed we had no choice but to continue fighting until our strength forced them to accept Israel as a fait accompli. With our victory in the Six-Day War, we could now achieve our destiny of liberating the Land of Israel — by settling Judea, Samaria, the Golan, Gaza, and the Sinai. Flotilla 13 was now playing a key role in this elemental struggle.

On July 10, 1969, enemy commandos made their way across the Suez Canal in dinghies, and at Mezach near the breakwater at the southern entrance of the canal, they infiltrated our lines and attacked our armored corps. Set aflame, eight of our soldiers died in their tanks, nine were wounded, and one was captured alive. Flotilla 13 would deliver Israel's response.

Just after dusk on July 19, the day before Neil Armstrong landed on the moon to take a "small step for man and a giant leap for mankind," we commandos of Flotilla 13 gathered in Ras Sudar, a Bedouin region of labyrinthine desert canyons in the Sinai south of the Suez Canal, in those days one the most strategic stretches of water on earth. If my friends and I could slip through Egyptian defenses and eliminate the soldiers on Egypt's Green Island, or Al Jazeera Al Khadraa, a reputedly impenetrable fortress like something out of the movie with Gregory Peck and Anthony Quinn's *The Guns of Navarone*, we would deliver a new plague on the House of Egypt. British military engineers had erected the fortress during World War II to protect the Suez Canal, the ultra-strategic lifeline of the British Empire. The resounding message would be that no matter how well fortified, no Egyptian position was beyond our reach. No enemy soldier, not even elite commandos hidden away in the Pyramids of Giza, could go to sleep or take a piss without the nagging fear that we could show up, guns ablaze.

The raid was to be the first such attack on this scale in the history of marine warfare. Our goal was to knock out a radar station, destroy the 37mm cannons and four 85mm antiaircraft artillery pieces, both heavy and light, and kill most of the combatants on the island. Our amphibious battle plan called for swimming and then diving toward our target through waters notorious for punishing currents before shifting over into assault mode the minute we divers poked our heads out of the water just under the walls of the enemy barracks. Not the American SEALs or the Italian Decima Flottiglia, nor their British, German, or Soviet counterparts, had ever gone, like a caterpillar emerging from its chrysalis, from diving to close-range commandos.

We trained at the Gesher police station, which had been turned into a replica of Green Island. Gesher was where my father had been stationed in 1948. According to our intelligence reports, Green Island, shaped like a dog's leg and not much larger than a soccer field, was protected from hostile forces by three coils of razor wire surrounding eight-foot-high walls jutting up from the water. The walls featured windows like of a turreted medieval fortress through which soldiers could shoot at an invading force. More than a dozen machine-gun nests covered a wide roof atop the walls. Down below, facing the interior of the island, an enemy garrison of at least eighty soldiers and forty elite members of the al-Saiqa Thunderbolt Forces manned concrete bunkers. I realized only in researching this book that the name al-Saiqa comes from a military unit established by the pharaoh Ramesses II; everyone in these parts, it seems, is obsessed with ancient history.

After raiding us nine days earlier, the Egyptians were determined to thwart our attempts at revenge. Our group of sea commandos, together with the equally elite Sayeret Matkal, or Unit 269, the special forces team usually assigned to carry out intelligence operations inside enemy territory along with operations to rescue hostages, would motor halfway to the island in twelve rubber Zodiac dinghies. At that point, in four teams of five, the flotilla men — carrying rifles, grenades, hundreds of rounds of ammo, and walkie-talkies — would dive in and navigate underwater the rest of the way. In our black wet suits, we couldn't be detected underwater.

We were to arrive by approximately 12:30 AM and no later than 1:30 AM. If we hadn't reached the island by then, we were to abort the mission because we wouldn't have time to complete it before the first light of dawn.

The only way for twenty commandos to have a prayer against such a large contingent of trained adversaries was the element of total surprise. We were to earn our motto: "As the Bat Emerges from the Darkness." The island's fortifications had a single vulnerability that we aimed to exploit. After landing, we would shoot our way onto the roof and clear the northern part of the fortress so that Unit 269, arriving on the island a few minutes after us, could pass through our rooftop beachhead and race to the far end of the platform, cross the concrete bridge, eliminate the Egyptians in their barracks, and continue with the sabotage mission. Once the fighting was finished and we blew up the island's artillery positions, an extraction team would carry our wounded or dead back to the Zodiacs.

I can still hear the parting words from chief of staff General Haim Bar-Lev, second in command only to our eye-patched minister of defense, Moshe Dayan, as he wished us luck on our mission. He was seated in a folding chair, the red glow of a cigar wedged between the middle and index fingers of his left hand. "Guys," he began, smoke corkscrewing up from his lip, "if you see that there's fierce resistance, if people start getting wounded, just retreat." He picked tobacco off his tongue. "This is not the time for victory at any price," he concluded before rising abruptly and heading for the exit.

"*What the hell!*" I mumbled under my breath. Did he really just say "not at any price"? Did the general, who was sending us on this either-us-or-them operation, truly not realize that once we opened fire there would be no turning back? If there were still Egyptians alive when we tried to leave the island, from the roof they would easily pick us off. Did he even understand the mission he was sending us on?

When the IDF crushed the Arabs on every front and liberated Judea and Samaria and the myth-shrouded Sinai in 1967's Six-Day

War, we in the naval commandos accomplished nothing. Six from our group were captured by the Egyptians and ended up as POWs, and the rest of us simply failed to carry out our mission. This sense of failure hung over me as I called to Haim, who was to be my human ladder, enabling me to summit the roof of the fortress, and to Zalman "Zali" Rot, another friend from Kibbutz Afikim in the Jordan Valley, who was to fight alongside me. "Listen up," I said, "forget about Lieutenant General Bar-Lev. There's nowhere to go. It's us or them."

Haim flashed a wry grin as if to say, *Let's make it them.*

We picked at our final meal before climbing into trucks and driving half an hour up a sand-and-shale track to Ras Masslla, the launching point. I recall staring out the back of the truck at the darkening sky, a couple of stars and some satellites traversing above. Neil Armstrong, I thought to myself, was up there somewhere.

It was silent in the truck, the only sound the rumble of the engine. Maybe I'm imagining it, but I recall Dani Levi, with his trademark graveyard humor, belting out a few ironic bars of Dylan's "The Times They Are A-Changin'": *You better start swimmin', or you'll sink like a stone . . .*

"Shut up, Dani!" someone snapped. Silence returned, leaving us alone with our fears.

At 8:30 PM on the dot we arrived at the launching point. We hopped into the dinghies and loaded up our ninety-pound combat belts with guns, a dozen stamped-steel magazines (each one holding thirty rounds), grenades, our diving equipment, and fins. Two hours on the rubber boats took us to within a mile of Green Island.

Unit 269 watched as we looped the straps to our heavy packs around our shoulders and slid silently, our combat diving tanks first, into the dark, warm waters of the Red Sea.

The currents were stronger than we'd anticipated, and to avoid them we descended to the unplanned depth of sixty-five feet, perilous for divers using closed-circuit rebreathers, heavy as anchors. With only a small illuminated compass and our lieutenant Dov

Bar's hand signals leading us through the pitch-black waters, we inched closer to the island, one painful stroke at a time. Nearing our target, we swam back to the surface, where we could just make out the black colossus looming a hundred yards ahead. We were dangerously behind schedule. It was clear that the chances of reaching the island by 1:30 AM, the point at which orders were to abandon the operation, were nil. I recall the way light from the half moon showed exhaustion on the others' faces. Dov's eyebrows arched into a menacing pyramid, nostrils pinched and determined. "I know there are some of you who think we will go back if we don't reach the island in time. No *fucking* delay will keep us from fighting tonight. We have only one direction in front of us," he said, pointing out to the ink-black waters, "*kadima* — forward — even if we reach the island in the morning."

We dove back down to make our approach and arrived under the north tower, where we soundlessly stripped off our diving equipment and fins. We arrived at 1:38 AM, already an hour and eight minutes behind schedule, but the delay in reaching the island turned out to be a godsend. The high tide bought by the extra time permitted us to dive all the way to the rocks on which British military engineers had erected the high concrete walls. Around my shoulder and chest, I slung the AK-47 and a harness heavy with a dozen magazines. Though weary from the dive, I was relieved that at least the fighting against the current was behind us. I inhaled the briny air. It was showtime.

The first group, led by First Lieutenant Ilan Egozi, who had been one of the POWs in Egyptian hands after the Six-Day War, cut through the outer lines of barbed wire. One of the sentries on the roof must have heard them slice through the thicker inner coil because we noticed a red light go on in the guardroom as we filed quickly through the gap in the wire. I saw the guard leave the room and creep toward us with a flashlight. Afraid we'd be spotted, Egozi lifted his weapon and fired at the guard, to us a featureless figure in the night. The crackle of this first gunfire seemed louder than a sonic boom. Upon seeing his comrade's body hit the ground, a second sentry lobbed a grenade in our direction. A shrapnel shard as big as a silver dollar hit Egozi, who struggled back to his feet and returned fire.

From the roof eight feet above, we heard footsteps and muffled snippets of Arabic. Within seconds volleys of enemy bullets flew into the water and ricocheted off rocks. The only thing in my mind, less a thought than an instinct, was to scale the wall and get on the roof. Any delay, even by a few seconds, and we'd be trapped between the sea and the wall, defenseless against the al-Saiqa commandos.

With Haim and Zali following me, I shot through the barbed-wire fence at the north wall while running up the concrete ramp to the eight-foot wall surrounding the fortress. I turned and motioned to Haim, who assumed his position as human ladder. It was only then that I realized I had lost a boot while racing up the concrete ramp. I peeled off the other one and climbed barefoot onto Haim's sturdy shoulders. The extra height permitted me to crane my neck over the edge and scan the roof, which was illuminated periodically by muzzle flashes. Some of the Egyptian soldiers raced from their barracks to the machine-gun nests; others — it seemed like half the garrison — headed directly toward us, firing everything they had, from heavy machine guns to rocket-propelled grenades. The din of explosions swelled to a roar.

My head jerked to one side — suddenly I saw stars. Shrapnel had struck just below my hairline, though I hardly noticed as I rooted into my bag for a grenade. Regaining my balance, I pulled the pin and lobbed the grenade in a perfect arc. It landed inside a machine-gun nest but failed to explode. I tried a second one and it, too, was a dud. So was a smoke bomb. It was while grabbing for one more grenade that I noticed it was damp. Seawater must have rendered the goddamned grenades useless.

I shouted over the din to Zali, "Follow me!" Directly ahead of us was a guard post emplacement manned by two soldiers, their heads swinging from side to side, caught in the bedlam. If we could just capture the post, I thought to myself, we'd have a direct line of fire into the onrushing commandos. I leaped off Haim's shoulders and crouched onto the platform, where Zali joined me.

Bootless, I sprinted with Zali toward the two Egyptians. The trigger on my AK-47 was hot to the touch. One squeeze and my first target staggered backward before doubling over and falling sideways. Zali blasted the second sentry in the chest.

We raced to the guard post and crouched next to the two dead bodies. All around us rocket-propelled grenades slammed into concrete walls, kicking up bits of rock as sharp as daggers. The captured post provided enough protection to spray more bullets at the Egyptians; those who didn't drop scrambled for cover. This enabled more of our commandos to climb onto the wall and join the battle. In our meticulously rehearsed plan, the Unit 269 team should have been arriving any moment.

Ahead of us was a machine-gun nest. "We'll have to take it," I shouted into Zali's ear just as another grenade erupted close enough for us to feel the vibrations. "Fuck!" Zali groaned, dropping his weapon and holding up his hand. One of his fingers was missing, blown clean off, and his severed thumb had fallen behind the head of a dead Egyptian.

"Can you still shoot?"

Sweat streaming down his face, he swallowed hard and nodded. "Could be worse," he said. "Still got three."

Out of the corner of my eye I saw Haim and his group, until that point waiting at the bottom of the wall, crawl onto the roof. Haim turned to clear the second machine-gun nest on the northwest corner of the roof. He must have figured that if his group could get through the concentration of raking fire, they could take out those assets on their own.

To cover their progress, I threw one of my few dry smoke grenades. Now the Egyptians manning machine-gun nests couldn't see my friends sprint past them, nor could they see me, still barefoot racing over hot casements and spraying their nests with bullets. The rubble shredded the bottom of my feet, but adrenaline numbed the pain.

Most of us frogmen were finally on the roof fighting the Egyptians in a fierce face-to-face shootout like in a saloon in the Old West. Dov sent up another green flare, signaling to the 269 commandos to get to the island as fast as their outboard engines could carry them. Where the hell were they? If the 269 didn't show up soon, I thought to myself, we'd run out of ammo and the enemy would regroup before we could escape.

"Let's move," I said to Zali, pointing with my gun to the next machine-gun nest. With Zali following me, gripping his blood-smeared weapon, we raced pell-mell at the machine-gunners, dodging and weaving. Banging in my final magazine, I blasted away with my head exposed above sandbags. We advanced to the 85mm antiaircraft position. It was then that I noticed the Unit 269 reinforcements finally filing onto the roof. With my AK-47, I motioned for them to join us.

All of a sudden it was as if a mist surrounded me. The din of battle disappeared, and an uncanny calm settled over me. Just as with the wound to my forehead and the lacerations on my feet, I felt no pain as shrapnel passed through the major artery in my neck. In cerebral shock, I swooned and tumbled unconscious to the ground.

I'm still alive, I thought a minute or two later. I blinked away the dust and opened my eyes, only to see that I was covered in the blood spilling from my neck. I heard retching, louder and, all these years later, much more memorable than the roar of cannon fire. On my back and on the verge of another blackout, I noticed Zali firing at the enemy with his three remaining fingers. I looked around, but I couldn't figure out who was retching. Then it dawned on me: A month earlier, during a sabotage operation against a coastal Egyptian radar station in Adabiya, I'd encountered Egyptian fire while breaking through coils of barbed wire.[10] From close range, I'd fired, and two men fell; the targets, nameless and faceless, were eliminated. Or so I'd believed until one of the men began retching as if choking on blood. I'd shot again, and not just once or twice; I'd emptied a magazine until the terrible groaning ceased.

I finally realized that I was the one who was dying. *So is this what it's like?* I asked myself. No good-byes, no final words, my life over before the age of twenty-five.

Determined to make my final minutes count, I emptied the remainder of my magazine in the general direction of our enemies, invisible in the inky-black night. Once I saw the Egyptian canon post was in our hands, using my AK-47 as a crutch, I hoisted myself up and on shredded feet crossed the roof, volleys of bullets whizzing through hellish smoke and fire. I returned to where I had stood on Haim's strongman shoulders. Fellow soldiers helped me down from the roof and into the Zodiac, where I reached in my bag, pulled out a dose of morphine, and shot myself up.

I guess it did the trick because I don't remember feeling any pain and my recollections from the return are hazy.

What I recall from my half-conscious state was the way our unit's physician, Dr. Slavin, inserted a needle into my arm for the IV while soldiers carried my friends into the Zodiac, friends who seemed to be in even worse shape than I was. One soldier landed with a thump next to me. He wasn't moving. Had he passed out? Haim, too, was motionless, though I could feel the warmth of his body. "Wait," I slurred to the doctor. I didn't understand why he was patching me up when others clearly needed his help more. Slavin, nodding, turned his attention to my neck, muttering to himself. "The bastards," he said, referring to the military brass who'd sent us, "what a goddamned waste."

5

THE BLOC OF THE FAITHFUL

Inspired by my conversation with Meir Shalev, I got back in the car for another road trip, this one to the Golan Heights. The first leg of the trip took me past the Sea of Galilee and Kibbutz Ma'agan. As I approached the Golan, the clouds on the horizon were tinged with peach, probably from fields burning somewhere. The temperature outside topped a hundred degrees Fahrenheit. As kids, Srulik and I used to stare up at the Golan's jagged, rust-colored ridge and at the grass and brambles growing over the rocky soil then under Syrian control, imagining blasting away at enemy soldiers. In those days, what did I know or care about the territory's two hundred Arab villages, towns, and farms? I was a kid who went to class in a bomb shelter; Syrian rockets were what I associated with the Golan.

My drive took me past Hamat Gader, a water park built on the ruins of the Arab village of Al-Hamma. Already in the Roman days, it was a place famous for its baths.

Next I drove through Kibbutz Tel Katzir, the site of a 1967 battle in which the man I was slated to meet the following week, Pinchas Wallerstein, the organizational brain behind the settlement movement, had fought. Pinchas's brigade had come under artillery and machine-gun fire, and he'd been badly injured. My father came up from Ma'agan to help evacuate the wounded soldiers. Israel prevailed, and as a result we no longer had to drive armored tractors into no-man's-land. The Golan was ours.

The next week, with these images of the Golan battlefield fresh on my mind, I set out to meet Pinchas at his home in a West Bank settlement. Most of my left-wing friends, including my wife, Biba, have never understood why I sit down with West Bank settlers who, to leftists, are weeds and cancers, as Rabin once said and Ariel

Sharon more or less repeated ten years later, slowly choking off our democracy until we become an apartheid state. But my story includes *them*, too. I'm mindful of what Uri Elitzur, a right-wing settler-activist, once said in response to the hatred spewed toward his kind by the Israeli left: "You expelled the Palestinians in 1948. You did not allow them to return; you established communities on top of all their villages. After that you built a separation fence and then you came complaining to us, even though we never destroyed even a single village on the West Bank in order to build a settlement."

While the truth is a lot more complex than this, kibbutzniks and settlers both believe Jews have a right to the Land of Israel. People forget that it was the secular kibbutz movement, supported by the Labor Party, that first built settlements after 1967, an effort that for many years I, too, backed with every fiber of my being.

The road to Pinchas's town of Ofra, the crown jewel of our settlements in Judea and Samaria and the throbbing heart of Gush Emunim — the Bloc of the Faithful — took me past Megiddo, better known by its Greek name, Armageddon, and now home to a military prison across the road from a gas station and a McDonald's. With the Israeli Arab towns of Umm al-Fahm and Tira behind me, I crossed into the West Bank. If I had continued driving east, I would have reached the settlements in the Jordan Valley built by my friends after the Six-Day War.

Once I reached hill country, the air turned drier, so I could finally roll down my windows. The long strings of mountains on both sides of the road make up the heart of the biblical Promised Land. On one of the many hilltops I spotted Beit El, a sprawling settlement of red-tiled houses marking the site where Jacob had his dream: "Behold a ladder set up on the earth, and the top of it reached to heaven . . ." Every red-tiled house cutting into the hillside represented for me a continuation of the idealism I'd been raised with on a small banana plantation. Like my parents, today's messianic settlers are convinced they are liberating the Land of Israel.

Driving past the guardhouse at Ofra, I continued up a street of identical stucco homes with neatly trimmed hedges and sprinklers watering the grass. The stiff breeze made all the Israeli flags on the block snap — each house had at least one.

I rang the doorbell, and Pinchas, kippah clipped to what remained of his gray hair, greeted me warmly. "So good to see you again, Ami. It's been what, ten years?" With his plaid blue short-sleeved shirt and slacks, he could have passed for an ex–banking executive in a retirement community.

I followed him inside, where we sat at the kitchen table. A jar of Nescafé sat open on the counter next to the microwave and framed photos of kids and grandkids. Outside the sliding glass doors stood a clutch of scraggly pines, the kind settlers plant to quickly root themselves, literally and figuratively, to make a new place look like it's always been there.

Pinchas, like Dani, was well prepared for our conversation. Over a cup of Nescafé, he opened a thick hardcover book full of black-and-white photos of generations of Wallersteins. His father immigrated illegally from Poland in 1936, and like Biba's mother, Rachel, he got caught by the British overlords, who detained him in a refugee camp in Atlit: Today the headquarters of Flotilla 13 is in the same area. He eventually got out and ended up in the town of Kfar Atta near Haifa and close to the Mediterranean coast, where he somehow rustled up funds to buy a horse and made a living delivering bread to neighboring villages.

Unlike my parents, who left their religion back in Europe, Pinchas continued to practice Orthodox Judaism. During his military service before the Six-Day War, he worked the fields on a kibbutz, an experience that stuck with him because of the insanely hardworking kibbutzniks and their antibourgeois ideals. After his injury in the Golan, Pinchas spent a year in a body cast, dreaming of using his wounded legs again. When he finally got out of the hospital, he headed straight to the religious Kibbutz Ma'ale Gilboa, built on the ruins of the Arab village of Khirbat al-Jawfa. Like Kibbutz Ma'agan, Ma'ale Gilboa was imbued with a Zionist culture marked by hard physical labor, the songs of Naomi Shemer — "Hurshat Ha'Eucalyptus," The Eucalyptus Grove — and rebellion against middle-class individualism. The

Zionist imperative to build, to settle the land, and to defend the community informed everything.

I told Pinchas that I'd long seen parallels between the kibbutz movement and the religious, right-wing settlement movement Gush Emunim. "Is this just coincidence, or is there something more to it?"

Pinchas cracked a smile. "Have I ever told you that we got our heroes, Bar Kokhba and the Maccabees, from the kibbutz movement?" Of course, the secular part of the Zionist revolution — the way my parents erased the past two thousand years of rabbinic Judaism — Pinchas and his friends respectfully set to one side. What they got from us was how to dig into history books to find their "roots." Hasmonean leaders from antiquity like John Hyrcanus and Alexander Jannaeus, obscure figures familiar only to history buffs, archaeologists, and us secular Zionists, became their role models.

Because of his war injuries, Pinchas couldn't quite hack the physical labor required by kibbutz life, so instead of settling down at Ma'ale Gilboa, he traveled from kibbutz to kibbutz like a journeyman, imbibing the spirit of kibbutzim that in Mandatory Palestine functioned like forts in the Wild West — we called them Tower and Stockade settlements.

In 1969 he decided to get a university degree in agriculture. He flipped a few pages in the family album that was open on the table in front of us until he came to the photo of a striking young woman who became his wife. They met at the university, and like Biba she agreed to go along with the crazy dreams of a man who was, as Pinchas described himself at that age, "too young to be a city slicker. I wanted adventure, and I wanted to be a part of building the state." He just didn't know how to go about it when all of the kibbutzim in the newly conquered territories were being founded by my friends from the kibbutz movement, secular desecrators of the Sabbath. For the first three years of their marriage, Pinchas grumbled to his wife about being a kibbutznik without a kibbutz.

"It all began after the Yom Kippur War," he went on to explain. "Because of our losses, I was more frustrated than usual. I was sitting at home when I heard a knock on my door. It was Hanan Porat."

I nodded knowingly because I had studied Porat, a charismatic genius, during my stint at the Shin Bet. This was after Rabin's assassination, and I was eager to understand the ideology of the settlement movement, of which he was a leader. As a soldier, he fought in Jerusalem during the Six-Day War, helping capture the Temple Mount. In the Yom Kippur War, he was badly wounded. Soon after recovering, he launched the messianic Gush Emunim movement, based on the promise God made in Genesis 15:18: "To your descendants I give this land . . ."

"I didn't know Hanan at the time," Pinchas said, continuing the story. "But somehow he knew me and what I wanted. That evening I heard for the first time about a core group of other Torah-true believers eager to do something. Though hesitant to trust this perfect stranger, how could I say no, after all my bellyaching about there being no outlet for my dreams?"

Porat told Pinchas about his idea to build a religious settlement in the Arab town of Sebastia in the West Bank. The history of Sebastia is as twisted and gnarled as one of my olive trees. A short list of its founders, conquerors, and destroyers includes the Canaanites, the Israelites, Alexander the Great, John Hyrcanus, Pompey, Augustus Caesar (who gave it as a gift to Herod the Great), and a bishop in the crusader Kingdom of Jerusalem.

In 1975, though secular men like Dayan and Shimon Peres were still at the helm of the Labor government, it wasn't hard for a group of religious Israelis to get started on their quest. The IDF needed to build a fence around the ruins of an Ottoman-era train station to prevent Palestinians from looting the site, so Pinchas and his group, led by Hanan Porat, volunteered to help. Every morning for months they dug ditches and erected sections of wire, before returning to their homes in Jerusalem. At one point they took over a former Jordanian police station and set up camp there. Perhaps they were inspired by my father and his friends, who had taken over an abandoned British army camp to build Kibbutz Ma'agan.

"It's not as if we were squatters," Pinchas explained. "We told people inside the army and the government: If you're against what we are doing, we'll leave. They said nothing."

"A wink for you to go ahead," I added. Today I'm convinced the Labor government quietly created the space for settlements in direct violation of international law explicitly forbidding an occupying power from building on conquered territory. Had I been in the government, I would have done the same thing. The more settlements, the less likely a future American president would force us to hand back the land of our forefathers to our enemies, like Eisenhower had done in 1956 with the Sinai Peninsula.

As Pinchas tells the story, Dayan and Peres didn't think the Arabs would care if we built on barren hilltops, especially because the roads we built connecting Israel with new settlements also ferried Palestinian workers to jobs at Israeli factories. Sebastia was just the start of the settlement drive, of course. After Menachem Begin and the Likud Party took power in 1977, settlers were championed by the new government as pioneers for Zion.

Pinchas, though, cautioned me from making too much of the Likud. "Begin couldn't say enough about Judea and Samaria belonging to us, but he didn't know the first thing about settling and defending territory. Likud politicians, city folk for the most part, could go on and on about settlements in their speeches, but it wasn't in their blood. Do you think our rabbis were any better? Think again. At first, only a handful of them supported us. So we asked some of your friends at Kibbutz Merom Golan, people with experience, drive, and organizational ability, to help. They came to Ofra and taught us how to settle the land, acre by acre, ditch by ditch, house by house. How to create facts on the ground. It was only once we succeeded that the rabbis and politicians came around."

And Labor Party support continued through the decades. "Rabin, even if he called us weeds, built bypass roads, tunnels, and bridges that allowed us to thrive. After Rabin's murder, which shocked me as it did most people, I went on a hunger strike for three days when the army for some reason wouldn't let us pave a road. Shimon Peres, prime minister at the time, invited me to his office; and you know what? We got our road."[11]

So with the help of governments, both left and right, for much of his life Pinchas and his ever-expanding group have been reclaiming real estate they saw as rightfully ours, bestowed by none other than the mighty Word of God, the Bible itself: "And ye shall divide the land by lot for an inheritance among your families."

I was eager to get back on the road before rush hour hit Route 6. But before squeezing his hand and saying good-bye, I asked Pinchas what he would do if there were a national referendum and a majority voted in favor of a two-state solution: Jewish and Palestinian states based on the old 1967 border, with some minor adjustments. Would he resist evacuation?

Pinchas stood up solemnly, as if saluting a flag. "If the Jewish people in a referendum supported such a decision, I would regard the decision as the voice of God and would comply. Our national sovereignty is more important than the lands of Eretz Israel."

"More important than Sebastia and Ofra?"

"Ami, I'm a student of Jewish history. In my reading of the three thousand years since the kingdom of David, we forfeit our sovereignty whenever we fight among ourselves. So yes, I would heed the will of the majority."

When he said this, I reminded myself that he wasn't propounding a faith in the sort of nonethnic democratic commonwealth Herzl envisioned in *Old New Land*. The referendum he had in mind would include only Jews; Arab citizens of Israel wouldn't count. But at least, when pressed to the wall, he considers the unity of the Jews of Israel more important than the dream of reestablishing the Kingdom of David.

Not all of the settlers feel that way, of course. In the Shabak, I met with the most extremist messianic rabbis and told them that as far as I am concerned, Jewish terrorism and Arab terrorism are the same thing. The murder of an Arab civilian by a Jewish terrorist and the murder of a Jewish civilian by an Arab terrorist are the same crime: murder. I saw a kind of horror in their eyes when I would say this to their faces, and invariably they would try to educate me about the Chosen People and the Redemption of Zion. One settler leader and leader of a terrorist underground group, Yehuda Etzion, once described to me in great detail how he was preparing the altar and the laws of sacrifices for the Third Temple to be built on the ruins of the Dome of the Rock and the Al Aqsa Mosque. These are the people we should be really afraid of.

6

IF YOU WILL IT

On my way home I stopped by a hummus place just down the hill from Ofra that I used to frequent during my days in the Shabak. Though run by Palestinians, it's a favorite lunch spot for settlers, in their knit skullcaps and with their loaded pistols packed in holsters. As I bit into a falafel ball, perfectly crisp on the outside, with a creamy interior just the way I like it, I reflected on how much Pinchas and I have in common. The fact that I was born on a socialist kibbutz while Pinchas was raised religious is paradoxically immaterial; we were both raised to settle and defend land that we believed to be historically and rightfully ours.

Pinchas and I were also both wounded defending our ideals. In his case, months in the hospital set him on an odyssey to discover himself within the religious kibbutz movement. For me, the losses at Green Island coupled with the national trauma of the Yom Kippur War got me serving in Flotilla 13 for nearly twenty years and participating in countless commando missions against Yasser Arafat and his PLO terrorists. If I hadn't been fighting, I probably would have joined my friends in establishing new settlements.

I remember only snatches of conversation after being evacuated from Green Island in the Zodiac. Eyelids scrolling open, I saw the faces of nurses at Assaf Harofeh outside Tel Aviv staring down at me. "Ami, can you hear me?" one asked. She snapped her fingers, and I blinked.

I felt like Rip Van Winkle rousing from a quarter-century sleep. IVs hung on hooks, tubes fed into my veins, and over the wound was a bandage as bulky as a neck brace. Amazingly, I could talk, though doing so meant fighting through pain ricocheting from my neck to my eye sockets all the way to the base of my skull and down to my leg.

"Where are the others?" I asked, meaning Haim and my other mates from Flotilla 13. The nurse changed the subject. "Why are your feet all cut up?"

"Fought barefoot," I managed to spit out. Talking made it feel as if I had razor blades in my throat.

The wounds and lacerations were insignificant compared with learning that of the twenty frogmen who swam with me to the island, most were wounded, and three had been killed.[12] I had personally recruited and trained Haim and Dani, two of the dead. An inch in one direction or the other and the shrapnel would have killed me, too.

That afternoon Uncle Jonah, proud owner of the kibbutz's only private car, a Ford, drove my parents and Hava to the hospital. Judging by the way the four of them gawked at me after entering the room, I must have looked as if I'd been put through a meat grinder.

Though Imma's face betrayed her horror, Abba was stoic as ever. He grabbed my arm, entangled in the IV line, and, choking up, whispered, "Proud of you." Uncle Jonah gazed down at me with a glow of approval.

Imma's sobs swelled, her tears dripping on my bandages, while Hava just shook her head. What must my aunt, who survived Auschwitz, have thought about young men doing everything they could to kill one another?

When my family left, a bevy of nurses rushed in and crowded onto the bed; the hospital's only television set happened to be in my room. When I asked what they were doing, the head nurse looked at me as if I were an idiot. "Why, we're walking on the moon."

As we watched Neil Armstrong take his "one small step for man, one giant leap for mankind," I braced myself with one hand against the rail of the bed, every movement of the mattress causing more pain. What would be called one of the greatest events in human history barely registered with me because my friends were dead.

Over the radio a couple of days later, I heard General Moshe Dayan speaking at their funeral. "On the fallen soldiers' shoulders rests the price of victory," began his commemoration. In a riff on

Theodor Herzl's motto, "If you will it, it is no fairy tale," he comforted the Israeli people. "Dreams have become the realities of independence, homeland, Jerusalem, and of settlements in the mountains and in the deserts, of planting trees and flowers; but also the reality of blood and sacrifice." I agreed with every word. The death of my friends merely strengthened my resolve to show the Arabs they couldn't drive us out of our homeland.

My next stop was Kay House, a military rehab center. One morning in early August 1969, my commander, Ze'ev Almog, came to check on my progress and to fill me in on what was happening with Flotilla 13. Ze'ev was a handsome man with blue eyes and a quiet voice. Not only did he stand out for his abilities as a commander, but he also came from a different background than most of us kibbutzniks. He grew up in a religious family, went to a religious school, and joined the army through Bnei Akiva, the religious Zionist youth organization.

A dim orange light filtered through the curtains, and the room had not yet become a steam bath from the sun's midday rays. I hadn't slept much that night, waking up several times because I was so anxious to get back on my feet and train with my comrades at our base in Atlit.

Ze'ev requested that the nurses step outside and closed the door behind him. In his clipped military cadence, he leaned in and told me, "We have a problem. A big problem."

Egypt's strongman Gamal Abdel Nasser, it seemed, had reacted to Green Island by doubling down on his War of Attrition strategy. In Cairo he declared our raid a "criminal aggression" and presented the fins and oxygen tanks we'd left behind at Green Island to the international press. He then turned to the Soviets for weaponry, including modernized antiaircraft systems and MiG-23s. Through speeches delivered in his melodious Arabic, the mustachioed pharaoh, called "Al Rais" or "the Boss" by subordinates, had roused the Egyptian masses and the Arab world to the mission of ridding the region of the Zionist scourge. The Arab world, led by Egypt, refused to accept the existence of Israel, and vowed its destruction.[13]

Ze'ev, his eyes fixed on me, explained that General Dayan had decided to respond by hitting Nasser even harder. Bar-Lev and Yeshayahu Gavish, the commander of the Southern Command, had begun drawing up Operation Drizzle, an elaborate ruse that called for our troops to masquerade as Egyptians in six Soviet-made battle tanks and amphibious armored personnel carriers, all captured from Arab forces during the Six-Day War. In a mini-D-Day, the first such operation in the short history of the State of Israel, our forces would cross the Gulf of Suez and wreak havoc on Egyptian military installations. Because of Green Island, the Egyptians had stationed two Chinese-built P-183 torpedo boats on high alert facing Ras Sudar on the west coast of the Sinai Peninsula, across the Gulf of Suez from Egypt's mainland. For the IDF to move tanks and troops to the other side of the gulf on landing craft, our unit of sea commandos would need to sink the P-183s, taking them out of play and creating a distraction north of the disembarkation point. Our mission would be audacious in the extreme. Covert intelligence determined that the vessels were armed with heavy machine guns, seventeen-inch torpedoes, the latest detection electronics, and plenty of charges for uninvited underwater intruders. To plant explosives on the armored hull of a P-183 required a team of combat divers using midget submarines to get close enough to dive, carrying the mines, to the target. But with much of our commando group dead or, like me, hobbling around in hospitals or rehab centers, who was going to carry out such a mission?

"This should be a cakewalk for you guys," Bar-Lev had assured Ze'ev, even though we had never undertaken such a complex and difficult operation. Just remember one thing, he added to make sure Ze'ev understood the gravity of the situation. Operation Drizzle was scheduled for September 9. By then our team had better sink the ships; otherwise there would be no Drizzle. Containing and deterring Nasser hinged on the success of Flotilla 13. We were the "tip of the IDF's spear."

The mission, as Ze'ev explained it, would require two SUVs (submersible underwater vehicles) each with four men: two to navigate and two divers to attach limpet mines (named after a sea snail that clings to rocks or other hard surfaces) to the hulls of the P-183s. Rafi Milo, the commander of the midget-sub unit, would lead the effort.[14]

"Who else will be on the team?" My heartbeat quickened. For nearly a month I had been cooped up in a hospital and a rehab center with a black-and-white TV and rounds of poker dice as my only diversions. I had to get back into a wet suit.

Ze'ev listed five names.

"Count me in," I said.

Ze'ev had a blank look on his face, as if he didn't understand.

"I'm joining the operation."

"You're out of your fucking mind, Ami." His response was understandable — I still had bandages around my neck, and turning my head felt like I was getting my throat slit.

"You can't pull this off without me." He had just six of the eight men he needed, and only two sabotage experts qualified to dive from subs.

The wrinkles around his eyes narrowed as he focused intently on me. "You can hardly walk," he said.

To prove him wrong I leaped to my feet, swallowing hard to conceal the pain. "Anyway," I added, "the operation doesn't require me to run a marathon, does it?"

A day later I was released from convalescence and returned to Atlit.

Though my comrades and I succeeded in sinking both ships — it's anyone's guess how many enemy sailors died that evening — we lost three of our own men when the SUV that was not transporting me unexpectedly blew up on the way back to base. Rafi, the commander of the commando training course, had returned to the service just a few days earlier to direct the operation that included Shlomo and Oded, friends and fellow fighters. I was present at the military funeral to hear Moshe Dayan give a eulogy fit for Pericles. "Soldiers," he said in front of mourning parents and friends, "build houses and sometimes they don't return to them."

7

THE FUTURE IS IN OUR HANDS

The last time I saw my childhood buddy Srulik alive was just after the Six-Day War, in an open field near Ramallah in the newly conquered Judea and Samaria. While our air force, armored divisions, infantry, and commandos blitzkrieged our enemies on every front, Srulik and his company mostly fought in the Sinai. At one point he arrived to fight in the Ramallah and Jerusalem area. After the war ended, his company marched triumphantly through the stunned Palestinian city of East Jerusalem.

Two years later, in 1969, he left the military to spend time with his wife and newborn child, only to return a few weeks later when General Dayan, needing his best fighters during the War of Attrition, personally requested that he rejoin as an officer in the tank division.

In May 1970, two months before the cease-fire that would end the War of Attrition, I was in the Sinai, having just returned from an intelligence operation inside Egyptian territory, when news came of Srulik's death by Egyptian fire. Though we'd seen so little of each other since our teenage years, I felt as if I'd just lost a brother. I got permission to leave my post and attend the military funeral, replete with orations. As usual, I kept my tears to myself. It used to infuriate me to see uniformed soldiers weeping at military funerals. Soldiers in uniform were there to comfort parents, wives, and children, not to feel sorry for themselves. They would have plenty of time to cry later, in private.

At the *sheloshim*, the gathering to mark the end of thirty days' mourning, held at our kibbutz, an elementary school teacher, noticing my uniform, pulled me to one side and, in a hushed tone, asked if we could talk. Children in her elementary school class, the teacher said, had been sending letters and care packages to soldiers on the Egyptian front. One boy extolled Srulik in the typically patriotic fashion: “You are protecting me — you are protecting us all against the enemies . . . You must kill all the Arabs.”

Unlike most soldiers, myself included, who never bothered responding to letters and gifts, Srulik sent a reply that arrived a couple of weeks later. The teacher pulled the letter from her pocket and handed it to me. It was postmarked the day after my friend’s death. Attached to the letter was a note from the IDF explaining that the writer, Captain Guttman, died the same day he composed the message. She told me she burst into tears in front of her classroom when she read to them what he had written.

I unfolded the letter slowly and began reading. He thanked the child for his note and the gifts but then swerved into unexpected territory. “Let me tell you one very important thing,” he wrote in his elegant penmanship. “You shouldn’t believe that all Arabs are bad. They, too, have families. They are just like us. We don’t want to kill them, we want peace.”

I read the letter over and over, repressing the urge to cry. I readily admit today that, at the time, I couldn’t fathom how Srulik could have written those words. The Arabs wanted to wipe us out, and it was only our preparedness, guts, speed, and intelligence that kept them from pushing us into the sea. Did the fact that he was a father change his attitude toward our enemies and allow him to see them as human beings?

A year later I met Biba, my wife, who with her dark features and stubborn will is as intoxicating to me today as she was the day I met her at the University of Haifa. I had considered joining my pals in building new kibbutzim on the 1967 war booty. However, I knew that Israel needed an effective seaborne commando force if we were to continue fighting enemies seeking our destruction, so I opted to stay in the military. Besides, it was my secret ambition to command Flotilla 13, something I kept to myself, having been raised by socialists who believed that talk was idle. Strong people act.

To pursue such a future, though, I needed to get myself an education. In those days kibbutzniks refused to take the matriculation exam required for university admission because such qualifying tests smacked of the elitism of the class-based society from which the kibbutz movement sought to liberate mankind. We learned to master necessary skills, not to be tested. The University of Haifa, however, offered a program designed to allow kibbutzniks who'd finished twelve years of schooling to slip through the back door, and I enrolled.

Then one day there she was, with her dark-brown take-in-everything eyes, sitting next to me in Intermediate English on the first day of class. The first time we sat together for lunch in the cafeteria, my heart pitter-pattering like an infatuated schoolboy's, I discovered that we came from parallel worlds. Biba grew up on Kibbutz Merhavia, founded in 1929 by Eastern European intellectuals, academics, and writers who believed that culture and ideas were just as important as fruit trees and guns. In those days she worked in her kibbutz's cowshed and loved animals. While from an early age she wanted to study social work, working in the cowshed opened her to the idea of pursuing veterinary studies. In the end, she chose to become a social worker and raise a family on the kibbutz.

Despite our similar backgrounds, winning her over was harder than most military operations. She had served as an officer in the Sinai and swore she'd never go out with a military man.

After a few dates, she put her skepticism to one side, and we rented a cramped apartment a couple of miles from the harbor in Haifa. Upon finishing the program at Haifa, I decided to continue my service in the navy and went to an eighteen-month naval officer's course. Once I had that behind me, Biba and I had an impromptu wedding at Kibbutz Merhavia. The party ended at dawn, when my comrades, most of them drunk, were chased off the grass where the wedding took place. Biba and I spent the night in a hut.

The following day, once we finished cleaning up and removing the wreckage left behind by my friends, I went to Haifa to take a test for commanding a fast gunboat. For less than a month I commanded a Dabur, a 60-foot gunboat, in Haifa, followed by an eighteen-hour "honeymoon" on the beach before I went down to Sharm-el-Sheikh on the Red Sea to take over command of a gunboat squadron, a big step up from a commando knife and AK-47. With hundreds of miles between Merhavia in northern Israel and the Sinai, my only contact with Biba was through the occasional phone call and letters. I wrote so infrequently I might as well have been on an Apollo mission.

Compared to my service during the War of Attrition, my second stint in the northern Sinai was a beach holiday. Instead of fighting, I spent long evenings at the commander's bridge staring at the sea and the monotonous landscape: dust devils and tumbleweeds traversing endless sand, jagged red desert mountains, black Bedouin tents dotting eroded desert hills, skeletal goats nibbling on thornbushes. My men and I smoked cartons of cigarettes and drank cases of Maccabee beer. I also discovered the sea again, its beauty and its cruelty. In the Red Sea at high tide or during storms, you can't see the coral islands that can both dazzle you and sink your ship.

I escaped the boredom for a few days when I traveled to Jerusalem on Israeli Independence Day in the spring of 1972. A photo from that day shows me in a freshly laundered white uniform, collar unbuttoned Israeli-style, standing at attention in the presidential mansion on Jabotinsky Street in Jerusalem. In the background you can see a stained-glass window of the prophet Elijah ascending to heaven. My pants are starched, the creases razor-sharp, with a perfect one-inch cuff falling like a curtain over navy boots.

I am facing President Zalman Shazar, Prime Minister Golda Meir, and the eye-patched Minister of Defense Dayan as they pin the yellow-ribboned Medal of Valor on my chest for my actions at Green Island. My parents are sitting in the first row — Abba beaming, Imma expressionless. The medal is Israel's highest decoration given to those who display the "ultimate heroism against enemy fire." I was its first recipient since the Six-Day War.

That summer, alongside the Suez Canal in the far western Sinai, I saw a performance of the antiwar play *Malkat Ambatya*, Queen of the Bathtub, by Hanoch Levin, Israel's Bertolt Brecht, the most thrilling diversion my men and I had from our tedium. In Israel right-wingers had disrupted performances of the play by tossing stink bombs; some called for Levin to be locked up in an asylum, Soviet-style. In the Sinai we hooted at the spectacle. In one scene, citing "state security," the Israelis try to give the Ten Commandments back to God. In another, Golda Meir, the eponymous Queen of the Bathtub, clutches her foreign minister Abba Eban's crotch to prevent him from offering a peace proposal. Meir's defense minister Dayan had famously quipped, "Better Sharm el-Sheikh without peace than peace without Sharm el-Sheikh." The Sinai was ours, and it appeared in that moment that we would never let it go.

In a heated discussion with the crew on the ship, I defended Hanoch Levin and other leftist writers. It was only because of us, I said to the men on the boat, that writers could ridicule us and political leadership. That was what democracy was all about.

By the late summer of 1973, I had had enough of the monotony in the Sinai, especially while my former colleagues from Flotilla 13 were turning their dinghies and guns toward Arafat and his gang hiding out in Lebanese refugee camps. At twenty-eight I was too young and ambitious, too hungry and thrill-seeking, to be sailing for long days and nights scaring off drug smugglers, infiltrators, and Egyptian intelligence squads crossing the Gulf of Suez to collect intelligence for a war that we didn't yet know was about to erupt and change our lives forever. I decided to attend another command and staff course in Tel Aviv, where Biba and I could live together as I qualified to take command of a missile ship and hunt down PLO terrorists.

Three weeks following my move to Tel Aviv, on the Thursday before Yom Kippur, Judaism's holiest day, intelligence reports detected Egyptian troop movements. But that evening in a speech, the head of the Military Intelligence Research Department, Brigadier General Shalev (no relation to Meir) — the man responsible for assessing military intelligence — determined there was no danger of renewed fighting. We could fast and repent our sins in peace.

As usual, the entire country shut down on Yom Kippur. Around noon the phone rang. Languidly, I picked up the receiver.

"Ami here."

"Sir, you have orders to return to Sharm-el-Sheikh."

"What's this all about?" I thought it might be a prank.

"Sir." There was a long pause. "War is about to break out."

War? Nasser's successor, Anwar Sadat, the bookish fellow with a black prayer dot on his forehead, was attacking us? I was stunned into silence.

"A car will pick you up in thirty minutes." Click. I stood still, holding the receiver in front of me like it was going to explode. "Finally," I exclaimed, "a real war!" Green Island, in my opinion, was a fine operation but not a full-fledged war. The 1967 war was, of course, the real thing, but the only action we commandos of Flotilla 13 saw ended in fiasco. Now I had the chance to fight in honest-to-goodness warfare, the kind legends are made of.

I raced around the apartment, stuffed clothes in a duffel bag, kissed a dumbfounded Biba good-bye, and dashed to the curb to meet the driver, who picked up another officer at a kibbutz near the city of Afula after collecting me. By the time we arrived in Tel Aviv, war was already under way. Military radio reported air battles between our forces, with Egyptian MiG-21s attacking our airport in Sharm-el-Sheikh. In fact, the scale of the air war was such that our entire fleet was needed to engage the Egyptians, and we would have to drive to Sinai. My first command in the war was of three buses filled with unruly reservists rumbling overland to Sharm. Driving through the night, I couldn't sleep, afraid it would be 1967 all over again, with the Soviets and Americans imposing a quick cease-fire. *If this goddamned jalopy of a bus doesn't speed up, I'll miss my war!* This time the Egyptians had been the aggressors, catching us off guard with a sneak attack, and I was determined to make them pay dearly.

At 7:00 AM we reached our base to find smoke spiraling up from what used to be our hangars and barracks. My men, hitherto cocky on the bus, were frozen with fear. The supposedly impenetrable Bar-Lev Line — a chain of fortifications made of concrete, stone, and sand built along the east bank of the Suez Canal following the Six-Day War and named after the cigar-smoking deputy chief of staff who had overseen its construction — had been breached, and Egyptian forces were pouring into the Sinai. It proved about as effective as the Maginot Line, built by the French after World War I to deter a German invasion. The danger of being surrounded and wiped out was palpable.

Losing the Sinai wasn't our only fear that day in 1973. With the Syrians attacking the north, the very survival of Israel seemed at risk. Orders from the Ministry of Defense were confusing and contradictory — only after the war would we find out just how panicked Dayan had become. For the first few days I had no real idea of the magnitude of the catastrophe. All I knew was that the IDF had been defeated along the canal.

For the duration of the fighting, chaos at the Ministry of Defense forced me to operate outside the usual chain of command. At my request, Zev Almog, the commander in the area, put me in charge of preventing Egyptian commandos from attacking Israeli bases along 180 miles of the Sinai coast.

With a mini-armada of five ships, and an additional ship soon to arrive from the north, my handpicked crew, most of them graduates of marine school, and I swung into action. During the first week of the war, our main task was to destroy the Egyptian gunboat *De Castro*, because it controlled the northern Gulf of Suez and threatened Israeli ships stationed in Ras Sudar. The ship was a lot larger and faster than ours, and with far more firepower: two multibarreled 23mm cannons, one in the bow and one in the stern, as well as light machine guns on the sides of the bridge. Ignoring orders, I went on the attack with two "Dabur" boats; it was the simplest and most basic form of face-to-face combat, a shootout. The way we maneuvered our ship brought the enemy ship around to be a perfect target. We shot first, striking the artillery positions, and after this direct hit we let loose with enough volleys of fire to sink the *De Castro*.

During the next three weeks of fighting, we returned to the marine base at Sharm in the Gulf of Suez only twice, mainly to rearm. Meanwhile, we sank dozens of Egyptian vessels, most of them trying to transfer weapons and fighters to the Israeli side of the gulf.

My men, who fought valiantly and courageously in these face-to-face battles, were not motivated by abstract notions of Zionist patriotism and of love for the Land of Israel. Nor did they have faith in our military leaders. No, they fought with such ferocity because, after years of training, they believed in themselves, their comrades, and the commanders of the ships who led them in battle.

Nineteen days after hostilities began, American president Nixon and Soviet dictator Brezhnev, in one of their détente deals, forced the Israelis and Egyptians into agreeing on a cease-fire. One of my men had died during the fighting, and many were wounded. The toll was both physical and psychological. I dropped twenty-five pounds during the engagement. Others would face PTSD, the first time I'd see how trauma can trip up the mind.

At the end of the war I was given command of naval operations at the base of Ras Sudar in the northern Suez. In the new position I was responsible for landing craft, naval ships, and hundreds of men. One day, as I was coming to grips with the new responsibilities, I received a welcome surprise.

"Ami, you've got a visitor!" one of my men said. "She says she's your wife."

I rushed to the port, where Biba was stepping off a Hercules airplane.

It was dizzying to see her, but my rapture was tinged with anxiety. Since our wedding night, she had put up with infrequent visits, bad pay, and a Spartan life. I hadn't written to Biba once during the war. I guess I was afraid that if I wrote, the evil eye would doom me just as it had Srulik.

When I asked Biba why she was there, she told it to me straight: "You might die in this war, and if I can't do a thing about that, there's something I can do."

"Which is?"

"Have your child."

I followed the good example of my unruly crew and broke protocol to let her stay.

Three months later, in early 1974, I returned to Biba and to the Flotilla 13. If the successes of our Arab enemies during the Yom Kippur War spurred Pinchas and his religious friends to launch their aggressively expansionist settlement movement, they had the opposite effect on the old guard of kibbutzniks and socialists. The message we took from the catastrophe was that there were limits to Israel's power and that hubris can lead to catastrophic and humiliating results.

Years later, when young people about to be drafted asked me about the Yom Kippur War, I didn't mention details of the war itself. Rather, I told them how during that conflict I lost the naive faith I'd had since boyhood in the State of Israel as embodied in the prime minister, who, throughout my childhood from the time I was ten, had been David Ben-Gurion. When I was a boy, Abba told me how the "Old Man," as he called Ben-Gurion, lived in a big white building in Jerusalem, where he sat behind the door of a room at the end of a long hallway on the second floor, carefully pondering decisions that he knew would affect each and every one of us. Now I wasn't sure there was anyone in charge.

In the months following the war I experienced death as never before. Thousands were dead and wounded, and the country was filled with bereaved wives, children, and parents, including many of my friends. I realized, too, that if I died there was one person whose entire world would be destroyed — Biba.

What made this confrontation with death so bitter was the hubris of our leadership. Golda, Dayan, Shalev, Bar-Lev, and a host of others had treated war as a kind of parlor game. Golda and Dayan had never even raised the option of negotiations with the Egyptians to the cabinet. Dayan had outright rejected any diplomatic solutions that involved handing back territory: "I shall reject concessions of any kind and if the Arabs ask for war, they shall have it."

Later, when I read Barbara Tuchman's *March of Folly* about the Vietnam War, I asked myself why I, too, had been marching in a parade that led to disaster.

8

FATAH-LAND

It was getting late, and Dr. Yehuda Melamed was expecting me in Ein Hod, the artists' village on the other side of the low-slung hills from Kerem Maharal, so I pulled my Prius out of the gravel driveway and drove for twenty minutes as the sun set along the coastal highway. There was still enough natural light for me to maneuver without headlights past a life-sized brass nude of a dancer and through the village entrance into Ein Hod. Somewhere close to the old mosque, now a martini bar modeled after Cabaret Voltaire in Zurich, I turned onto Yehuda's narrow lane.

Parked in front of his house, I admired the view as I stepped out of the car. In 1948 commandos from the Palmach conquered Ein Hod, Hebrew for "spring of splendor." The Arab inhabitants fled to land half a mile up a hill and founded the town of Ein Jud, a village that only a few years ago received state recognition and gained access to a regular supply of electricity. In Ein Hod the state settled Jewish refugees from Algeria, and in the 1950s a group of Israeli artists moved into the Arab homes and wouldn't budge.

Yehuda, big-chested behind his I♥NY T-shirt, came bounding down a set of stone stairs, arms stretched wide for a bear hug. These days he is the director of the Institute of Hyperbaric Medicine at Elisha Hospital in Haifa. He's also a classical music aficionado who's conducted the Army Symphony in Johann Strauss's *Unter Donner und Blitz*. He's given public lectures on one of my favorite childhood books, Jules Verne's *Twenty Thousand Leagues Under the Sea*; other hobbies of his include gardening, winemaking, and, as I was about to experience, storytelling.

We sat on high-end leather sofas, French doors flung wide open to the outdoors, the scent of cypress pines — planted by the

Jewish National Fund — wafting in from the valley below. It was hard to reconcile my memories of Yehuda as a doctor in a wet suit wielding an AK-47 with the man in front of me, sitting in a home that could have graced the pages of *Architectural Digest* — he might say the same of me if he saw me splashing in the pool with my grandchildren.

On a long mahogany table, obviously handcrafted, he laid out a bottle of his own vineyard's Cabernet Franc and a bowl of olives harvested from his nearby grove.

There is something almost Homerian about my friend, a man deep into his seventies who runs about like an athlete, roars with laughter, and pounds his fist on his knee to make a point.

I gave him my standard riff about his being a part of my life story and of the story of Israel. In particular, our years fighting together in Lebanon with Flotilla 13 made him the best candidate to help me tell aspects of my life story I might have forgotten. We polished off a bottle of wine as he gave me the backstory that preceded his joining the special forces in the summer of 1974.

Before medical school he had served as an officer in a commando unit in the south and received a citation for an intelligence operation in which he participated. By the time the Yom Kippur War erupted he was just finishing his residency and was sent to serve as a doctor with Ariel Sharon's unit in the Sinai. Their base took the brunt of Egyptian rocket fire because the Egyptians knew that defeating the IDF hinged on eliminating his unit. It had been a slaughterhouse, and he'd had to treat hundreds of wounded. Rockets rained down day and night. "It was like that scene in *Apocalypse Now*," he said, "when the Vietnamese village gets blasted by helicopter gunships to the accompaniment of 'Ride of the Valkyries.' It was a miracle anyone survived."

After the war he returned to civilian life. He did six months at a regular hospital but couldn't hack it. "I told the head of my department, 'This isn't working for me. I don't want to work in a hospital.' Convinced I had PTSD, he gave me a long holiday. What did I do? I returned to the Sinai, to the same base where I had served during the war. There in the desert, I had a lot of time to think. I decided to go back to the military as a doctor in an active combat unit. I asked around, and when people told me Flotilla 13 was the most dangerous place to serve, I knew that was what I needed."

And that was where we met. After the War of Attrition and the Yom Kippur War, it was clear that changes were needed in the structure of the naval commandos. To help carry out these changes, I returned to the unit from my position in Sharm-el-Sheikh. With the fight against the PLO heating up, I quickly realized that we needed a fresh approach to recruitment, training, equipment, and armament. Though war had nearly bankrupted the country, funds were made available because the stakes were high.

The reason for our sense of urgency was Yasser Arafat, the guerrilla leader with a thick black mustache and checkered keffiyeh. Arafat and his Fatah faction within the PLO were putting a new wrinkle on what had until that point been a traditional conflict among states. His band of terrorists took advantage of the failing state of Lebanon to turn UN-administered refugee camps into an armed fiefdom. Arafat's men, calling themselves freedom fighters, smuggled weapons into refugee camps from wherever they could get them, often by sea from Cyprus. Arafat's Fatah, along with competing terror groups, began to carry out attacks on Israel by sea.

Arafat's stated agenda, modeled on Algeria's successful campaign to drive the French from their country, was straightforward: "The Palestinian revolution's basic concern is the uprooting of the Zionist entity from our land and liberating it."

A month after the cease-fire agreement with Egypt, PLO terrorists hijacked TWA and Pan Am airliners. Not long after that, PLO operatives in Gaza murdered two Israeli children with a grenade. An even more gruesome bloodbath took place when a rival ring of terrorists, from the Marxist-Leninist Popular Front for the Liberation of Palestine (PFLP), slipped across the border on the road to Moshav Avivim near our frontier with Lebanon and fired bazooka shells at a school bus, killing twelve, including eight children.

One of our missions was to disrupt the smuggling routes to Arafat's bases. Another job was to sabotage weapons depots inside the camps. Unlike in classic warfare, where armies fight on battlefields, our enemies were nestled in densely populated areas. We were fighting people without uniforms among a population where we couldn't easily distinguish between combatants and noncombatants. A man could be a pharmacist in the daytime and at night turn into a terrorist holed up in the basement of a UN-run school. Since fleets of aircraft and tank divisions were crude instruments for this sort of fight, top military brass began to see the commando groups as their go-to guys for cloak-and-dagger pinpoint actions. Paratroopers dropped by helicopter fought in the mountainous region of Lebanon. Flotilla 13, on moonless nights, operated against the terrorist bases along the coast.

In the old world of war, you fought knowing full well you might die, and that was the price the individual soldier risked paying for a decisive victory. But in Lebanon there were no surrenders, no decisive military actions, no final victory. After one operation there'd be another, and another, and another. Our mission wasn't to eliminate all the threats, because the potential supply of enemy fighters was inexhaustible. The idea was to prevent terrorist attacks against Israeli civilians by hitting a target and disappearing before everyone else in the refugee camp began firing at us.

In building my team, I didn't want Son-of-Sam psychotics itching to mow everyone down. I wanted hard-charging yet sensible men able to exercise restraint — to know who to kill and who to spare — as they emerged from the sea, faces smeared with camouflage paint, and stormed into the terrorists' backyards, up their stairs, and into their bathrooms if need be. It was just as King Solomon said, "By ruses — *tachboulot* — shall thou wage war" (Proverbs 24:6).

When Yehuda turned up and asked to join, medical bag in one hand and AK-47 in the other, he was exactly the kind of guy I was looking for.

We went on numerous operations together. The most dangerous missions had us swimming through churning seas and, once ashore, unpacking grenades, Berettas with silencers, and submachine guns with phosphorus bullets from bags. We'd then race to our target.

One time, following intelligence from the Mossad and the Shin Bet, we hit a guerrilla base and killed fifteen terrorists just hours before they planned to slip across the border and kill our civilians.

"You remember the boy?" Yehuda asked, suddenly changing the subject.

"Which boy?"

"That kid at the Al Rashidiya camp. Don't you remember? After the operation, right before we swam back to the Zodiacs, you asked me if you'd done the right thing."

He was referring to an incident from 1975 that I hadn't thought about in years. Orders came to sabotage a building used by a PLO commander in the Al Rashidiya refugee camp south of Tyre, a city founded during the Iron Age that had become home to nearly twenty thousand Palestinian refugees and a militant hotbed.

Missile ships took us as far as Lebanese territorial waters. From there we sailed in rubber boats until we were close enough to swim the rest of the way. We arrived on land late at night. Yehuda joined the larger of the two groups — more men meant more potentially wounded men for him to patch up later. I hurried with my fighters down rutted paths, past concrete shanties, broken-down cars, and closed shops. We set explosive charges outside the building that, according to intelligence, was the terrorist headquarters and raced back toward the beach to take cover before the blast.

The detonation woke up the entire camp. Loud voices rang out of the surrounding buildings, and no doubt guerrillas, machine guns ablaze, were heading in our direction.

It was then that I heard what sounded like a young boy howling. Maybe the blast had blown him out a window. Spotting him on the ground ahead of us paralyzed me. By stopping, I endangered all of us, but I couldn't let the boy bleed to death.

The sounds of gunfire seemed to get closer and closer, as if half the armed men in the camp were up on their feet. In the inky-black night, none of us made a sound. I ordered one of the fighters who trained paramedics to work on the boy, and fast. With voices approaching, we had to get the hell out of there.

When we got back to the beach, we found Yehuda's group waiting for us.

"We had begun fearing you'd been ambushed," Yehuda recalled as we sat on his comfortable leather sofas. "Then, just before jumping into the water, you grabbed me by the shoulder like this . . ."

Yehuda reached over the table and squeezed my shoulders with his big hands. "It was so dark," he continued, "I couldn't see your face, but I heard the emotion in your voice. I remember it so well because it was the only time I ever heard you talk that way. You told me how you ordered your paramedic to treat the boy, and you wanted to know if you'd done the right thing to take the risk. Those extra minutes put everyone's life in danger."

"Do you remember what you said?" I asked him.

"I think I just gave you a hug."

I held up my empty glass for a refill and gestured for him to continue with his storytelling.

"Do you remember the briefing we had with Eitan before the operation in Tyre?" Yehuda asked. "The time you told him to screw himself. I still think about it all the time."

Chief of staff General Rafael "Raful" Eitan was a farmer, carpenter, veteran of the Palmach, and ferocious fighter, with a mind bursting like a hand grenade with operational ideas. He was also a hardened bigot. Once, on a missile boat before an operation in a refugee camp, someone asked him how we were supposed to identify the target. Raful, with a smirk, answered, "If they aren't holding birthday party balloons, they're terrorists." Fire away!

During the briefing just before the 1980 operation in Tyre, Raful ordered us to eliminate one of Arafat's senior operational commanders. Two years earlier this commander had dispatched a group of terrorists in a Zodiac dinghy to kill Israeli civilians, including children. We had every right to go after him because he was continuing to send terrorists across the Israeli frontier.

Our intelligence for the operation was superb: We knew exactly what he looked like and where he sat each evening in the same café on the dock in the harbor. The plan, slated for August 5, was for us to take dinghies to within half a mile of the beach and use binoculars to make a positive ID. From there we would swim to shore, climb onto the breakwater, and two snipers would take him out.

Raful added a twist to the plan. After ensuring we'd hit the target, he wanted us to mow down everyone else in the café with guns and MAGs and set explosive charges on the breakwater.

"Sir," I told him, "that's not happening."

"What's that supposed to mean? It's an order."

"Sir, this operation is about killing a terrorist, not families in a café or kids running around on the breakwater." Unlike the terrorists we hunted down, the hit squads I'd led carried out our tasks without transgressing my personal moral strictures, such as they were in those days. My model was the Japanese Samurai, a noble fighter with an internal code of conduct. My Hebrew Samurais did our killing in a targeted, precise, and intelligent manner.

Rolling his eyes, the general doubled down. We had to "secure the retreat."

"Sir, if we open up with massive fire, everyone in the entire region will know we are there." It was much better to take out the man with a few bullets from a sniper rifle fitted with a silencer.

Raful continued to insist on an indiscriminate slaughter, and the argument, before dozens of our fighters, turned heated. My jaw agape, I stared at him, with his receding hairline and cheeks red from too much sun. The mocking tone of his words, as if we were exterminators talking about vermin, made his order all the more impossible to carry out. He honestly saw no difference between surgically taking out a terrorist and committing a bloodbath against civilians.

"Sir, if you want everyone dead, you don't need us. Dispatch the air force. They'll drop a one-ton bomb on the pier and it'll all be over."

Alert to the low value he placed on Arab lives, I laid out my counterarguments with care. It was more effective, I said, to target only the PLO commander, and no one else. Two shots by a sniper, fired from the breakwater at night, would be nearly impossible to trace. A clean operation will produce fear, and our enemies will think we are all-knowing, all-powerful. *If you raise your hand against us, someone's going to find you and make you pay.*

In the end we carried out the mission my way, and we put the man temporarily out of action — he was wounded, not killed.

I left Yehuda's at around midnight, and over the next couple of days working the fields with Biba, I thought a lot about that debate with Raful. Yehuda made it sound as if I were a great humanist staring down a cold-blooded killer, but I knew better. In one essential matter, I was no different from Raful in those days. Both of us were convinced we stood on the side of justice, that our fight was noble, and that our enemies deserved our bullets because they stood in the way of our rightful control over the Land of Israel. It took an experience far from the battlefield to shake me from this belief.

9

MY "FANTA MAN" MOMENTS

In 1981, I finished my term as commander of Flotilla 13 after more than two and a half years and returned to the navy, which soon sent me, along with Biba and the kids, to the US Naval War College in Newport, Rhode Island. It was the first time in years Biba didn't have to raise our two sons Nir and Guy more or less alone while working full-time as a social worker in Haifa while at the same time I was getting my Master's at the University of Haifa, and it was a fine career move for me. We got a house close to the base and settled into American life.

Courses at the war college opened up for me a new world of strategy and geopolitics. Ronald Reagan was in the White House, and the Soviet Union, what Reagan dubbed "the Evil Empire," was mired in Afghanistan. The Berlin Wall still stood, a literal reminder of the figurative Iron Curtain separating communist countries from the free world, and the threat of nuclear war was palpable.

A seminar on submarine warfare taught me just how important it is to have the right sensors to detect threats. A submarine lurking just below the surface of a calm stretch of water could pack enough explosive power to destroy Manhattan a dozen times over. I saw subs as nuclear-tipped versions of sea commandos: silent, stealthy, and deadly. And you can't do anything to stop them if you don't see them coming,

The course I remember best was on military strategy, including the institutions tasked with monitoring the ethics of warfare, such as the World Court, the Geneva Convention, and the International Red Cross. Until this point, I'd taken my "ethics of warfare" from classic stories about gallant warriors — the Maccabees and the Samurai masters — not from training in international law. My refusal to intentionally target civilians had been grounded in my education on the kibbutz and a personal moral compass, not theories on human rights.

My classmates included senior naval officers from Muslim, and mostly enemy, states. I met an Egyptian submarine commander, a commander of Sudanese patrol boats, and a Jordanian naval officer who later became commander of the Jordanian navy.

One day a Pakistani colonel came to me and, without preamble, issued a warning: "Don't permit the Israeli–Palestinian conflict to become a contest between Judaism and Islam." His voice was a low rumble, the way a torpedo sounds just before it strikes. "Don't lift the lid off that Pandora's box. We can live with Israel, and your fight with the Palestinians is of no interest to Pakistan. Just don't fool around with the Islamic holy sites or use religion to justify your claims. That would tear apart the entire world."

"Religion has nothing to do with our conflict," I assured him with a pat on the shoulder. "In Israel religion is a private matter and will never be used by politicians."

How wrong I was.

I was perhaps most influenced at the war college by the theories of nineteenth-century Prussian thinker Carl von Clausewitz, the father of military-strategic studies, and in particular his dictum that the "original means of strategy is victory — that is, tactical success; its ends . . . are those objects which will lead directly to peace." Israel's treaty with Egypt certainly validated this maxim. Never once, though, did I consider that it might be my job to make peace with terrorists. Their tactic was to target women and children, and my mission remained to eradicate them.

On June 3, 1982, shortly before Biba, the boys, and I planned to pile into our Ford LTD for a cross-country summer vacation, a terrorist sent by Abu Nidal, the head of a Palestinian terror outfit and a hated rival of Arafat and his PLO, approached the Israeli ambassador at the Dorchester Hotel in London and put a bullet through his head. I wasn't privy to the debates inside the Israeli cabinet about how to respond to the attempted assassination. All I heard about were the results: heavy Israeli strikes against PLO targets in Lebanon, killing two hundred, and the PLO retaliating with rocket fire over the border in the Galilee. The next day, June 4, Prime Minister Menachem Begin issued an order to destroy the terrorist infrastructure in Lebanon, with Minister of Defense Ariel Sharon leading the charge. Begin declared that the purpose of the invasion was to "avoid another Treblinka." Arafat, in Begin's words, was the "Hitler of Beirut."

Sharon, an aggressive tactician, mobilized the country to invade Lebanon and oust nettlesome Arafat and the PLO. Unbeknown to me at the time, Arafat and the PLO actually had nothing to do with London. The assassination was being used as a pretext for a massive operation that leaders like Sharon had long been eager to launch.

I received orders to return to Israel at once. Before I left, my roommate, Sam Hans, the commander of Norway's fleet of submarines and the future deputy commander of the navy, cornered me. "Why in the devil do you want to conquer Lebanon because of a botched assassination attempt against one man?"

"Hans," I replied without thinking, "we Israelis count differently than you Europeans: You count your dead on one hand — one, two, three — while we count ours starting with the number six million. Imagine if six million and two Norwegians were killed. You'd be like the Vikings. Of course you'd want to go to war."

From his baffled gaze, I realized that we had different perceptions of reality. "Ami, your ambassador didn't die, and the Palestinians aren't Nazis."

It was only on the flight back to Israel that I asked myself why had I reflexively dragged the Holocaust into the conversation with Hans. It certainly couldn't have been because I grew up hearing about it; I didn't. Had I unconsciously created an equivalency between Nazis hell-bent on liquidating Jews and PLO fighters who refused to acknowledge Israel's right to exist? Perhaps, but so what? I ordered a drink and tried to get some sleep.

During the fighting, I commanded the naval base in Ashdod and was in charge of landing operations in Beirut and elsewhere. I helped blockade Lebanon's ancient Phoenician ports. I followed orders, as any officer would, to bomb our targets. How much collateral damage — deaths and injuries to noncombatants — these shells caused was impossible to calculate, and anyway I was there to fight, not philosophize. Had I not just learned from my course on Clausewitz that as an officer seeking tactical victories, I was contributing to the strategic aim of peace? Besides, unlike terrorists, we were not *deliberately* targeting civilians.

My first insight into the true nature of our conflict with the Palestinians — my first "Fanta man" experience, you could say — came off the coast of Israel, just north of the Green Line separating it from Gaza. When the Lebanon front quieted down, I had been reassigned to the stretch of water from the city of Hadera, located between Haifa and Tel Aviv, to the Egyptian border in the south. From 1982 through 1985 my brief was to prevent smugglers and terrorists from breaching Israel's borders.

From my base in Ashdod, I prevented such attacks by monitoring the closed military zone off the Gaza Strip. Gaza's smooth, flat coast offers no natural deep harbor and no protection from winds. This means that fishermen often had to cast their nets far from shore to avoid the waves and currents. One day while on patrol, we came across an old man in a rickety boat floating toward the Israeli city of Ashkelon. I steered my boat toward him to block his path and my men shot warning bullets into the air, but he didn't change course. We shot again. He continued ignoring us. I banked south so that our boat was on his starboard side, close enough for me to see his sinewy arms and skin blackened by the sun like Santiago in Hemingway's *Old Man and the Sea*. Since, shamefully, none of us spoke Arabic, we could only gesture to tell him to turn around.

"*La*," he said. No. I didn't need a translator to understand he wasn't budging.

One of my men held up a gun to deliver the message that we'd open fire if he didn't return to Gaza.

The bare-chested old man spread his arms out wide, his charcoal eyes resolute. *Be my guest*, was the message his gesture conveyed, as if he had nothing to lose.

The consequence for a Palestinian who refused orders in a military zone was often death. But what would opening fire on an old man who just wanted to feed his family do for Israel's security?

I walked to the bow to think, and when I came back, my men were waiting to see what I would do.

Goddammit, I remember mumbling to myself, *just move your boat!*

He cast his net as if we weren't there. Raful Eitan always said that Israeli soldiers stormed enemy positions because they feared their comrades more than their foes, and for an instant I was fearful of showing weakness in front of my men, of losing a battle of wits with a toothless fisherman. But kill a man just to show who's boss? Would that make me stronger or weaker than the old man?

I turned to my men and said, "Let's get the hell out of here."

Not long after, in 1987, the First Intifada broke out.

An IDF soldier in Gaza lost control of his truck, careened off the road in the Jabalia refugee camp, plowed into a crowd, and killed four Palestinians. The uprising that erupted in response to the tragic accident struck me a bit like the Yom Kippur War in that it seemed to come from out of the blue. After a brief tenure as a commander of a missile-ships squadron, at the time I was already a brigadier general and the naval commander of the north. While sailing in the Northern Command operation ship, I was stunned to hear General Dan Shomron, the new IDF chief of staff, say that the Intifada was a mass uprising and not something the military could eradicate with bullets. Like firefighters outnumbered by a wildfire, all the army could do was try to contain the flames. It was for the politicians to deal with the root cause.

I wasn't used to hearing such defeatism. I was less surprised to hear Minister of Defense Rabin order soldiers to beat Palestinians into submission. Another general, Rehavam "Gandhi" Ze'evi, referred to Palestinians as "lice." I read about broken bones and other heavy-handed acts that only plunged us deeper into conflict. In *Haaretz* the journalist Ari Shavit described the "Gaza Beach Detention Camp" with its dozen watchtowers and the "horrific screams" he heard at night because Shin Bet agents were trying to "break some youngsters in the interrogation ward."

Years earlier, when I was commander of the Ashdod base, I spent time on shore in Gaza getting to know the fishermen. We drank coffee at a café near the harbor, and I tried — in Hebrew, which many of them spoke — to explain our orders to men whose ancestors had been fishing those waters since the Iron Age.

With their smiles and their hummus, I thought the Palestinians had come to terms with us. I figured they knew we were doing the best we could in a tough neighborhood. Unlike the French in Algeria, we weren't colonists; we were liberating land that had belonged to us since antiquity. As for the Palestinians, we were "enlightened conquerors." We built them universities and roads and introduced modern agriculture.

In a prime example of colonial wishful thinking, I assumed poverty, not patriotism, was driving the Palestinians to violence. If we could just prop up their economy, they'd submit to our rule and would eventually seek peace on our conditions.

One day in early 1988 when I was deputy head of the navy, with a driver, my trusty AK-47, and in a jeep that wasn't bulletproof, I set out to meet a group of fishermen. We set out around noon. From the naval base at Erez we took a route that straddles the Green Line between Gaza and Israel that would take us through to the harbor. We exited the main settlement road, separated from Palestinians by razor wire and neck-high stacks of sandbags, and turned onto a pitted two-lane track toward the Sha'ati refugee camp.

We entered the camp, and I gave the driver directions to the meeting place at the harbor. Smoke from burning garbage hung in the air. Pirated electrical lines were strung from hovel to hovel, and sewage puddled in front of a crumbling UNRWA school. Suddenly a throng of people surrounded our vehicle from all directions. Some were old men in donkey carts, but most of the mob were women and kids on bicycles.

This human roadblock was the first indication that I'd have to postpone my chat with the fishermen. Then came a much stronger sign, a hail of cinder blocks from buildings on both sides of us. Raining debris bounced off the roof of the jeep. Not too far away, Samson had pulled down the temple of Dagon, and here I was about to get stoned to death by kids and grandmothers. One Molotov cocktail and the jeep would be our funeral pyre.

I'll never forget the eyes of a boy no older than fifteen glaring at me with hatred. His look, which felt like a declaration of war, struck me harder than the shrapnel had on Green Island. Since we couldn't back up into the narrow alley, I told the driver to haul ass through the hailstorm of stones.

Only later that night did I have time to reflect on what happened. Twenty years after Meir Shalev had his Fanta man moment in the West Bank, I saw myself through the eyes of this kid. On the kibbutz I was raised to hate the oppressor and to value human dignity and freedom above all else, and according to those values I had to agree with the boy in the camp: I was a hateful occupier and oppressor of millions of Palestinians who aspired to political independence.

Who am I? I began asking. The Maccabees were in my blood, as was Masada and those words in our Declaration of Independence: "The Land of Israel was the birthplace of the Jewish people. Here their spiritual, religious and political identity was shaped."

But how was I to square this with that look of hatred in the boy's eyes? I still didn't know.

10

THE KING'S TORAH

Biba thought I'd finally gone off the deep end when I told her of my plans to go to Jerusalem and speak with Rabbi Yitzhak Shapira.

"What could you possibly hope to get out of him?" she asked.

As a devoted reader of the *Haaretz* literary supplement, Biba was well aware of the rabbi's notorious book, *Torat Hamelech — The King's Torah* — in which Shapira doesn't just sanction ethnic killing, but encourages it. He claims that his argument rests on the moral foundation of centuries of rabbinical exegesis: "If we kill a Gentile who has sinned or has violated one of the seven commandments — because we care about the commandments — there is nothing wrong with the killing."[15] Shapira goes even further by greenlighting the killing of non-Jewish babies who are still suckling at their mothers' breast because he says Arab babies are likely to grow up to commit the same sins as their parents.

My dealings with Shapira and his sect within the Lubavitcher community began during my Shin Bet days, when part of my brief was to prevent Jewish terrorist attacks, like the assassination of Yitzhak Rabin. In September 1996, I visited him at Joseph's Tomb in Nablus, where he was head of the Od Yosef Chai (Joseph Lives) yeshiva. One reason for the visit was to discuss the attacks carried out by settlers in Yitzhar, a village south of Nablus, against neighboring Palestinians. Acts of retaliation had followed, terror begetting terror.

Over the years I've maintained an interest in the rabbi and his circle because I realize they are an inseparable part of Israel's fate, and I want to avoid the future Amos Oz feared: "The fiefdoms of Yiddishkeit will annex region after region, and we will stand deaf and dumb."

If I was going to execute my mission with this book, I needed to understand how Shapira could find justification where I saw a crime. At the end of the day Shapira and I are both Israeli Jews, and if we can't sit down and speak frankly, we'll never figure out how to extricate ourselves from the trap we're in.

The rabbi lives in a dilapidated building a twenty-minute walk from Ben Yehuda market, where a Hamas suicide bomber murdered a dozen people during my time at the Shin Bet. I pulled up to the curb and tried to gather my thoughts. As best I could, I wanted to enter the rabbi's office with an open mind.

Mounting the stairs, I found the rabbi waiting for me in front of his door, slight and frail. His wispy gray beard and the dark lines around his eyes suggested a visitor from the world to come. Shod in Birkenstocks, he led me into his empty study. He shrugged off the room's clutter, saying playfully: "I have twelve children, Mr. Ayalon, and don't get me started about my brood of grandkids!" This rabbi, who is regarded by many to be the finest disciple of St. Louis–born guru Yitzchak Ginsburgh, spoke in a soft, lilting voice.

"Call me Ami."

A photo of Rabbi Ginsburgh, whom I ordered hauled in for questioning after Rabin's assassination because, in my opinion, his teachings incited violence, was the only decoration on the room's otherwise bare walls. "If a Jew needs a liver," Ginsburgh had asked rhetorically, "can you take the liver of an innocent non-Jew passing by to save him? The Torah would probably permit that. Jewish life has an infinite value. There is something infinitely more holy and unique about Jewish life than non-Jewish life." Some of Ginsburgh's hotheaded students interpreted his teaching on the biblical concept of "revenge" as a license to take the law into their own hands and kill Palestinians they considered terrorists.

"Before we start," Shapira said, "when was the last time you laid tefillin?"

I mumbled something about my bar mitzvah. The truth is, I'd put on tefillin — small leather black boxes containing parchment scrolls inscribed with Torah passages that Orthodox Jewish men strap to their heads, just above their foreheads, before praying — only a few times in my life. The first was before my bar mitzvah, on a visit with my father to an observant friend of his living on a moshav. Abba wanted to show me how a religious family lived in Israel, to teach me to honor Jewish religious customs even if we didn't practice them on the kibbutz.

"Do you mind if we put on tefillin? I always find it the best way to clear the mind and soul."

I was strangely relieved the rabbi didn't consider me an interloper in his world of the Torah. With my nod of approval, he wrapped my arms with leather straps and fitted the prayer box over my forehead. "*Baruch atah adonei* . . ." Like a young kid in synagogue, I kept my eyes open and marveled at Shapira as he prayed. How on earth had this man living like an ascetic in his simple apartment twisted Judaism, a foundation for humanism, into a tract like *The King's Torah*?

Once the rabbi was finished with the prayers, I unraveled the leather strap from my forearm and explained the reasons behind my request to meet. He nodded benignly while I spoke, and when I asked him about his biography, his eyes sparkled.

Born in Kfar Pines, Shapira was among the first settlers to move to Hebron, in the West Bank, after 1967. Soon after that he pitched in to help establish the settlement of Ofra. He later moved to Yamit, the settlement my friends established in the Sinai. Once the peace agreement with Sadat handed the Sinai back to Egypt, he returned to Judea and Samaria. The settler movement saw the peace agreement with Egypt as a warning and vowed to do whatever it took to prevent a similar evacuation from the West Bank. Radicals formed a Jewish underground movement and committed acts of terror against Arabs; a few even cooked up an apocalyptic plot to blow up the Dome of the Rock.

The rabbi eventually found his way to a new settlement built around the personality cult of Rabbi Ginsburgh. In the world of the Lubavitchers, closeness to God was measured against proximity to "Rebbe" Menachem Schneerson, and no one in Israel was closer to the rebbe than Ginsburgh. The rebbe had asked Ginsburgh to carry his blessings and prayers to Ariel Sharon in his besieged military base during the Yom Kippur War.

Again with the rebbe's blessing, Ginsburgh set his eyes on Joseph's Tomb, smack in the middle of the West Bank city of Nablus, with its 120,000 inhabitants, and cheek-to-jowl with a refugee camp that, in more recent years, has been a hotbed of Hamas support. In the early 1980s his followers built the Od Yosef Chai yeshiva next to Joseph's Tomb.

Shapira spent ten years with Ginsburgh, living in the nearby settlement of Yitzhar, and was there when he published *The King's Torah* in 2010. Ginsburgh and other top rabbis in the religious Zionist camp celebrated the book as a masterpiece of Talmudic commentary, while mainstream Israel condemned it. The Israeli newspaper *Maariv* called it "The Complete Guide to Killing Non-Jews."

Before exploring the labyrinth of his theology, I wanted to talk to Shapira about the Palestinians. I concealed nothing, sharing with him my belief in a two-state solution to our hundred-year war with the Arabs who share the land of Eretz Israel with us. To my surprise, mentioning the Palestinians did not cause him to suddenly harden or grow belligerent. "Let's make a deal," Shapira said, his mystical expression unchanged, "if you tell me what you believe, I'll tell you where we see eye-to-eye. Maybe we'll find that I'm a leftist just like you."

"Sounds fair. But for the record, I'm not a leftist or a rightist. If you want to label me, call me a pragmatic humanist."

"All the better," he said with such relish that I expected him to start clapping, "because I consider myself a humanist, too. Now, if you could define for me what it means for you to be humanist, we might discover we are two peas in a pod."

Casting a quick glance at the framed photo of Ginsburgh, I gave him my view of humanism, which I take to be the bedrock Jewish belief that individuals, their dignity and freedom, are at the center of human society. Man is the master of himself.

"My parents and other kibbutzniks like them," I went on to say, "never for a minute considered Zionism anything other than humanistic. Saving the Jewish people meant for them to build the State of Israel as a place rooted in equality and the protection of rights, a society that has returned to the vision of our prophets and is dedicated to the values of our Declaration of Independence. They just had one blind spot: the Arabs. It's not as if they despised them. The way they brought us up, it was as if they simply didn't think about them at all."

My ultimate goal is to maintain my parents' humanistic values, and I have concluded that the only way to do so is to preserve a Jewish majority in the State of Israel. I shared with Shapira my belief that the peace process started at Oslo offers a chance to preserve Israel's identity as a Jewish and democratic state.

Midway through my monologue, his smile vanished, and his eyes scanned up to my face and down to my chest, like I was in a police lineup. The muscles on my back seized up, but he remained calm, like a boxer who is confident he will knock out his opponent, however many rounds it takes.

"Tell me, Ami," he said without a hint of rancor, as if he were a therapist and I was in need of counseling, "in your view, is Orthodox Judaism humanist or anti-humanist?"

"That depends. I know plenty of Orthodox Jews, such as Rabbi Jonathan Sacks in England, whose books I've read, as well as Hebrew University professors Moshe Halbertal and Rabbi Binyamin Lau, who I assume would define humanism the same way I do."

"Thank you, Ami. Now I understand." The rabbi placed his palms on the table and then retracted them and ran them through the sides of his closely cropped hair. He paused with his eyes closed, reopened them, and then, bowing his head almost as if he was praying, grabbed the water glass next to the tape recorder with both hands and emptied it in one long gulp. "I must tell you," he finally said, "that in our view of things, what you just said is not humanistic at all. It is quite the opposite."

"How so?"

"First to the question of historical objectivity," he said. "Oslo didn't hand a part of the Land of Israel over to Arafat because we were colonizers; that would have been impossible because you can't colonize what is rightfully yours. We gave our land away in search of peace and security, and the Palestinians responded with murder, death, destruction, and pogroms."

While I believed the rabbi was describing a skewed version of history, I didn't reply because I didn't want to get sidetracked by a quarrel. I was there to listen. To be sure, Palestinian terrorism was the main reason many Israelis had lost confidence in the Oslo Accords. Yet for Palestinians wishing for an end to our occupation and the establishment of their own state alongside Israel, the past twenty years have brought only more settlements and more Israeli army incursions, a deepening occupation. In their eyes we are the betrayers, the unreliable negotiating partner. Pain and suffering on both sides have made it impossible to recognize what we are doing to each other.

The rabbi began fiddling with the tape recorder I had set in front of him, as if he wanted to be sure it captured his every word. "There is another reason what you said is not humanism," he said. "Humanism is about justice, is it not?"

I nodded for him to continue even though my mind was still stuck on our self-righteous inability to understand what motivates the Palestinians.

"We all know that there can be no contradiction between justice and the Torah," he continued. "How, then, can justice require the Jewish people to turn against the Torah by betraying the Land of Israel?"

He didn't say this in the tone of a fanatic demanding blind belief, and yet he presented his position as a sort of unassailable truth. I wasn't certain I was following his every rhetorical step, but there was no mistaking that his Zionism was radically different from the one practiced by my parents' generation of humanists, who believed it was our duty to shape our destiny rather than to wait for God's command or for the arrival of the Messiah.

It was time to change the subject. Sometime after I left the Shin Bet, the organization arrested Shapira. I asked him why.

"Because of *The King's Torah*," he said with a placid smile. "The Shabak arrested me in the middle of the night and interrogated me, but never charged me with a crime," a fact he was evidently proud of.

"Can we talk about the book?"

"*Be'ezrat HaShem*."

I repeat to myself his pious response: with the help of God.

"Good," I began, "because there are some things in it that I don't understand. There's a section where you permit the killing of Arab babies because we know they will grow up to be terrorists." I was thinking of the passage "There are reasons for killing babies even though they have not violated the seven sins, because of the danger that will arise if they are allowed to live and grow up to be as evil as their parents."

The rabbi writes in the present tense as if offering theological advice to yeshiva students before they get drafted into the army. The plain meaning of his words seems clear, and yet I wanted to give him the benefit of the doubt. I held out the possibility that there might be some cabalistic level of meaning that a nonbeliever like me failed to decipher.

He reached behind him and pulled from the bookshelf a copy of his 230-page burgundy-colored book, which is subtitled *Laws of Life and Death Between Israel and the Nations*. He set it on the desk between us.

"Now, what is it you don't understand?"

"Like I said, the bit about killing babies. How do you square this with Thou shalt not kill?"

"There's nothing to square."

"Seems to me there is."

"There isn't because, according to the Torah and the consensus of our sages, the absolute prohibition against killing applies only to Jews. This law does not extend to goyim."

"Wait! What you're saying is that killing non-Jews is no problem?"

"According to the Torah, no. The commandment against killing refers to fellow Israelites."

Before a conversation, I usually do my due diligence. I study a person's background and seek to understand his mentality. But never in my wildest imagination had I contemplated that Judaism, the original cornerstone of humanism because it introduced the concept that every human being is created in God's image, might sanction cold-blooded murder along ethnic lines. Sure, I knew about the legends of Joshua and the Children of Israel eradicating the Canaanites. But for me such biblical tales have about as much relation to actual history as Gilgamesh or the story of the Big Bad Wolf. To me Jews as a people are defined in works by the likes of Martin Buber and Rabbi Jonathan Sacks, who speaks of "an exodus story of various diverse peoples leaving oppression, crossing a wilderness and joining together to help create a promised land."

For years I've been telling people that Judaism is the source of humanism. At the Navy War College, I proclaimed to my friend Hans from the Norwegian navy that while we were bringing humanism to the world, his horn-wearing Viking ancestors lived in caves and sailed out to sea. And now this rabbi, as steeped in Jewish sources as I was in naval doctrine, was telling me that the Sixth Commandment prohibiting murder was an internal tribal code.

I was too flabbergasted to respond.

"Now let me explain why this is humanistic," he said as if any reasonable person, once exposed to his reading of the Torah, would agree.

His logic, if you can call it that, went like this: If Jews are fighting against Jews, the biblical prohibition against murder stands. The gentiles, lacking the light of the Torah, have a different set of rules that places naked self-interest above all else. It's as if we Jews are exempt from the Darwinian struggle for survival, while everyone else is locked into a merciless battle, tribe against tribe, nation against nation. International law, the rules of warfare, the Geneva Convention, and the entire history of human rights are window dressing for this elemental egotism. If Jews are fighting goyim, we must adapt to their rules. This means that if the goyim threaten us, it is just and morally necessary — according to their own rules — to kill them first, not just terrorists or soldiers, but women and children, the old and the young, even newborns. For him it doesn't matter if the target is a militant; the war is between Jews and non-Jews, and in this fight the gloves are off.

What an upside-down mad hatter's world you inhabit, I thought, but to keep him talking I simply said, "Yes, I see."

He put on reading glasses, flipped through the pages of his book, and began rattling off quote after quote with the speed and accuracy of an expert sniper. What I gleaned from his homily was again a flat denial of any neutral standard for human behavior, and the reduction of all non-Jewish reality to the merciless rules of the jungle. Only Jews, chosen by God to establish a homeland in the Land of Israel, have carved out a sliver of true morality, and to protect our lives and our land we must play by the rules of the goyim.

Rocking back and forth in my cheap folding chair, I decided to tell him the story of the wounded boy in the Lebanese camp whose life I sought to save at the risk of endangering my own and those of my men. In my Torah, I implied by recounting the tale, there is an elemental difference between fighters bearing arms and civilians, between those who want to kill us and those who want only to live.

Instead of responding, he returned his gaze to his book, his lips still moving.

I became acutely aware of my surroundings, of the tefillin boxes on the shelf, Ginsburgh's mystical stare from the framed photo on the wall, the smell of Eastern European food wafting in through the open window, the sweat from my armpits. The room resonated with a quiet sense of reverence rarely found in loud, frenetic, elbow-jabbing Israel.

Before I escaped back to my home on the slopes of Mount Carmel, there was one last question I wanted to ask, perhaps the most essential one. I can abide a rogue theologian; one rabbi alone doesn't threaten the State of Israel, and he has a right to speak his mind. His ideas could become lethal, however, if they made their way into laws enforceable by Israel's courts. "I have heard," I told him, "that you and members of the Knesset are writing a constitution for the State of Israel."

With his steadfastly placid expression, he said that while he couldn't delve into the secret details of the plan, together with Rabbi Ginsburgh and members of the Jewish Home Party he was looking for ways to introduce a Torah-based legal system as a long-term solution for exercising Jewish rights over the Land of Israel. In other words, the gentle rabbi and his friends wanted to erect a theocracy. For Israeli Arabs and the Palestinians under occupation, this would complete what I would call the process of apartheid and turn Israel into a pariah state rightfully despised by the rest of the world. Never in my life, not in Flotilla 13, not during battles and operations, not as commander of the navy, and not as head of the Shin Bet after the murder of Yitzhak Rabin, had I met a more dangerous enemy to our democracy and experiment in self-determination than this "man of God" and father of twelve.

Driving out of Jerusalem, I reflected on my conversation with Rabbi Shapira and marveled at his friendly demeanor and modesty. Despite his fame, Shapira led a simple life, as if he had taken a monk's vow of poverty. I was surprised to discover that I found things about the rabbi to admire — in particular, his willingness to speak frankly with a man who had once dragged in his teacher for interrogation.

I tried my best to see things from his perspective. He and his ilk say they are fighting for the soul of Israel because they believe the Jewish people stand for more than the Sodom and Gomorrah of Tel Aviv and Haifa. Such a sinful waste — is it not? The Chosen People tanning on the beach rather than praising the Lord of Hosts. Without our obedience to Adonai, the Jewish people would have disappeared ages ago. Is it too much to ask to want the Jewish state to be Jewish? Is it unreasonable to work night and day to herald the coming of the Messiah and the restoration of King Solomon's Temple?

Yet despite his holy airs, Rabbi Shapira terrifies me. We live in the same country, speak the same language, participate in the same democratic political system, and sing the same national anthem. But an ever-widening chasm separates us intellectually and spiritually. The rabbi bases his thinking on religious laws that might have made sense in the Iron Age. But those laws, written for a different time, have to be updated to account for modern conceptions of law and rights, and this is something he refuses to do.

On the highway driving home, seeing a large logo sign for the pharmaceutical giant Teva reminded me of Israel's prodigious capabilities in software, biotech, and solar technologies. In the early 2000s, while partnering with Professor Nusseibeh to launch People's Voice, I was the chairman of the board of directors for Netafim, a drip irrigation company launched by a kibbutz in the Negev that is helping feed hundreds of millions of people worldwide. Today Israeli geeks and technologists, many of whom were inspired by the kibbutz movement's vision of building a better humanity, are tackling some of the world's most pressing problems.

The Judaism I uphold is no less progressive. On my moshav the secular and religious members respect each other. On holidays I join the believers in services at the synagogue around the corner from my home. My sons read the Torah during their bar mitzvahs; we celebrated my grandson's bar mitzvah at the Western Wall. But Rabbi Shapira's theocratic plot to change the laws of Israel would undermine our legal system and turn an Arab living in the Land of Israel into a *ger*, or resident alien. If he and his friends in the Knesset have their way, our much-lauded Start-Up Nation will betray the values of our Declaration of Independence and land us with other rogue states on the wrong side of history.

11

DR. KHALIL SHIKAKI

The following day I returned to Jerusalem with Biba, her friend Chen, and her husband and my close friend Orni Petruschka. Orni, a nephew of the novelist A. B. Yehoshua, is a former fighter pilot in the Israeli air force, a graduate of the Technion in Haifa and of Cornell University, a successful high-tech entrepreneur, and my partner with the People's Voice. It was Orni who facilitated the press interview that gave the inspiration for the making of the Academy Award–nominated documentary from 2012, *The Gatekeepers*. Directed by Dror Moreh, the film features five other former Shin Bet heads and me candidly discussing our contrarian views about the organization's, and Israel's, successes and failures since the Six-Day War.

A Palestinian driver was tasked with meeting us at the American Colony Hotel in East Jerusalem and taking us through the Qalandiya checkpoint to the office of the Palestinian pollster Dr. Khalil Shikaki in downtown Ramallah. Each time I cross into Palestinian territory I need to apply for a permit from the IDF. Sometimes I get one, sometimes I don't. The security chiefs no doubt worry that I'll end up in a Hamas dungeon somewhere in a refugee camp, hands and ankles duct-taped together.

The line at the checkpoint was backed up, which gave me the chance to get to know our driver, Ihsan, and to hear his assessment of the political situation in Jerusalem. In flawless Hebrew he told me how little faith he had that life would improve for Palestinians. His kids are studying at German universities. "What kind of future do they have in this country?" he asked. I had no ready reply for him.

Although I met Khalil for the first time at the same meeting in London where I met Sari, I'd studied him and his work since early in my tenure at the Shabak. I had found our spy toolbox — the wiretaps, electronic surveillance, informants, and interrogation rooms — lacking, because no amount of intelligence-gathering can predict a popular and unplanned outbreak like the Intifada. I began to listen to what Palestinian writers, poets, and social scientists were saying about their own people. The opinion polls Khalil and his team carried out at the Palestinian Center for Policy and Survey Research were professional, scientific, and revealing.

I also found Khalil personally fascinating. He and his brother Fathi, a pediatrician, had responded to the Israeli–Arab conflict in radically different ways. In 1948 their parents fled their homes in Zarnuqa, a former village near the city of Rehovot. Khalil studied political science at the American University in Beirut before going on to get his PhD at Columbia University. Fathi, meanwhile, cofounded the terror group Islamic Jihad, with support from Iran. Shortly after Fathi's group carried out a suicide attack against Israeli soldiers at the Beit Lid Junction in January 1995, his name ended up on our hit list.

Later that year, in October 1995, a couple of months before I took over the Shabak, the Mossad tracked Fathi to Malta. Two hit men, riding a blue Yamaha, shot him in the head after he bought a gift for his wife at Marks & Spencer.

Passing through Qalandiya, I noticed signs of recent rioting: teargas canisters, rocks strewn about, and what looked like bullet casings. Graffiti portraits of Yasser Arafat and the imprisoned Palestinian Marwan Barghouti decorated the Separation Wall, which runs through the checkpoint and cuts off the West Bank from Israel.

The border police manning the checkpoint barely looked at us. "Okay," they said, waving us through. I cracked the window, and the stench of burning garbage flooded the car. A bright-red sign, in Hebrew, Arabic, and English, warned us like tourists on a safari that we were "risking our lives" by entering a Palestinian-controlled area.

We drove for another twenty minutes or so before reaching the office building in downtown Ramallah, where Khalil's office is located on the second floor. After ushering us inside, Khalil apologized for having to meet in such a formal setting. "We have no electricity at home," he explained. Blackouts and dry water taps are a daily occurrence in the Palestinian West Bank, an archipelago of apartheid-style Bantustans split up and surrounded by territory controlled by Israel. "As soon as power is restored," he said hopefully and in colloquial American English, we could "move the party" over to his house in the village of Atara, where his wife was preparing a feast.

Stocky and broad shouldered, Khalil has iron-gray hair and a square chin well engineered for absorbing whatever blows come his way. Yet he doesn't display any of the signs of a man living under an oppressive occupation, neither ours nor the Palestinian Authority's corrupt dictatorship. After greeting Orni, Chen, and Biba for the first time, he eased himself into a chair and motioned for the three of us to sit as well.

He nodded along as I acknowledged in detail how much his work as a pollster had influenced me during my years in the counterterrorism business. The analysts working for me during my time at the Shabak, professionals who had mastered Arabic well enough to pick up the slang spoken over tapped phone lines, never provided the same level of intelligence as Khalil's small team of people going door-to-door in refugee camps, equipped with clipboards and questionnaires. Khalil once told me, and I think he was right, that his public opinion polls could have alerted us that the First Intifada was about to erupt — if only my predecessors had been paying attention.

I also wanted to explore what, for me, had been an enduring mystery. Though I had known Khalil for years, we had never discussed the circumstances that led to his brother's death. Sitting around a long conference table under tubes of fluorescent lights, I asked myself why one brother, Khalil, opted for peaceful means of resisting tyranny, while his brother the pediatrician raised his sword?

I decided to ask Khalil about his upbringing. What was it that formed him as a person, a scholar, a researcher, and a humanist?

In his answer he mentioned how his years studying at the American University of Beirut, before the civil war, had introduced him to an open, free, cosmopolitan culture. Living in New York and studying at Columbia for his PhD — fellow Palestinian Edward Said taught there at the time — completed the journey he had begun in Beirut. He emerged as a scholar committed to using ideas and reason to liberate his country from occupation and feudal backwardness.

I sought to establish a connection by revealing a relevant feature of my own past. During my first days at the Shabak, Hamas had carried out a series of suicide attacks, murdering dozens of Israelis, including the daughter of a friend. I knew my biggest challenge would be to comprehend the source of the hatred and desperation behind such barbaric attacks. But how? It was clear to me that Israel could not defeat terror without understanding the psychology and culture of the terrorists — what produces and fuels hatred and violence? But it was equally obvious to me that it was difficult to get reliable information, and hence to develop an accurate picture of a world I knew nothing about.

"That was the point at which I discovered your polls," I said.

"And what did they tell you?"

"That Palestinians wanted peace with us, if we'd only lift our boots from your necks."

"And that was how people felt," he said, "back when there was a viable political process that people trusted." When Rabin and Arafat shook hands in the Rose Garden in front of President Clinton, most Palestinians accepted and supported the idea of two states for two peoples.

Orni, the ex–fighter pilot, had been listening keenly without comment. "And what about today?" he now asked.

Khalil leaned back in his chair and raised his eyebrows; for maybe ten seconds he seemed lost in thought. Finally, he cracked a half smile and responded. "Look, people behave according to what they expect. In our last poll we found that most Palestinians no longer support a two-state solution; they want a single state between the Mediterranean and the Jordan River. They want to go back to 1948. We also conducted a poll among Israelis. For the first time since I began polling Jewish Israelis seventeen years ago, most Jews no longer have faith that politicians will reach a two-state solution. For once, Jews and Palestinians agree on something."

Khalil asked his secretary to get us a copy of the report, titled "Israel and the Palestinians: Sliding Toward a One-State Reality," which had been produced for the Crown Center for Middle East Studies at Brandeis University.

"As you'll read here" — Khalil gestured to the report — "Palestinians no longer think Abbas and his cronies are serving their interests. Ten years ago only a minority considered our leaders to be collaborators with the Israeli occupation; now 60 percent do. The security coordination, in particular, is widely seen to be a joint Israeli–Palestinian plot to prevent our independence."

There was a hint of melancholy in Khalil's voice. Biba, noting the change in tone, asked why he believed people had lost hope.

"Back in the 1990s everyone knew how corrupt Arafat's regime was. Corruption wasn't just a by-product of Arafat's incompetence; he used corruption as a means of building loyalty. Every vegetable monger in the souk knew this. I got a glimpse into the slime because the Council on Foreign Relations asked me to write a report that assessed the strength of Palestinian public institutions. Let me tell you, it was a horror show. Point is, despite all the corruption, most people trusted Arafat because he never took a dollar for himself."

"And today?" Biba asked.

"Today? Just look around Ramallah at how many shiny black Mercedes there are belonging to government insiders. I'll tell you a story. Not long ago our government arrested some Hamas activists for holding illegal arms, then released them due to family pressure. The minute they got out of jail, Israel killed them. You can guess what the rumor mill did with this."

"They must have said your security forces lined them up against a wall, and let us be the firing squad," I said.

"That's right. It gets even worse. In a move straight out of Kafka, our government is still pressing charges against the men in the courts, though they are dead. Just this past Monday there was a big antigovernment demonstration in Ramallah because of this."

Khalil grabbed for a shot glass of strong Arabic coffee and stirred in a packet of sugar. "The polls we do are political — we want to wake up our leaders," he said. "I know them all personally. How do you think Abbas got his job? It was because the Europeans, shocked at my corruption report, put Arafat under fire to hire a competent prime minister. These days I tell Abbas and his men: 'To keep people's support, you have to show more backbone. Stand up to settlers, blockade the settlements, and without using violence stand up to Israeli colonization.'" Khalil tossed back the coffee and smacked his lips. "And they also have to do something about our crooks."

Per Oslo, Area C, which is most of the West Bank, is under full Israeli control, and the Palestinian police can't so much as hand out a traffic ticket. And since Israeli cops don't venture into those areas, much of Area C has become a paradise for organized crime.

"How does our government respond?" said Khalil. "With words and slogans, and maybe Abbas makes another speech in front of the UN. You ask me why people are giving up on the two-state solution, well, now you know. They'd rather have a single state between the Mediterranean and the Jordan River because at least for its citizens, Israel has the rule of law."

"Which means the end of Israel as a Jewish state," I said.

Khalil poured himself another cup of coffee. "Ami, my dear friend," he said, "most Palestinians don't even think that far ahead. They just want out from under the boots of the IDF."

Khalil's wife phoned to tell him that the electricity was back on in Atara and lunch would soon be ready. Our driver followed Khalil north out of Ramallah into the hill country made famous by Raja Shehadeh's *Palestinian Walks*. The crimes against these ancient hills, which as Shehadeh says in 1967 would have been recognizable to Jesus Christ and Rabbi Hillel two thousand years ago, are many: settlements, Israeli bypass roads, IDF bases, and a sprawl of unregulated Palestinian construction have laid waste to the landscape.

Atara is situated on the spine of a high mountain ridge half a mile above the sweltering coastal plain, and I felt the first cool breeze in a month. The village, like so many in our part of the world, sits on strata upon strata of history from the Iron Age through the kingdom of Judea, the Persians, Greeks, Romans, Byzantines, and Mamluks. The nineteenth-century American explorer and biblical scholar Edward Robinson associated the village with the Ataroth from the Book of Joshua. Local Muslims pray at a shrine to a Sufi dervish. Christians in the area flock to a pile of rocks dedicated to Saint Catherine, a fourth-century martyr killed by a Roman emperor.

The bones of saints didn't lure Khalil and his wife into buying their plot of land, with its hilltop view of the distant Mediterranean. They came here, Khalil explained, because of his wife. Her family arrived from Bosnia a hundred years ago, established a village on the port of Caesarea, only to end up as refugees in the West Bank city of Tulkarem. Stories her parents told her of the gentle waves of the sea, invisible from their shantytown, turned her into as fanatical a lover of water as I am. When she and Khalil got married, she insisted that they build a house on a hill so high they could see the coast.

From the top balcony of their home, Khalil and his wife, wearing a silk hijab and fitted jeans, pointed to the hazy western sky and assured us that on a clear day they could see the beachside Israeli luxury hotels. After our tour of the house we sat down to lunch served Palestinian-style: a main course of chicken and rice accompanied by multiple salads, hummus, falafel, stuffed zucchini, and peppers. I again put off asking Khalil about his assassinated brother — it didn't seem like a suitable lunchtime topic — but I silently marveled at the fact that this friend heaping food onto my plate had grown up with a boy who in March 1996 dispatched a suicide bomber that killed the daughter of a friend of mine.

12

THE SPOILERS

Most of the books that line our shelves at home are Biba's. Books of psychology and social work butt up against her father David's works of scholarship and literary criticism. Works of fiction, mainly in Hebrew, occupy the bulk of the shelf space. My books on military history and strategy are in the dining room, easy to reach from my workplace at the long wooden table. The morning following the visit to Khalil, I pulled out a couple of books that I'd brought back from my time at Harvard's Kennedy School in the early 1990s. One book I find myself thumbing through more often than I should because of what it does to my blood pressure is Barbara Tuchman's magisterial *The March of Folly: From Troy to Vietnam*. Back in the 1990s I highlighted the line "Chief among the forces affecting political folly is lust for power, the most flagrant of all passions."[16]

Another volume I pulled from the shelf that morning, also on the syllabus at the Kennedy School, was Neil Sheehan's classic study of the Vietnam War, *A Bright Shining Lie*. Notes scribbled in the margins, and the texts I highlighted in yellow and blue, capture my state of mind during that 1992–1993 academic year. "The truth," I wrote on the inside of the back flap, "is often only perceptible to 'outsiders.'" I think reading Sheehan's book was the first time I became aware that outsiders to the military hierarchy, such as journalists and academics, are equipped with different "sensors" than military officers or politicians that enable them to see through the lies and other stories we tell ourselves when tangled up in war.

I don't mention the Palestinians once in my notes, even though I now realize that one could have called Israel's attitude toward them "a bright shining lie," too.

My stint in Cambridge, with Biba and our three sons along for the adventure, came at a thrilling time to be alive: The Iron Curtain had fallen, apartheid in South Africa had ended, and opinion polls had Bill Clinton, a young, liberal, visionary politician, poised to win the upcoming presidential election. The atmosphere was intoxicating.

Some of the smartest political scientists on earth were puzzling out the post–Cold War world on Harvard's campus. Samuel Huntington was putting the final touches on "The Clash of Civilizations," his monumental essay, which would appear in *Foreign Affairs* in 1993. The article was written largely in answer to the publication of *The End of History and the Last Man* by Huntington's star student, Francis Fukuyama, that had inspired impassioned debates over Turkish coffee at Cafe Algiers on Brattle Street. "*Just don't hold your breath*," I told people when they quoted from the book that "the universalization of Western liberal democracy is the final form of human government."

Just as I was finishing up my master's degree, my colleague Ehud Barak, who was serving as chief of the General Staff, called me up in the middle of the night with an offer to head up Israel's navy. To be the admiral of the navy was the culmination of thirty years of service, and I felt a sense of honor and responsibility I struggled to capture in words.

My swearing-in ceremony back in Israel provided another opportunity for my parents to pose for the camera with me. This time even Imma showed her pride and, I suspect, relief. The office job at naval headquarters next to an old Templer settlement in Tel Aviv would keep me out of harm's way.

Yitzhak Rabin, who replaced Shamir as prime minister, had promised Israeli voters during his campaign that he would never talk to the "liars and bastards" in the PLO. A year into the job, however, he surprised us all by calling a meeting of members of the IDF General Staff to tell us the former archenemy had become his partner, and he was going to make peace with Arafat. The State of Israel and the PLO would recognize each other as the legitimate representatives of their respective peoples. Arafat and his Fatah men would be permitted to return to what they would surely call "liberated Palestine."

Their government, called the Palestinian Authority, would administer a part of Gaza and the city of Jericho, and in time they would extend their rule over more territory. We would eventually clear out of every place except for military installations and settlements. But what did "security zone" mean? As they say, God, and the devil, are always lurking in such details. Within five years, we were told, final status talks would settle the thorniest issues, such as Jerusalem, security, borders, Palestinian refugees, and Jewish settlements.

We members of the General Staff looked at one another, too stunned to respond. How the hell was this supposed to work? Did the prime minister really expect us to implement and enforce the terms of a back-channel peace deal that had been cooked up in a Norwegian forest without any input from security experts?

At the heart of our unease, even if no one dared say anything out loud, was the basic human difficulty of imagining an enemy to be a partner. How could we roll out the red carpet to Arafat, the man who turned Jordan and Lebanon into terrorist hotbeds? The Italian journalist Oriana Fallaci once said about Arafat that he "always plays the double-cross, lies even if you ask him what time it is." And now we were supposed to trust him as a partner?

The Oslo Accords were just as mind-boggling for me as for thousands of others in the military because I had waded through fedayeen terror swamps to fight Fatah close up. Yes, during the Intifada, I had come to recognize the futility of trying to control Palestinian populations in Judea, Samaria, and Gaza. I knew politicians would have to square the circle of the Jewish people returning to their ancient land with the cruelty of our rule. What I had never considered was that Arafat and his band of terrorists would even be considered as part of the solution. For years I had sailed almost all over the region — the Adriatic Sea, the Western Mediterranean, Tunisia, Libya, and pretty much every other Arab country — to kill these very men. Just five years earlier, following Rabin's order, I had joined a hit against Abu Jihad, Arafat's deputy and cofounder of Fatah.

When Rabin sat us officers down and explained the deal, he addressed many of my concerns. I remained skeptical, but I trusted Rabin, a hawk, not to do anything that would compromise Israel's security. What I worried about was how we would deal with Palestinian organizations that opposed the agreement, including Hamas, a leading force of terror in the Occupied Territories.

An unrelated question was how on earth we would contend with Jewish settlers who would feel betrayed, and rightfully so, that their own political leaders and every Israeli government since 1967 had lied to them. At a conference where he lectured, I asked Shimon Peres, then foreign minister, how he intended to deal with the inevitable protests. In my question I mentioned the Jewish underground, a terrorist organization that grew up as a response to the peace treaty with Egypt and the withdrawal from Sinai.

"Look," he said, "I'm a bus driver and I have to take the bus and all its passengers to a safe place. Sure, there might be some passengers in the back of the bus who put up a fuss. But I can't ask every traveler what he thinks. My job is to keep my eye on the road."

"But you changed your destination while driving, after they bought a ticket. They chose you as a driver because you promised to take them somewhere. They deserve at least to speak their minds. As far as they're concerned, you kidnapped them and now they feel like hostages being delivered to a destination they didn't choose." Peres shrugged and changed the subject.

Because the navy patrolled the waters off Gaza, Oslo was now partly my problem. Would Arafat get use of the sea off the Gazan coast? How could we prevent his people from smuggling in arms? What would happen if we stopped a ship inside waters Arafat controlled? Soon enough, we would have to sit down with PLO men, experts at smuggling weapons, and plan a common security system.

As many of us feared, terrorism spiked as soon as the ink dried on Oslo. In the 1980s, during the Intifada, terrorist attacks, including a suicide bombing carried out by Islamic Jihad, were sporadic. Hamas, until the late 1980s what seemed to be an Islamic charity, set out to derail Oslo by murdering Israeli civilians. In a 1993 attack near Beit El, Hamas bomb maker Yahya Ayyash packed explosives into a Volkswagen van, wounding eight of our soldiers.

Whatever halfhearted measures Arafat took to keep a lid on Islamic terror disappeared altogether in February 1994 when the American-born settler Dr. Baruch Goldstein, graduate of the Albert Einstein College of Medicine, revenged Palestinian terror attacks around Hebron by emptying the magazine of his government-issued Galil rifle into the kneeling bodies of Muslims during Friday prayers in the Cave of the Patriarchs in Hebron. Twenty-nine were killed and 125 wounded. The slaughter took place on Purim, the Jewish Halloween celebrating evil Haman's destruction. Goldstein's intention was partly revenge for Hamas terror; mainly, he wanted to end Oslo by triggering a religious war.

Hamas at once lashed out at Arafat, burning him in effigy in a dozen refugee camps that were its strongholds. A slew of Hamas suicide revenge attacks followed in the late summer and early fall, culminating in a massacre on Dizengoff Street in Tel Aviv. An unemployed man from Gaza boarded a bus and detonated the suicide belt strapped around his waist, killing twenty-two Israelis and injuring fifty more, the first successful suicide attack in Tel Aviv. In all nearly forty Israelis died at the hands of Hamas in 1994. Not since the War of Independence had so many Israeli civilians died in terror attacks. Like every other Israeli, each time the phone rang I was terrified I'd learn that one of my kids or Biba was a victim.

In late 1994, I was with Ehud Barak in Rabin's bare upstairs office in the Ministry of Defense in Tel Aviv, wrapping up a discussion of Israel's long-term security. I pushed the navy's position, which was for a modern submarine fleet capable of projecting Israeli power and deterrence regionally. Barak didn't agree. He thought we needed greater land defenses, while I countered that our main enemies weren't going to crash through our borders in tanks. In the end Rabin came down on the side of the navy.

After the discussion the prime minister asked to see me alone. Barak nodded before shutting the door behind him. I was standing at attention with my hands behind my back and Rabin, less than a year before his murder, told me to take a seat.

"Coffee?"

I nodded. Rabin poured out two cups, lit up a cigarette, and cut to the chase. "Ami. I'd like you to take over the Shin Bet."

"Excuse me, sir?" Amazingly, I avoided spitting up my drink.

"Listen, you've completed your stint as commander of the navy, and the issue of the submarines has been settled. I need you at the Shin Bet." He tapped ashes into his empty coffee cup while waiting for my response.

I sat there too stunned to respond. This was nothing like Barak calling me in the middle of the night to offer me a post for which I'd been preparing my entire career. To ask someone like me to command the Shabak made so little sense that I didn't know what to say.

"Just think about it, Ami," Rabin said.

Rabin didn't need to explain why the Shin Bet needed fresh blood. In the year and a half since he had pumped Arafat's hand in the White House Rose Garden, a legion of demons had descended upon the Land of Israel in the form of Hamas and Islamic Jihad on the Palestinian side, and Baruch Goldstein on ours.

Rabin didn't blame Arafat for the bus bombing and was determined to pursue peace "as if there is no terror" and to "fight terror as if there is no peace process." But his approach proved to be a double mistake: he failed to present Arafat with the ultimatum that if he didn't put up a serious fight against terror, there would be no peace process. At the same time, Rabin's strategy swelled the ranks of our right wing, especially the settlers, who now numbered a quarter million. A photo montage at an anti-Oslo rally featured Arafat's keffiyeh wrapped around Rabin's forehead. A different placard had Rabin wearing a Nazi uniform and a swastika armband. "With blood and fire, we will expel Rabin," young toughs chanted, their fists lifted in defiance. Settler newspapers likened Rabin's partnership with Arafat to Marshal Pétain's collaboration with Hitler. At one rally, the young politician Benjamin Netanyahu, joined by Ariel Sharon, looked on without comment as crowds carried a coffin on their shoulders and chanted for two hours, "Death to Rabin."

With the Shin Bet failing to stop the worst outbreak of terrorism in Israel's history, Rabin needed someone new at the helm, an outsider who could shake up the agency.

I sat stone-faced, fidgeting in my chair, my palms clammy. *Why me?*

We remained silent for God knows how long — maybe a minute. *There's no way*, I was thinking. I knew enough about the Shabak to know that as its director you're deployed not at sea, but down a sewer. I still operated largely in a simple world of friend or foe. Putting a bullet through a hostile adversary in a uniform was a very different thing from hauling a blindfolded shopkeeper, or a kid, into a cell to extract information, either through finesse or under duress. In those days of mass protests against Oslo, the job would also require spying on fellow Jews. I had read Orwell as a kid and had no appetite for playing Big Brother.

"Mr. Prime Minister," I finally said, looking him directly in the eyes. "Thank you for your confidence. I just don't think I'm the right man for the job."

Rabin nodded, stubbing out his cigarette.

One year and a slew of terrorist attacks later, at the US Naval War College in Newport, Rhode Island, I was so lost in thought, staring out French doors at Narragansett Bay, that I didn't even notice the approach of the marine attaché at the Israeli embassy, his footsteps pounding the floor with a military cadence.

I was in a cheerful mood that Indian summer afternoon of November 4, 1995. It was the day before the opening of the International Seapower Symposium, the biggest gathering of the heads of the world's navies. I was proud to represent Israel in this exclusive fraternity of admirals. The American chief of naval operations, Admiral Mike Boorda, the first Jew to reach such heights inside the US Navy, in his double-breasted uniform with gold stripes on the sleeves, had invited me to the symposium. Some years back, when Mike was a US Navy commander, he visited Israel and I was his host. We'd struck up a friendship. Seamen, both fictional and real, from Odysseus and Captain Ahab to Admiral Nelson and the Florentine explorer Giovanni da Verrazzano, who first sailed into Narragansett Bay in 1524, share a certain stoicism that comes from facing the primal elements of nature.

The marine attaché was about to remind me that being an Israeli is like sitting on a ship knowing a torpedo was about to strike, just not from which direction.

"Admiral," the marine attaché said with uncharacteristic formality for an Israeli. He grabbed my shoulder and I swung around to see him, tall and strapping in his crisp blue suit. With his pale face and shaky voice, there was a grim-reaper air about him. He had once been the captain of a missile ship under my command. I felt my stomach knot up.

"Yes, what is it?"

"The prime minister has been hit in a terrorist attack."

"Rabin?" *Did a Palestinian terrorist get to Rabin?* I asked myself.

"Word just came that he has been shot."

"What the hell are you talking about?"

"At the peace rally in Tel Aviv."

"Rabin . . . shot?"

"Sir, he was pronounced dead a few minutes ago."

I froze, my jaw agape. In the military you grow so accustomed to the dark art of war that you can stand tearless next to the grave of a friend or light up a cigarette after stepping over the body of an enemy. But the violent death of a prime minister tore me from my moorings. Still today I can feel the way my eyes widened, my skin tingled, and my hand involuntarily moved to my chest.

"Shot!" I stammered, stumbling backward.

I regained my balance. "Hamas?" I asked him. "Islamic Jihad?" A crazed Islamist, camouflaged as a peacenik, must have somehow slipped through Rabin's security detail. A terrorist penetrating Israeli security would have been a catastrophic failure for the Shin

Bet, the agency that, among other things, is responsible for protecting the prime minister.

"Sir," he said, shaking his head. "The killer wasn't a Palestinian; he was a Jew."

"A Jew?"

"An Israeli Jew."

"What the fuck," I murmured to myself. The idea that a fellow countryman could pull a trigger on our prime minister had frankly never entered my mind. Of course, I knew Jews were capable of terror: In the early 1980s members of the Jewish underground had tried to assassinate mayors of Palestinian cities, had killed Palestinian students at Hebron University, and had plans to plant bombs on Arab buses. Another of their schemes was to blow up mosques on the Temple Mount. But such terrorists in my mind belonged to a lunatic fringe, *and* they targeted Arabs, not Jews.

I canceled the meeting I had scheduled with Admiral Boorda for later that afternoon and rushed by embassy car to JFK Airport to catch the next New York–Tel Aviv flight. A sleepless night on the plane gave me plenty of time to ponder the unthinkable.

13

BUS LINE 18

In his cell Rabin's assassin, Yigal Amir, the fine-boned Israeli-born son of a kosher butcher of Yemeni heritage who had served as a combat soldier in the Golani Brigades and studied law at the Bar-Ilan University Faculty of Law, asked the police guards for a glass of schnapps to toast his deed. From his perspective, killing Rabin, which *The New Yorker* called one of "history's most effective political murders," was cause for celebration.

Amir had been present at the funeral of Baruch Goldstein, the doctor who gunned down Muslims in Hebron, and had vowed in writing to undertake the radical surgery needed to prevent the loss of Israeli control over Judea and Samaria. He based his decision on the ancient theological principle of *din rodef*, the "law of the pursuer," that condemns to death anyone classified as a "pursuer." In Amir's twisted mind and the mind of extremist rabbis, *din rodef* applied to Rabin because the Oslo agreement involved handing over parts of the Land of Israel to terrorists who would then kill Jews.

The Shabak had all this on file but still failed to stop the man agents dismissed as "a little Yemenite who said in the restroom that he would murder Rabin."

I didn't yet know any such details. But newspaper accounts of settlers offering up prayers of thanks for Rabin's murder while millions of Israelis, including settlers, lit candles in memory of their martyred leader made clear just how divided the country was. I had always assumed Israel, like ancient Israel, or Sparta, was a society united behind a settler-warrior class motivated not by greed or self-interest but by our nation's shared ideals. Despite the divisions that only deepened year after year since 1967, it never entered my mind that a Jew could murder a prime minister.

It was only now, for the first time, I understood that our country was made up of competing tribes. Nor were we kibbutzniks, the reincarnated Maccabees who served in the elite units and settled the most exposed and dangerous lands, any longer the vanguard. Israel had changed and was now an apocalyptic place splintered into warring factions.

Rabin's funeral in Jerusalem brought the world's heads of state to Israel, including President Clinton and former head of the Soviet Union Mikhail Gorbachev. As commander of the navy I drove to the home of Rabin's widow, Leah, in Tel Aviv to offer my condolences during the shiva, the traditional weeklong period of mourning. While I was there Arafat turned up in his green field uniform. Out of respect, he left his "freedom fighter's gun" back in Ramallah and removed his keffiyeh. With his bald head the ex-terrorist looked small and harmless, like a retired postal worker. Teary-eyed, he said to Leah of her dead husband, "He was a hero of peace, and he was my friend." Underneath Arafat's multiple masks — revolutionary, gangster, nation-builder — was apparently an emotional man.

"My husband," she replied, "regarded you as his partner in peace."

Meanwhile my retirement from the navy was in less than two months, and I had no idea what I'd do next. What I didn't want to do was become an arms dealer or military adviser to some junta leader in Africa or Latin America like so many other retired officers; in fact, I wanted to get away from the military altogether. By temperament, I'd never fit comfortably into the hierarchies and conformity of military life, and I'm not the type to relive my glory days by donning the old uniform for parades and reunions. I had been in the war business long enough to prefer my family, or for that matter porpoises and dolphins and other creatures of the sea, over men with weapons. So on January 1, 1996, I packed up the uniform, stuck my citations in a shoebox, and replaced my khakis with a pair of jeans and a T-shirt. I could finally be a good husband and father and join Biba in walking the dogs and pruning our olive trees and reading books about scuba diving in the Seychelles.

This sublime freedom lasted precisely one week.

At around ten in the evening, I got a phone call from Avi Gil, a friend I first met when we studied at the Kennedy School together and one of the negotiators of the Oslo Accords.[17] In those days Avi was the director general of the Prime Minister's Office, which meant he worked for Shimon Peres, who had taken over from the murdered Rabin and served as interim prime minister until new elections slated for the end of May. Like Truman after Roosevelt's death, or LBJ after Kennedy's, he was the man in charge. Peres had already ordered the IDF to withdraw from Nablus, in keeping with the terms of the Oslo Accords. While Palestinians already controlled Jericho and parts of Gaza, handing over Nablus was fraught with risks: The Tomb of Yosef, a Jewish holy site, was located in the center of the city, and the refugee camps surrounding Nablus were Hamas hotbeds and launching pads for suicide bombers.

From Avi's tone of voice, I braced myself for something unpleasant. "What's up?" I asked.

"Ami, Peres wants to talk to you."

"Peres?

"That's right. The prime minister."

"Talk to me about what?"

"You'll find out once you get here."

"First thing in the morning."

"Come now."

"Now?"

"Now."

No longer having the use of a government driver, I hopped in the car and sped off. On the steep uphill drive to Jerusalem, I tried not to speculate on the reasons for the summons. Whatever it was, I sensed it wouldn't square with my newfound freedom.

Avi was waiting with the acting prime minister at the official residency of the foreign minister, where Peres was still living, the shelves of which were filled with books in the variety of languages the polyglot Peres spoke. Peres, who belonged more to my father's generation than mine, had a long and checkered career. Before becoming a driving force behind Oslo, he had been a major backer of the settlement movement within the Labor Party. The architect of what he called a "new Middle East" was now scared. As a fifty-year veteran of Israeli politics, he knew the suicide bombings that continued apace would play into the hands of those opposing peace, which was the reason for the summons. He began by telling me that the head of the Shabak had resigned out of a sense of responsibility for the slack security that had enabled Yigal Amir to kill Rabin. He then repeated nearly word for word what Rabin had asked me a year earlier about taking over the Shabak. Peres was well aware of the main objection I raised when Rabin offered the job — why me? — and had an answer prepared. The Service needed a different mind-set, he said, someone who could see Palestinians as not just terrorists but also partners in the political process. It needed an outsider like me.

With the Shabak reeling from its failure to protect both the prime minister and Israeli civilians from terrorism, this time around I felt it was my duty to accept.

"Mr. Prime Minister," I said in the most solemn voice of my life. "I'll need to ask my family. Can you give me twenty-four hours to decide?"

"Of course. Take a day."

It was still dark out when I returned to Kerem Maharal. Biba was waiting up, and our three sons were asleep. One by one I woke them and asked them to meet me down in the kitchen. As I brewed a pot of tea and listened to my sons' footsteps on the stairs, my heart ached. I wanted more than anything to become a family man for the first time in my life. But I knew I couldn't.

Once everyone had a hot drink in their hand, I told them about Peres's request.

Biba, with the same stoic spirit she displayed when I would disappear for long missions at sea, said she would support whatever decision I made. My youngest son, Roy, not yet in high school, was nodding off — he just wanted to get back to bed. The only thing that bothered him about the job offer was that we might have to cancel a ski trip we had planned.

My attention turned to our oldest son, Nir, just finishing up his four years in Shaldag, a top-secret air force commando unit. "Forget it, Abba," he said, a hint of bitterness in his voice. "It's like you've just crawled into your tent after finishing a forty-mile march with all the gear on your back, and now they ask you to get up and set off on another mission. Tell Peres to find a different sucker."

Our second son, Guy, months away from beginning his own military service, piped up with an emphatic counterargument to his brother's. "*They*," he said in a voice that seemed to come from deep inside his gut, "*they* murdered Rabin." He didn't say who he meant by "they," but it was clear to me that "they" were all the Jewish and Palestinian terrorists determined to destroy a better future for both peoples. "Abba, you can't allow *them* to get away with it. Abba, you have no choice." I felt the same way.

Although I was already retired from the navy, I needed a month to tie up loose ends there. As a parting gift from the chief of staff, I was presented with the 9mm Browning pistol a Fatah terrorist once pointed at my head during the takeover of his ship in the open sea. For some mysterious reason, he didn't pull the trigger.

Preparing for the new post was a process fraught with the uneasy sensation that I no longer understood my own country. How could someone raised to believe that we, not God, led ourselves out of captivity in Egypt understand religious Jews interpreting Rabin's murder as an act of divine intervention?

Following a tradition dating back to the 1940s within the Shabak — sometimes referred to as the Service — my code name was supposed to be my first initial, in my case the Hebrew letter alef. The only reason I didn't become Alef, and hence maintain my privacy and that of my family, was that several Israeli newspapers bypassed the censors and published my name in an announcement of my nomination to the post. Within an hour a stream of photographers stood on the street outside our home waiting for me to show my face.[18] Biba called out from the living room that there was someone on the phone.

"Who is it?"

"How should I know?" she snapped. She was still fuming about the plague of paparazzi across the street.

"Ami here."

The man on the other end introduced himself as Noam Livnat. His sister, Limor Livnat, was a well-known Likud political leader. Livnat, who lived in the settlement of Yitzhar, was a self-declared "radical right-wing messianist" and a follower of Rabbi Ginsburgh.[19] Yigal Amir was an avid admirer of his. He asked if we could speak "before the Shin Bet brainwashes you about us." I figured I had nothing to lose, and possibly something to gain, by sitting down with a member of a community I would soon be tasked with infiltrating.

Right after hanging up, I got a second call, someone from the Shin Bet who asked me not to leave the house or to talk to strangers on the phone. "Sure," I said. I knew immediately that my conversation with Livnat had been tapped.

For years I had been the absentee husband and father who occasionally walked his dog at daybreak. With my name made public, people in the grocery store across the street looked at me sideways. Now I was the man standing between them and terror. Quite different stares hit me at the vegetable stand in the neighboring Arab town of Fureidis. Opinion polls among Israeli Arabs showed that for them the Shin Bet was like the East German Stasi — an instrument of state terror.

I was so conspicuous that after Biba refused to have a bodyguard posted in front of our house, the government insisted on building a high white fence around the yard to create a closed compound. An agent turned up one day to give us instructions on how to open and close the gate. We weren't supposed to get our own mail from the mailbox or walk outside to scoop up the morning edition of *Haaretz*. Makeup artists instructed me on how to go incognito; to this day I've held on to the box of wigs, glasses, makeup, fake beards, and ridiculous hats I used while on the job.

I met Livnat at one of the roadside cafés along the Tel Aviv–Haifa highway. The man was tall, with inky-black eyes and a bushy reddish-brown beard. He wore the standard Orthodox uniform of a knitted kippah, dark slacks, and a white button-down shirt with tzitzit — prayer strings — peeking out below the hem. Sitting in a wheelchair, he pushed himself to my table in the back of the restaurant. He conspicuously lacked the pistol many settlers carry.

As Livnat spoke it became clear immediately that he had asked for the informal chat out of concern the Shabak would unleash its vengeance against settlers. I made a point of locking my eyes on him, listening respectfully to what I considered dangerous nonsense. He told me there were two Shin Bets, the good one that fought the Arabs, and the bad one that persecuted him and his fellow believers doing God's work. He seemed to think I was about to start dropping black hoods over the heads of thousands of fellow Jews and dragging them into interrogation rooms.

Livnat told me I should reserve the dungeons for the Arabs. "As a Jew, your job is to defend us against *them*."

Reading about settlers and their mind-set was one thing; sitting across the table from someone who truly believed that God had given him power over Arabs was something entirely different. It was the first time I had ever heard anyone defend what can only be described as apartheid: two sets of laws, rules, and standards, and two infrastructures. If Arabs behaved themselves and acquiesced to our dominion, we'd allow them access to water and a bit of electricity. The fact that we hadn't yet driven them over the Jordanian border was, to his mind, a sign of our benevolence.

"*Hold on a second*," I told Livnat, though I wasn't sure it was worth trying to talk sense into him. "My job is to stop people, Jews as much as Arabs, from committing violence." I also threw in some comments about international law and basic morality. He wasn't at all happy with my refusal to go along with the idea that a thumb belonged on the cosmic scale tipping the balance in favor of the Jews because, according to God and history, the Land of Israel belonged to us.

Days before my nocturnal meeting with Prime Minister Peres about taking the Shin Bet job, our agents booby-trapped a cell phone used by Yahya Ayyash with three ounces of explosives. The so-called Engineer was one of the founders of Hamas's underground Izz ad-Din al-Qassam Brigades and responsible for the deaths of about a hundred Israelis in terrorist attacks. Blowing off his head was my predecessor's swan song.

During the swearing-in ceremony, all I could think about were Hamas's inevitable plans to avenge the attack. I was so on edge that when President Ezer Weizman ribbed me, joking that it was the first time he'd ever seen me in a jacket and tie, I could barely muster a chuckle.

Also humbling was how little I understood about the Shabak. To quote Avigdor Feldman, the human rights lawyer who took the Shabak to court in 1999 for torturing prisoners: "In the interrogation facility, the Shin Bet is king, and no one, not the Prison Service and not the Israeli Police, is allowed in without permission from the Shin Bet person in charge." What was true for an interrogation facility was even more so for the organization as a whole. Every other director had risen up through the ranks. Until now, it had been a closed network, its secrets jealously guarded. I was an alien, an outsider hired to be a change agent.

On the first day of my service, a Friday, I convened all the division heads at Shin Bet headquarters in northern Tel Aviv. I'd met only a couple of members of the senior command, all of whom were men, during joint military operations with the navy. By this point I had pored over the history of the Service. While I understood that our interrogators and handlers weren't by default sadistic bone-breakers but in fact highly trained professionals, they had also been trained to work in what I came to call the sewer — the shadow world of terror groups — where anything goes. "In the war against terror," Avraham Shalom, my predecessor at the Shin Bet, declared in *The Gatekeepers*, "forget about morality."[20]

Reading about some of our past misdeeds made my skin crawl, even if we wore kid gloves when compared with similar organizations in the United States, France, and England.

I opened the staff meeting by telling those present the truth as I saw it. "Gentlemen," I said, "I do not know this organization. I don't know how to recruit agents, and I don't have a clue how to gather intelligence. But paradoxically, I am responsible for everything that happens here, and all of us will have to work together to bridge the gap between my lack of knowledge and experience and the degree of responsibility I have. If you think I am wrong about something, I want you to tell me.

"But old strategies have failed," I continued. We were no longer fighting the PLO, I reminded them, stating the obvious: Our enemy was now Islamic terrorists.

More specifically, to prevent Hamas from murdering Israeli civilians, we needed to infiltrate its military wing, the Qassam Brigades. Our failure until then was the consequence, I was convinced, of not having the right sensors. "So we'll examine everything: the methods of intelligence collection, the methods of recruitment, the methods of prevention. We'll question every single convention and axiom. What works, we'll keep; what doesn't, we'll ditch. The one thing I'm not willing to hear," I went on, "is, *This is the way we've always done things*. We will turn over every stone in this organization. We may find out at the end of the process that most of the stones are where they should be, but the house will look different."

I concluded my remarks by reminding the men sitting upright and alert in their seats that Israeli lives, and the fate of the peace process, depended on us doing our jobs.

Three days later, shortly after six in the morning, I waited behind the white fence surrounding our house — it was forbidden for me to wait outside on the street — for the driver to pick me up and whisk me off to Tel Aviv. With one ear I listened to the army radio station while my thoughts turned to the work I would need to do. The fact that a Jew had gunned down Rabin meant I had to pay a lot more attention to Jewish terrorism than my predecessors had, not a pleasant prospect given that Hamas posed as great a threat as ever. In all my years in Flotilla 13 hunting down PLO guerrillas I never could have imagined that one day I'd be tapping settlers' phones. For years I had seen in settlers the continuation of my parents' Zionism, and now here I was seeding their groups with informants.

At around 6:45 on my way to Tel Aviv, I was about to make a phone call when a news alert of a suicide bomb attack came over the radio. "Hold on a second," I told the driver, who pulled over to the side of the road. The target had been the Egged Line 18 bus on Jaffa Road in Jerusalem. Since the end of the nineteenth century, Jaffa Road has been one of Jerusalem's busiest arteries, with shops, falafel stands, cafés, the bus station, and the Mahane Yehuda vegetable market.

"Jerusalem," I told the driver, who flipped on the siren and flashing lights and sped up the steep mountain highway. Even with sirens blaring, we made slow progress through the heavy traffic. Rusted brown half-tracks from the 1948 War of Independence sat along the side of the road. Beyond those, just over the forested hills, was Tel Gezer, the supposed site of Joshua's decisive battle against the Canaanite king Horam of Gezer.

Once in the city, we raced down Jaffa Road past lines of cars blocked by police and crowds of Israelis. I jumped out of the car into a scene of carnage. Smoke billowed from the roof of the scorched bus, peeled away by the blast. The dead and wounded had already been cleared from the scene, which was still drenched with blood. One dazed man on the street later told a journalist: "It was like entering the gates of hell."

My team was now tasked with identifying the murderers of twenty-four people; two more died from their wounds within days. From the charred head and ID card collected at the scene, police forensics experts working with us determined the bomber to be Ibrahim Farahneh, a nineteen-year-old from the al-Fawwar refugee camp near Hebron, a kid dispatched by Hamas, whose charter declared at the time, "Israel will exist and will continue to exist until Islam will obliterate it."

Survivors recalled that Farahneh, wearing jeans, a T-shirt, and a baseball cap — an outfit bought in the market on Selah a-Din Street in East Jerusalem to make him look like a student — had sat quietly in the back of the bus holding a black duffel bag on his lap. Just as the Line 18 bus approached the central station, he sprang to his feet, shouted *Allahu akbar* — God is great — and pressed the button attached to the strap of his backpack to detonate twenty pounds of explosives.

It was our job to penetrate and uproot the Hamas terror network, a daunting challenge because Hamas, like insurgent groups from the Vietcong to the Algerian FLN, was organized into cells. Because most individual members of a cell didn't know the identity of the people pulling the strings, there was no way to track an individual bomber, dead or alive, back to the mastermind.

What added to the challenge was that, until the beginning of Oslo, most terrorists belonged to Fatah, the Palestinian Islamic Jihad, or the Popular Front. Hamas, a marginal charity, wasn't on our radar, and we had almost no agents inside the organization. We lacked the requisite sensors to detect the activity below the surface — in basements, garages, and mosques. It would be our job to develop them, a process I knew would take months if not years.

Within a couple of days we received information pointing us to a Hamas student group at a teachers' college in Ramallah, whose members had been recruited from a mosque in the al-Fawwar refugee camp just south of Hebron. Our information also told us that the same cell behind the Mahane Yehuda bombing was planning further attacks, and soon. The operational plan that ended up on my desk was to capture the students on Friday when they returned home to the village of al-Fawwar near Jerusalem.

But the terrorists didn't go home that Friday.

On Sunday, a week after the first attack, I was once again in the backseat of the government car on my way to Shin Bet headquarters when I heard the radio report of a fresh attack on another Line 18 bus in Jerusalem. This time a young suicide bomber murdered nineteen civilians near the Generali Building on Jaffa Road.

On the way to Jerusalem, between telephone calls, I felt to my bones that one of the students from the teachers' college had carried out the bombing. We had all the intelligence we needed to pull them out of their classroom in Ramallah, but we hadn't acted fast enough. This, my first major failure as director of the Service, made me dizzy with frustration. I'd had lost friends in combat, I'd lost fighters under my command, but never had I felt such a deep sense of failure.

Back at Shin Bet headquarters, I asked my team why we had failed to scoop up the students before they could act. The answer they gave me was that there hadn't been enough time to plan an operation and capture them inside the college before Friday. Typically, they said, launching an operation required several days of planning, from putting the team together to consulting various experts, and so on.

"Stop!" I insisted, slapping my hand on a nearby table. "I don't know how to recruit agents and gather intelligence," I fumed, "but I know operations. That's what I did for thirty years. To tell me that twenty-four hours isn't enough time to plan this kind of operation is bullshit." In the commandos, if we could receive information on a terrorist cell on Tuesday, and by Wednesday put a bullet through someone's head in a terrorist camp in northern Lebanon, why couldn't the Shabak, an organization with a hundred times the resources, arrest a couple of kids in the same amount of time?

My recriminations came as a shock to people accustomed to seeing themselves as the blue bloods of the Israeli security system. But too much was at stake for me to care about their feelings.

It seemed as if the eyes of the entire country were on me. The next day, which was Purim, I was summoned to appear before the Knesset's Foreign Affairs and Defense Committee to give a report. How could I guarantee an end to such atrocities? Why hadn't I already arrested or killed the terrorists?

At a cabinet meeting of the government ministers I was again asked when the attacks would end. My frank response, based on intelligence reports I'd been reading deep into the night and on my intuition, was that I could not guarantee that there weren't dozens of suicide bombers on their way to explode in the streets of Israel.

My gut had been right. While on my way back from Jerusalem, I received news of a fresh attack at a crosswalk outside of Dizengoff

Center in Tel Aviv. A suicide bomber sent by Fathi Shikaki's terror group, wearing a twenty-kilogram explosive belt packed with nails, killed 13 civilians and wounded 125, some severely. Many of those killed were girls in Purim costumes. I would later learn that Bat-Chen Shahak, the daughter of my friend Zvika, a decorated soldier who'd finished an officer's course with me and who fought under my command during the Yom Kippur War, was among the dead. It was her fifteenth birthday. Just as with the Jerusalem attacks, I raced to the Dizengoff Center to meet the survivors in person.

That July, on the Beit Shemesh–Beit Guvrin road, close to the old cease-fire line between Jordan and Israel, terrorists began opening fire on passing cars, killing thirteen Israelis in a series of sniper attacks. Our agents traced the attacks to an Islamic Jihad cell from the village of Beit Zurif. Our people were right about the village, but we were watching the wrong terrorists. Hamas, not Islamic Jihad, had carried out the killings. We were still not smart enough.

When I asked the department heads about this intelligence failure, and how we could correct it in the future, one fellow referred me to the "files." "Everything," he said, was in the "files."

"Where are these files?" I snapped. "Show them to me."

An embarrassed silence filled the room. As in a Kafka story, we went down corridors, descended several flights of stairs, and finally entered a cavernous room filled to the ceiling with large cabinets jammed with cardboard binders. I couldn't believe my eyes. Each time an agent met with an informant, the information would be duly typed up and filed away. Even if our mountains of inert files contained potentially useful intelligence on quick, highly adaptive, and disciplined terrorists, we'd never find it in time to prevent tomorrow's bus bombing. The Shabak seemed to be stuck in the Dark Ages. To quote Yuval Diskin, the man I appointed to direct counterintelligence for the West Bank, the Shabak had plenty of "muscle" and an "underdeveloped brain."

Part of the problem was that most of the files were filled with materials on Arafat's secular PLO supporters, not on the hundreds of teenagers waiting in line to strap on a suicide belt for the sake of Islam. Even if our mountains of dusty files contained potentially useful intelligence on militants, we'd never find it in time to prevent the next bus bombing.

I decided that this was the moment to put our operational capabilities on a radically new footing, an especially urgent task because fresh attacks kept coming. Looking back, I can say that that decision led to a dramatic shift in the Shin Bet's approach to information. Information, hitherto often lost in rooms of files, became a vital part of its operational decision-making process. We went from being a muscular organization to a thinking organization, a smart organization.

14

ENTERING THE SEWER AND FINDING A PARTNER

Sitting in my office late at night, I'd often pick up a piece of shrapnel from a suicide bombing to remind myself why I was spending so much time away from Biba and our boys. In the case of the first Line 18 attack on Jaffa Street, the explosive began as a buried ordnance in the Sinai Desert, an unexploded shell from the Yom Kippur War. Someone who knew what he was doing dismantled it, extracted its explosives, and gave it to smugglers to carry into a West Bank refugee camp. There, in a back room, a student from the engineering college who should have been devising technologies to enhance life packed ball bearings into a suicide vest. Who were the masterminds behind these cells, and what were they after besides revenge for our killing of the Engineer? Surely they realized that exploding buses would never drive us out of the Land of Israel.

In the commandos and later in the navy, I knew nothing about the people I killed, nor did I have to. They were merely targets. In the Shabak, I no longer had this luxury. To defeat the enemy, I had to know everything about him, including the source of the pain behind his hatred. To understand the mind-set of terrorists, I had to study their context — their families' stories, who their neighbors were, the people with whom they prayed in the mosque. Was his, and sometimes her, brother or uncle in one of our prisons? Had a friend been killed by us? None of this meant, of course, I had to identify with their beliefs. But to design an effective counterterrorism strategy I had to learn and understand.

Many of these human kamikazes, I discovered, came from families who became refugees in 1948. The family of Ibrahim Farahneh, who exploded himself on Bus Line 18, originally came from 'Ajjur, a village we demolished to make room for Jewish immigrants from Iraq after our War of Independence.

In my first two weeks on the job as head of the Shabak, fifty-nine Israeli civilians had died and more than two hundred had been wounded in suicide attacks and shootings, most at the hands of Hamas. With the country under siege, Prime Minister Peres summoned me to his office on Balfour Street, on the opposite side of Jerusalem from the holy graves and hallowed stones of the Old City. I knew Peres would grill me to find out what I was going to do about it.

When I entered his office at the Office of the Prime Minister, my nerves on edge from too much caffeine, Peres rose to greet me. He reminded me of my father and my uncle Jonah, both of whom he knew well from his time as a member of Kibbutz Alumot, which overlooks the Sea of Galilee. Peres was a statesman and a smooth talker, European to the bone. On that day he was also keenly aware of the abyss over which he dangled. Oslo had been his initiative. Rabin, who had supported the process, had been murdered, and now Israelis were being slaughtered by the dozens. Opinion polls showed the Likud's Bibi Netanyahu and national-religious parties to the right gaining in popularity. If Peres couldn't stop the attacks, fearful voters would give his job to a right-winger who promised he could.

After a few pleasantries about how glad he was to have me on his team, the prime minister got down to business. Who on our side was responsible for failing to prevent the attacks?

"I am, Mr. Prime Minister." By this I meant that as director of the organization responsible for preventing terrorist attacks, I was personally to blame for our failure to do so.

"How can we stop these attacks?" he asked.

"How? We'll have to start by putting the Shabak on new footing." We had entered a new era — in terms of politics, technology, and security — but the Shabak was stuck in the past. The Oslo Accords had made Fatah, the old enemy, into a partner. Our new enemies were the Islamist groups, primarily Hamas, hitherto a religious social movement without national political aspirations, which, in response to our occupation, crafted a fundamentalist religious nationalism and was now leading the wave of terrorist attacks, and the Palestinian Islamic Jihad, which, despite suffering a debilitating blow with the death of its leader Shikaki in Malta, remained a threat.

To defeat these enemies, we had to rebuild the Shabak from the ground up. And since there wasn't time to hire and train an entire new staff, we had to do so with the same people. It was like tearing down one building and using the old stones to build another one. Thankfully, we were working with deeply committed, well-trained professionals who understood the stakes.

Peres promised a blank check from the government. *Money is no object*, was the message. *Do what it takes.*

I thanked him for his support before explaining that money wouldn't be enough. "Ultimately, ending terrorism depends on politics." I quoted Chief of Staff Dan Shomron, who at the beginning of the First Intifada told our politicians that Palestinian terrorism wasn't a military phenomenon and as such the army couldn't defeat it. All the army could do was fight back the flames to create breathing room for the politicians to launch a political process.

"To hunt down the terrorists, we are also going to need Arafat," I added with a grimace, because such a thought violated decades of Israel's sacrosanct rely-on-no-one-but-ourselves military doctrine.

This, of course, was the logic of Oslo and explicit in Rabin's handshake with Arafat. But Arafat wasn't doing nearly enough, in part because he lacked motivation. Rabin's policy to pursue terrorists as if there was no peace process, and the peace process as if there was no terror, meant that Arafat paid no political price for the ongoing terrorist attacks. Our advice at the Shabak to the prime minister was to drop this approach and press Arafat's back to the wall.

In a few weeks, per Oslo, we were supposed to hand over control of the Arab neighborhood of Abu Sneina in Hebron to the Palestinian Authority, or PA for short. Arafat would become responsible for the security of this liberated area. I advised the prime minister to tell Arafat he wouldn't get that part of Hebron, or anything else, unless he worked with us. To make my point, I reminded him of the story of the *Altalena*, a ship owned by the Jewish paramilitary group Irgun during the War of Independence. In June 1948, Ben-Gurion ordered the IDF to sink the ship, in order to enforce his policy of there being only one Jewish army. "Arafat has to do an *Altalena*," I said. Arafat, who shared the Nobel Prize for Peace with Rabin, needed to crack down on terror, even if it meant going after Palestinian militias.

Peres nodded.

Although I was new to my job, my ill-fated jeep trip to the Gaza refugee camp years earlier taught me that we couldn't defeat those who oppose us with tanks or interrogation rooms. Despite our military might, we would never completely crush Hamas on our own. In the end only Arafat could defeat Hamas, because almost all Palestinians still lined up behind his vision of national independence. So if the PA worked with us to fight Hamas, we couldn't stop at Abu Sneina. We'd have to follow through on the terms of Oslo and withdraw from over 90 percent of the Occupied Territories.

With no end in sight to the bombings, the prime minister took the Shabak's advice into his first meeting with Arafat and gave him an ultimatum: "We can't continue like this. If you want a political process, you have to create security." He put off the withdrawal of Abu Sneina until Arafat proved his seriousness in fighting terror.

Around this time I got a late-night phone call from Yossi Ginossar, a former top officer in the Shabak who had become a businessman on such good terms with Arafat that he served as his secret emissary to Peres. The prime minister's message to Arafat obviously had gotten through because Yossi told me the chairman wanted to pass on to me some highly sensitive intelligence, and that it couldn't wait until morning. I had to come to Gaza right away because Arafat, an outlaw on the run most of his life, preferred to work in the dark.[21]

Upon my arrival at the Erez checkpoint, the Israeli entrance to Gaza, at 3:00 AM, Arafat's Presidential Guard, former gunmen I had once stalked from Tripoli to Tunis, spirited me off to the Presidential Palace. Upstairs in his office Arafat sat behind what looked like a poker table. The lightbulb hanging from a wire must have been a ten-watt job because the office was shrouded in shadows. A spare field jacket hung from a hook, and a few books were stacked on a shelf. A pistol weighed down a stack of papers. On the wall was the red-and-black PLO emblem with two swords crossed over the Al Aqsa Mosque in Jerusalem — the monument Arafat had been promising his people, and himself, that he would by gun or by olive branch snatch back from us.

The chairman, stirring honey into a cup of tea, sized me up with his bulbous dark-brown eyes. He then stood and gave me a surprisingly limp handshake — I had expected something more vigorous from the Palestinian Castro.

"Sit, sit, sit," he said in his thickly accented English. With a snap of his fingers, Arafat summoned platters of food, which he then piled onto my plate. The kind of intimacy he showed made me squirm in my seat, and I steeled myself against the hypnotic charm he famously exerted. Standing in the back of the room was Mohammed Dahlan, Arafat's strongman in Gaza. It was the first time I'd set eyes on him.

We ate and drank for an hour before Arafat, with exaggerated theatrical effect, spoke vaguely about some Hamas attack without providing details. The performance was a ruse; he was, in fact, sizing me up. I left Gaza that night without the top-secret intelligence I'd supposedly been summoned to procure. But I understood his message, which I assumed was meant for Peres: that he was acting determinedly against Hamas and the Islamic Jihad military underground.

Following this strange face-to-face with Arafat, I had to establish effective cooperation with the Palestinian security forces, led by Dahlan in Gaza and Colonel Jibril Rajoub in the West Bank, which were at that time just being established. Because of the bad blood between most of our people and most of theirs, I had to make sure my relationship with Dahlan and Jibril operated at a personal and not just formal institutional level.

Playing on the kibbutz grass in 1947 with Srulik (Israel Guttman). *Courtesy of Ami Ayalon.*

Yitzhak Ayalon and Jonah Rosen, around the time they served as successive heads of a secret mission to smuggle Jews from Hungary to Palestine after World War Two. *Courtesy of Ami Ayalon.*

Palestinian refugees leaving a village in the Galilee five months after the creation of the state of Israel. © *Reuters.*

The author with a comrade-in-arms.
Courtesy of Ami Ayalon.

The author with fellow Flotilla 13 commandos. *Courtesy of Ami Ayalon.*

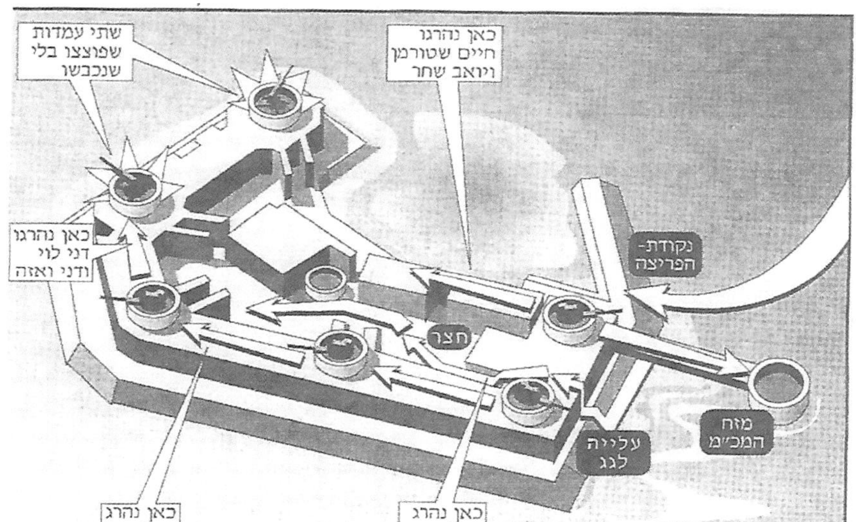

Green Island battle diagram, July 1969. *Courtesy of Ami Ayalon.*

Receiving the Medal of Valor, Israel's highest military honor, from Prime Minister Golda Meir on Independence Day 1972. *Courtesy of Ami Ayalon.*

The author with Zev Almog during a landing operation in Lebanon. *Courtesy of Ami Ayalon.*

Prime Minister Yitzhak Rabin in 1995 at naval headquarters after approval of the submarine project the author advocated. *Courtesy of Ami Ayalon.*

With Shimon Peres and Carmi Gillon in 1996 at the author's installation as Shin Bet director. *Courtesy of Ami Ayalon.*

The author with Bibi Netanyahu in 1997 at Shin Bet headquarters. *Courtesy of Ami Ayalon.*

Prime Minister Ehud Barak and the author at the end of term as Shin Bet director, May 2000. *Courtesy of Ami Ayalon.*

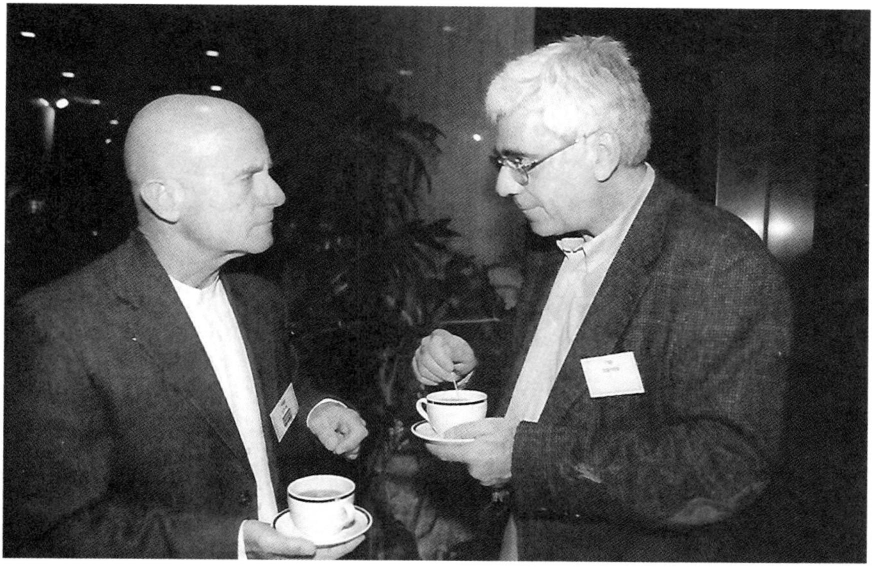

Sari Nusseibeh and the author in 2003 during the campaign to raise signatures to end the Israeli-Palestinian conflict. *Courtesy of Ami Ayalon.*

The author, Saeb Erekat, and Khalil Shikaki in Ramallah. *Courtesy of Ami Ayalon.*

Flotilla 13 commando training. *Photo by Ziv Koren.*

Aziz Salha, an unemployed nineteen-year-old, celebrates after throwing the beaten and stabbed body of IDF reserve Sgt. Vadim Nurzhitz into a seething mob in a squalid Ramallah neighborhood. *Photo by Chris Gerald/AFP via Getty Images.*

For my first direct encounter with Jibril, aka Abu Rami, I headed to the "Muqataa," an ugly cement edifice in Ramallah with the grace of an old parking garage. The British had built it as a prison in the 1930s. It was bizarre to be ushered through sterile, fluorescent-lit halls and into Jibril's office. If I had met him in previous years, it would have been for the first and only time, my face blackened and my AK-47 primed to execute him.

Jibril, who looked as burly as a linebacker, had long ago shed his battle fatigues; for our meeting he was dressed to the nines, with a necktie knotted just over his Adam's apple. Unlike Arafat, Jibril made no effort to charm me. "*T'fadal*," he said, gesturing at bowls of pretzels and pistachios on a table. "Take some."

"Colonel," I began after cracking a pistachio, "we're not here to make peace. That's the job of our leaders. But if we don't do our jobs, there will never be peace. We'll just keep fighting. I'm telling you, I'll stop at nothing to thwart terror."

Jibril's face remained expressionless throughout my monologue. I gathered from his laconic grunts that he trusted me as much as I did him — not at all. It surely wasn't easy for him to sit around a coffee table with a man who had spent his career sailing around the Mediterranean hounding, and in some cases killing, his friends and comrades. "Mr. Ayalon," he finally said, summing up his views, "I didn't sit in jail for seventeen years for Hamas to build a fundamentalist state." His message was clear: He was working with me because he was a patriot, which I liked. The impression he gave me was that he'd do what it took, including going far beyond our relatively tame Shabak interrogation methods, to clamp down on terror.

Dahlan, Jibril, and their forces, acting on Arafat's orders, packed Palestinian prisons with militant Islamists. Peres, though, found one reason after another not to withdraw from Abu Sneina.

If our laser focus on combating Hamas was aimed at saving Israeli lives, for Arafat, Jibril, Dahlan, and their men, turning on Hamas came out of an internecine war between those using negotiation as a means to win lands we conquered in 1967, and the fundamentalist Islamists using bombs to achieve their dream of driving the modern-day crusaders out of all of pre-1948 Palestine from the Jordan River to the Mediterranean. Dahlan, for instance, applied the screws to a Gazan dentist by the name of Ibrahim al-Makadmeh after discovering that he was a member of Hamas's military wing who had been given a mission to infiltrate the PA and undermine it from within. Dr. al-Makadmeh, whose parents fled the village of Yibna in 1948, sat in one of our prisons for eight years during the Intifada.

Cooperation between the Shabak and the Palestinian Authority didn't mean we let our guards down. Jibril knew we were still monitoring him and his men, just as we knew they were trying to monitor us, and each side sought to locate the other side's undercover agents. More than once Jibril planted false information during telephone conversations, knowing that we were snooping on the bugged line. We had expected this, and we weren't surprised. Even longtime allies, like the British and American intelligence services, do the same to each other.

Having said that, my trust in Jibril grew after I put him to a test. Not long after we first met, I pressured him into arresting his younger brother Sheikh Naif, an imam and head of the Hebron Beekeepers Union who also belonged to Hamas. Photos we had on file of him showed he had the same high forehead and small dark intense eyes as Jibril, plus the thick black beard sported by Islamists.

The sheikh was considered by his many supporters to be modest and uncorrupted. But once he got a microphone in his hand, he spouted anti-Semitic conspiracy theories. He once said that Jews, the "children of pigs and monkeys," were plotting to destroy the Al Aqsa Mosque and build the Third Temple on its ruins. Jews in his view were the main culprits behind the sexual revolution, socialism, psychoanalysis, and other ills of the infidel Western civilization.[22] He also incited his followers to violence by urging revenge for the *Nakba* and the daily humiliations and losses they had endured since then.

"Either you arrest your brother," I warned Jibril, "or we will." It was a lot to ask from a member of a society in which family ties trump ideology. In some quarters he was already being called an Israeli agent, a Shin Bet deputy, and a traitor.

Jibril continued cooperation with us even after we hauled his brother into prison. A month later his younger brother walked out of prison more popular than ever. I didn't expect more of Jibril than that. But the episode taught me that Jibril was willing to break national taboos for the sake of peace. From that moment, we understood each other. He wasn't going to become a Zionist, and I wasn't going to hoist the Palestinian flag. But we had to fight terrorism together.

15

SENSORS

Jibril wound up locking up more terrorists than we did. Since those days, Jibril and I have remained friends because, you could say, we belong to the same fraternity of fighters. We are also survivors of an era when a solution to our peoples' conflict seemed within reach.

Just to remind myself that once upon a time there was trust between our two sides, whenever a fresh eruption of violence breaks out, I'll ring him up or we'll arrange to meet. I'm never looking for secret intelligence; neither one of us has any to share.

A week after my terrifying talk with Rabbi Shapira, I decided to visit him in his office at the Palestinian Football Association in the West Bank town of Al-Ram, half an hour from Jerusalem and a storied place with roots dating back to the Iron Age. During the Crusades, King Godfrey gave it as a fief to the Church of the Holy Sepulchre.

A Palestinian driver took me in a Range Rover through the checkpoint. As we approached Al-Ram, I squinted to make out something activists had painted on the security wall. It was a text by the South African writer and antiapartheid activist Farid Esack: MY DEAR PALESTINIAN BROTHERS AND SISTERS, I HAVE COME TO YOUR LAND AND I HAVE RECOGNIZED SHADES OF MY OWN.

The Palestinian Football Association headquarters looks like a high-end medical complex. In front of the entrance three men were busy washing a black, late-model Mercedes sedan. Jibril's unarmed bodyguards led me to his office. When I entered, he rose from his desk on the far end of the long room and strode in my direction, arms extended. He wore a suit, and his shoes were as shiny as the Mercedes in the parking lot.

"*Ma nishma, Ami?*" he asked. His nearly flawless Hebrew reminded me once again of my failure to learn Arabic.

I told him about the book I was writing and asked him about rumors that he was planning a political comeback, possibly positioning himself as the successor to President Abbas. He just winked.

He worked to light a cigarette; his large hands fumbling with the lighter gave the impression of a dockworker or a middleweight boxer, and he looked as combative as a cannonball flying right at you. "What do the doctors say about the smoking?" I nudged.

"I don't see any doctors in the room, unless you've changed professions, Ami." He took a long drag on the cigarette.

We discussed the unrest on the Temple Mount, as always the place to look for rumblings of the next Armageddon. Jibril, speaking in his low, raspy voice like Brando in *The Godfather*, remained confident that the situation was under control. The Palestinian government had no interest in a popular uprising against Israel, an uprising that just as easily could turn against them.

A man with tea and cookies appeared and, just like the first time we met, Jibril pointed at the tray and growled, "Take some." We then bantered about old friends and acquaintances. I followed this up with a joke about placing bets on the Palestinian national team to win the next World Cup. He started to chuckle, a wheezing, wolverine guffaw I'd heard from him many times before.

"*Baruch HaShem*," he said. "Thank God!"

"How is Biba, Ami?" There was a tenderness in his gravelly voice. "She's still putting up with you?"

"Amazingly, she is."

I looked at him and, as always, found it difficult not to think about his brother, Naif — the sheikh who says Jews are monkeys — because the brothers look nearly identical: the same dark eyes, the same linebacker physique, a graying beard instead of a graying mustache. I've often wondered what was it like to have the Palestinian blood feud between Fatah's secular nationalism and the radical Islamists run directly through his family, or for that matter through other families like the Shikakis.

On the drive back to Jerusalem, passing again by the South African's words spray-painted on the wall, I thought about something Netanyahu had recently told *Newsweek*: "We will surround Israel with walls to defend against wild beasts."

Wild beasts! How would I have responded to a brutal foreign army capturing and occupying my country for fifty years?

I thought about Jibril and his thirteen siblings raised by traditional parents in a stone house in the dusty village of Dura, the ancient Adora that Josephus mentioned in his *Jewish Wars*. In Palestinian lore, Noah was buried in the town. Today there's a Jewish settlement called Adora a couple of miles north of where Jibril grew up.

At the age of fourteen, I was swimming in the Sea of Galilee with Srulik dreaming of playing the hero in battles near and far. Jibril, born in 1953, was fourteen when we conquered the West Bank. A year later the Shabak arrested him for helping smuggle Egyptian military officers, caught behind enemy lines in 1967, out of Palestine. He had his first encounter with Israelis when an IDF major came to arrest him and slapped his father across the face in front of the entire family. In the four months Jibril spent in a Hebron prison, he endured countless rounds of slaps, beatings, and other forms of humiliation and resolved to fight his captors. He also met Abu Ali Shahin, a top Fatah man who was a one-person university inside the prison, educating teenagers like Jibril to fight the occupation with whatever means they had — including arms.

Jibril got out, acquired his first Kalashnikov, and became a leader of the militant student group Fatah Hawks. At seventeen he tossed a dud grenade at Israeli soldiers, and our military court sentenced him to life in prison.

For seventeen years Jibril sat behind bars, where he learned Hebrew well enough to translate Menachim Begin's *The Revolt*, a story of the Jewish underground, into Arabic. We eventually released him in a prison exchange in 1985.

During all those years his younger brother steered clear of politics; he wanted nothing to do with Fatah and its secularism. Naif studied Islamic law in Jordan and settled into the life of a local religious leader and beekeeper. During the Intifada, he was drawn to the Islamic charity Hamas because of its work with widows, orphans, and families whose breadwinners sat in our prisons. In 1992, just before Oslo, at Chief of Staff Ehud Barak's insistence, Rabin ordered him and more than four hundred other members of Hamas and Islamic Jihad arrested, driven to the Lebanese border, and expelled. For a year he lived in a tent camp in the mountain village of Marj al-Zohour. The deportees spent that year living in the snow, mud, and heat conspiring to reproduce the Hezbollah model of jihad in Palestine.

Just after Oslo, Naif returned to his simple life in the West Bank: He traveled by bus, lived in a small house on a dusty pitted road, and dressed like the farmers who crowded his mosque to hear him preach. Jibril, meanwhile, was the second most powerful leader in the Palestinian Authority, just after Arafat. With his position came the trappings of power. But it wasn't Naif's modesty that turned people in ever greater numbers away from Fatah. Palestinians were flocking to the Islamists because terror had made it politically impossible for Peres to return so much as a single stony field to Arafat. Jibril's heavy hand in preventing Hamas from murdering Israeli civilians had yielded nothing.

In the years that followed, as the Palestinians received only scraps of the 90 percent of the territories Arafat thought he would get from us, Jibril went from being a hero on the streets, a tough ex-prisoner who did what it took to liberate his country, to someone perceived as tainted. In the eyes of many, Sheikh Naif, the fundamentalist preacher and anti-Semite, had inherited his brother's role as intrepid fighter for Palestinian freedom.

Back in 1996 stopping the Hamas kamikazes took time, and for most of my first year at the Shin Bet, more Israeli citizens died as a result of terror than any other time since the founding of the State of Israel. Bombs seemed to be ticking everywhere.

I spent most weeknights at a Shabak safe house in Tel Aviv. Late at night I'd sit and nurse a beer at Café Apropo on Ben Gurion Boulevard, trying to gather my thoughts. I had a lot to ponder. I had entered the Shabak as an outsider with a lot to learn from the veterans of the Service. At first I didn't touch the organization's inner culture, such as our code of ethics, even if I suspected it would eventually have to change. I knew I'd have to show myself to be a credible leader before I could broach a subject as sensitive as ethics.

When I was in the navy, the chief of staff and minister of defense had been above me; now I answered only to the prime minister. For most decisions — tapping phones, signing arrest warrants, delivering suspects over to interrogators to apply "moderate physical force," a legal euphemism for torture — there was no need to ask anyone for permission.

The café, at night packed with people whose lives I was sworn to defend, was a good place to think about the dangers of power. No one there knew who I was or that, with some exceptions, such as judges, journalists, and elected officials, suspicion alone was enough for us to violate people's privacy and rights, including everyone in the café. The waiter. The cook. The couple speaking Arabic in the corner. It was chilling to realize that the Shabak was by design a monster that protected democracy by systematically violating its most sacred principles of privacy and due process. I thought often of Orwell's *1984* and the words of James Madison: "I believe there are more instances of the abridgment of the freedom of the people by gradual and silent encroachments of those in power than by violent and sudden usurpations."

But my father immigrated illegally in the 1930s to build a New Man and New Society, not to have his son turn into the Israeli J. Edgar Hoover at his most imperious. My main task at the Shabak wasn't to kill terrorists, it was to preserve Israel as a free society. Back home on the weekends, Biba also kept me grounded. There was one thing this woman who put up with my long absences, my nervous pacing, and the box of disguises I kept in the closet would never tolerate: a husband drunk on power. At every opportunity she reminded me that I was still a guy who wears mismatched socks and leaves the toilet seat up. "I am the only one who sees you for who you are," she'd say.

In rebuilding the Shabak, I needed to acquire a deep understanding of our past efforts to combat terrorism: the strategies we'd tried, where we had been successful, and where we had failed.

The Shabak during the Intifada ten years earlier presented a case study in what not to do. Not only had brutalizing terrorist suspects failed to end the Intifada, but our cruelty had often fanned its flames and debased Israeli society. To avoid losing our humanity in the process of trying to save lives, what we needed, I concluded, was to draw a bold red line between permitted and prohibited techniques. A moral compass for the sewer.

I stumbled across a clue of where to draw the line quite by accident. From our own statistics I learned that during the Intifada, the level of terrorism was similar in Gaza and the West Bank. We faced the same people, the same slogans, the same exiled PLO leadership, the same refugee population with rusting keys to ancestral homes jingling in their pockets. But the level of violence in the Shabak interrogations in Gaza was higher. Our interrogators had the same training, the same procedures and background. So why did so many more prisoners end up in the hospital in Gaza than in the West Bank?

The researchers I tasked with figuring out this riddle failed to come up with a convincing theory. Finally, I called the head of the Interrogation Division. During the first intifada, he headed up a team of interrogators in the West Bank. "No clue, Ami," he told me at first. I told him he could think about it overnight and get back with an answer in the morning.

The next day I didn't hear from him — he probably hoped I forgot — so I rang him up. He told me he'd been up late thinking about my questions. "All I remember," he said, "is that my division commander, before sending us to interrogate prisoners, told us, 'In your mission today, remember that we are all human beings: free man and prisoner alike.'" In Gaza, where there was no such daily routine, prisoner interrogations were conducted according to the "club them into submission" school of thought. I began to think about how best to change the inner ethics of the Shabak. Thumbscrews were off limits, but what about shaking? Slapping? Blackmail? Bribery? Humiliation? Deception?

Placing clear limits on slaps and shackles was clearly the right thing to do, but a code of ethics would not be nearly enough to check Hamas. We also needed to find a way to understand the motivations of our Islamist enemies. Why would a perfectly healthy student strap on a suicide belt and kill people on their way to school or while sitting in a café? As a soldier I killed perfect strangers all the time, but they were combatants — I never knowingly attacked civilians, people I considered to be innocent bystanders. How could we re-create the organization to see our adversaries as individual human beings? Searching for answers, I read through a file put together by Dr. Matti Steinberg, an expert on Arab affairs previous directors had employed as an outside consultant and who, at that moment, was polishing up a political biography of Arafat. Many security organizations bring in academics as advisers. In practice, the radically different culture dividing the academic world from the sewer means that an outsider's advice usually ends up in file cabinets, unread and unheeded.

From the minute I opened the file Steinberg had produced, I knew he might be one of the sensors I was looking for.

In our first meeting I peppered Matti with questions on the history of Palestinian nationalism.[23] He told me straight out that I would never understand the Palestinians if I didn't read their national poets and familiarize myself with their songwriters, graffiti artists, and clandestine newspapers. Matti also added to my reading list Amira Hass, the *Haaretz* journalist who reported on Palestinian affairs from Ramallah and Gaza. "She'll give you a picture of the Palestinian street more revealing than anyone here," he said with his arms spread wide as if to take in the entire Shin Bet. Respectfully, he was saying that much of the Shabak's fifty years of work was irrelevant in an era of security cooperation with Arafat's Palestinian Authority.

Another key source for me, he continued as I scribbled down notes, would be Khalil Shikaki's opinion polls. It was also from Matti that I first learned about the work of Dr. Eyad Sarraj, the Gazan psychiatrist. Matti's point was a simple one: Forget about understanding terrorism if you are not willing to reach deep into its source — the ideological and theological ideas fed by past collective trauma.

Like a diver straining to reach the surface, I found myself manically making my way through Dr. Sarraj's reports, which were excruciating to read but also revealing. In one account Dr. Sarraj, his head held high, said to an IDF soldier threatening to beat him: "Be my guest. But before you do, I know there is a real human being behind that uniform, and I would like you to show me that person." The soldier bravely walked away.

Just as eye-opening was Palestinian literature, the "soul" of the Palestinians as Matti would say. For the first time I read *A Lake Beyond the Wind* by Yahya Yakhlif, a novel that recounts the final days before the author's family fled the town of Samakh in 1948. "A disaster was coming and there was a sense of the earth starting to tremble." As a kid, I harvested bananas on the land where Yakhlif once played soccer with his friends.

It was also my first encounter with the poet Fadwa Tuqan, whose words were as monumental for Palestinians as Nathan Alterman's verse was for us:

All I ask is to remain in the bosom of my country
As soil, grass, a flower.

The Palestinian national poet Mahmoud Darwish topped the reading list of Matti's crash course. Seven-year-old Darwish fled with his family in 1948 from their ancestral village in the northern Galilee, now a moshav. I found myself breathless reading "To Our Land":

To our land, and it is a prize of war,
the freedom to die from longing and burning
and our land, in its bloodied night,
is a jewel that glimmers for the far upon the far
and illuminates what's outside it.

At Café Apropo one evening, bleary-eyed from an eighteen-hour day, I read one of Darwish's finest literary feats, the Palestinian Declaration of Independence. He wrote it at Arafat's request in May 1988, the same year as my near lynching in Gaza. The document snapped me awake because Darwish had obviously used the Israeli Declaration of Independence as his model:

> In the heart of its homeland and on its periphery, in its places of exile near and far, the Palestinian Arab people have not lost its unwavering faith in its right to return nor its firm belief in its right to independence. Occupation, carnage and displacement have been unable to dispossess the Palestinians of their consciousness and their identity — their epic struggle has endured, and the formation of their national character has continued with the growing escalation of the struggle.

Why did Darwish quote nearly word for word our declaration of independence? Was he also writing for an Israeli audience? For me, his most revelatory lines were those related to UN Resolutions 242 and 338, the international legal undergirding of the two-state solution:

> On the basis of the international legitimacy embodied in the resolutions of the United Nations since 1947, and through the exercise by the Palestinian Arab people of its right to self-determination, political independence and sovereignty over its territory: The Palestine National Council hereby declares, in the Name of God and on behalf of the Palestinian Arab people, the establishment of the State of Palestine in the land of Palestine with its capital at Jerusalem.

My God! I found myself thinking. By accepting the resolutions of the United Nations since 1947, Arafat had long since broken from the Palestinian revolutionary ethos of doing to us what the Algerians had done to the French. By tacitly recognizing the State of Israel along the 1967 borders, he prepared Palestinian public opinion ideologically for the painful compromise necessary for a peaceful resolution to our conflict. Why hadn't we officers been handed translations of this in 1988? I asked myself. If we had recognized Arafat's strategic shift ten years earlier, we might not be facing Hamas's suicide bombers. What had we done instead back then? Rabin, as minister of defense and through the Shabak and the military government, had secretly supported Hamas based on the hope that the religious group would undercut the nationalists in the PLO. "We saw the fundamentalists mainly as an unthreatening social force," confessed one of our top generals.[24]

From Matti, I also received a chilling tutorial on Hamas and its Islamist brethren. For years Hamas's influence had been spreading because, in addition to its theologically driven fanaticism, it was the largest charity serving the Palestinian poor. The leader of Hamas, the wheelchair-bound Sheikh Ahmed Yassin, had been behind bars in Israel since 1989 because of his connection to terror and to his organization's military wing, Izz ad-Din al-Qassam. The sheikh symbolized the suffering and misery of the Palestinian people and preached the messianic dream of the ultimate victory over the infidels. He also had moral red lines that shifty Arafat lacked. Even from prison, he set the organization's policy and made it known when terrorist attacks were warranted.

There was no chance, Matti told me, that Hamas would ever come up with a document such as the Darwish-Arafat Declaration of Independence. The reason for this was simple: They based their politics on the interpretations of Islamic religious law that forbade any territorial compromise with us, to them the modern-day crusaders. In their reading of Islam, all of historic Palestine, including Tel Aviv, belonged to Muslims: The Hamas charter reads that its members "strive to raise the banner of Allah over every inch of Palestine" because, under the Israelis, "the state of truth has disappeared and been replaced by the state of evil." If Arafat failed to deliver on a Palestinian state, Matti warned darkly, the Palestinian masses would turn to the Islamists, and the gates of hell would open wide.

16

TUNNEL VISION

Once a month I met with Jibril and Dahlan to coordinate activities. Our efforts were paying off: We had considerably reduced the frequency of suicide bombings. While we deepened our intelligence penetration into Palestinian terrorist organizations, we had to build out our intelligence and counterterrorism efforts against Jewish terrorism, and we took on Jewish terrorism by recruiting settler informants. The most extreme of ideological settlers, those who had offered up prayers of thanksgiving at the assassination of Rabin, developed counterespionage in an effort to identify our agents in the settlements.

Targeting fellow Jews only compounded the cognitive dissonance of veteran Shabak agents who now had to listen to our former Palestinian foes, take their opinions into account, and even rely on them, which required unlearning what they had been indoctrinated to believe about the PLO since nursery school.

One day I encountered a very different sort of moral quandary. In developing a Shabak code of ethics, I asked the head of interrogations to make sure the language we came up with wasn't some incomprehensible jargon written by philosophers or poets but would make perfect sense to agents in the interrogation rooms. This fellow, let's call him "X," came to my office and told my secretary he wanted to discuss something important.

"Sure. Let him in." I had an open-door policy.

The interrogator, jug-eared with cropped dark hair, entered my office. I knew from his file that he was the grandson of a Yemenite Torah scholar and had been raised in a religious home. "Sir," he began, "you've been talking to us about what we do to the prisoners" — referring to the committee I had set up to propose guidelines for interrogations. "What I haven't heard from you is what you are doing to us."

"What are you talking about? I'm not doing anything to you!" With so much at stake, I had no patience for self-pity.

The interrogator shook his head because, clearly, I misunderstood him.

He explained. "Growing up, our house was full of books. They were everywhere, lining every wall. Books, music, ideas, that's what I was surrounded by. But since I joined the Service, I've been living around stench, screams, and violence. I don't know how I can keep doing this."

He might have been referring to one of our prisons, a former Russian Orthodox monastery variously called Tomb of God, Dark Night, and Slaughterhouse. One prisoner, the son of a Hamas leader, described it as "black and stained and dark, like the rat-infested medieval dungeons you see in the movies."[25] Or perhaps what he had in mind were techniques used by interrogators to squeeze out information to prevent the murder of our civilians, such as sleep deprivation or forcing people to maintain painful positions like the "frog crouch" for hours on end. (Though we applied such techniques far less often than in the past, there were still "ticking bombs" that required some physical persuasion.) Maybe he was thinking about our use of blackmail — sometimes we pressured members of Hamas to spy on their fellow militants in exchange for medical care they or their loved ones couldn't live without.

The very power he had over prisoners created an atmosphere of violence. It wasn't that he had empathy for our enemies; he didn't. It was his own humanity, the very thing I wanted him most to keep, that he was afraid of losing.

"Then why do you keep working with us?" I asked.

"Because I'm saving lives," he responded, his eyes moist.

I reached out and put my hand on his shoulder. "The minute you stop asking these questions, take your things and leave. I wouldn't want you interrogating terrorists." I then gave him a version of my talk to Jibril and Dahlan: Those of us down in the sewer were doing the dirty work so the peacekeepers could strike a lasting deal. We were, so to speak, the bridge across the Rubicon the politicians would have to cross to seal a political agreement. The other point I made was that, more than any law or regulation, what should help us draw the line between the permissible and the forbidden in the interrogation room was the daily reminder that the prisoner was a fellow human being.

The bridge across the Rubicon was sometimes wobbly.

One day several months into the job a former commando in my Flotilla unit called on an unsecured line to congratulate me on a targeted killing of a suicide bomber in Jerusalem who had played a role in the Dizengoff Center bombing. My friend had become a Labor politician and was at that time the chairman of the Knesset's Foreign Affairs and Defense Committee.[26] We had received information on an attack planned for the Jerusalem neighborhood of Gilo, which Palestinians consider a settlement because we built it on lands we conquered in 1967. The kill succeeded without injuring innocent civilians. While we were happy that the terrorist was no longer a threat, we certainly didn't brag about having a hand in it.

"What!" I clutched the receiver. "Who told you about the operation?" It turns out Peres himself had shared the information with him. With the body count eating away at his popularity, he couldn't pass up the opportunity to gloat over such a significant security success. "Don't say a word to anyone," I demanded.

"No worries," he assured me. "As a politician it's my job to lie; your job is to tell the truth."

The effectiveness of our security cooperation with Arafat and his men came too late to help Prime Minister Peres in the 1996 summer elections. Opinion polls had given Peres a clear edge over Likud's Bibi Netanyahu, and on the night of the election most people went to sleep assuming Labor had won. But the Hamas bombing campaign had done its work on our national psyche. While the number of attacks had dropped, the impression many Israelis had was that Oslo had led to more terror and that each concession we made created the ideal environment for Hamas and Islamic Jihad to send in their bombers. Voters turned to the right. When fear took over because of terror, we voted in leaders who promised to kill the enemy, not those who promised a better, more just world.

Netanyahu was a new kind of Israeli leader: young, energetic, and media-savvy. He also painted himself as an expert in fighting terrorism. In his first book, *International Terrorism: Challenge and Response*, he opines, "The impact of terrorism, not merely on individual nations, but on humanity as a whole, is intrinsically evil, necessarily evil and wholly evil." His follow-up, *Terrorism: How the West Can Win*, berates every shade of appeasement and accommodation as another 1938 Munich Agreement.

I was at the Likud victory rally on the day following Netanyahu's upset victory because one of my jobs was to make sure our new leader escaped Rabin's fate. Some of the settlers with whom I had been meeting, and secretly spying on, were at the rally. Thousands of black-robed Ultra-Orthodox joined the armed settler contingent.

Far from cameras and the scrutiny of public opinion, my brief was to tell the naked, unembellished truth to the prime minister. One thing I didn't have to tell Netanyahu, an MIT graduate, was that his upset election would never have happened without the help of Hamas suicide bombers. He also knew that keeping his job would depend on the Shabak's success at stopping terror. I therefore assumed he would listen when I told him that thwarting terror required continuing our security cooperation with the Palestinian Authority, which involved arming our former foes. Bibi would know better than I how to sell this to his right-wing base.

I had less confidence that he would adhere to the other terms of Oslo; namely, territorial withdrawals. The Hebron neighborhood Peres had promised Arafat remained under our control, and the new prime minister seemed in no rush to hand it over, which only stirred up Arafat's paranoia. He was, after all, a man who thought there were Shin Bet bugs under every rock. The fact that Sharon, a man who had destroyed entire neighborhoods of Beirut in an effort to kill him, was a top minister in the Likud government made him wary of a trap.

My first meeting with Netanyahu was in the official prime minister's office, designed in the graceful Bauhaus style of the 1930s, an architectural cousin of the Guggenheim Museum in New York. To enter, my driver passed through the beefed-up security wall we built following the assassination of Rabin, which made the residence feel like a bunker.

Upstairs in his office, I noticed Netanyahu's antiterrorism books on a shelf behind his desk. He opened the discussion with an astute analysis of Oslo and indicated his support for making the political process contingent on security cooperation. But despite his stated willingness to continue peace talks, he seemed to flinch when I brought up Palestinian expectations of territorial withdrawals.

"Arafat will have to get something in return for working with us," I said halfway into our meeting, explaining what Jibril repeated nearly every time we met: His boss was paying a political price for signing a peace deal with us and repressing Hamas. Syrian president Assad was calling Arafat the "prostitute of the Arab world." For sticking out his neck the way he was, he'd better get repaid. It was vital to reassure the Palestinians, in word and in deed, that if they kept up their security cooperation and continued cracking down on terror, we would hand over the territories he'd been promised. Sending in more tractors and cranes would only reinforce the suspicion among Palestinians that Oslo was a sham. I warned him that if Arafat felt we were stringing him along, he and his men would stop packing his prisons with their neighbors.

Yeah, yeah, yeah, Netanyahu said.

I left his office that day in the dark as to what he thought about my counsel. But when I saw his cabinet ministers doing their very best to undermine Oslo, I understood that the settler faction inside his government and his political base among the Greater Israel right wing held a lot more sway over him than we in the Shabak did. During one cabinet meeting, Minister of National Infrastructure Ariel Sharon told phony stories of Jibril hanging out with me in a Jacuzzi drinking champagne. Even as he spoke,

Sharon slipped me a note apologizing for the confection. It was politics, and I shouldn't take it personally.

In a public visit to Ariel, a settlement in the middle of the West Bank, Bibi declared to a singing and dancing crowd: "We will be here permanently forever," while promising the settlers he'd push for new construction on lands where Palestinians planned to build their future state.[27]

During our next meeting Jibril raised the alarm: "Your prime minister says he wants an agreement, and then he promises more settlements."

"*Maybe*," I said. "But it's also not easy for Israelis to forget the exploding buses. We still have a lot of work to do before you can claim that the Israeli government is not fulfilling its promises."

In his first weeks in office Bibi sought my advice on another delicate policy issue. Having campaigned on the promise never to hand over parts of "liberated" Jerusalem to the Palestinian Authority, he needed to show his supporters that he was the man for whom they voted.

He sought symbolically to reinforce Israeli sovereignty over the Muslim Quarter in the Old City by opening an entrance to an ancient tunnel first dug during the Hasmonean dynasty, before the Romans destroyed Jewish sovereignty over the Land of Israel. Once part of a water system, the tunnel had been excavated during the British Mandate, and until 1996 it was a popular Jewish Quarter tourist attraction because it ran along the Western Wall. Standing in the ancient drainage ditch gave believers the sensation of being close to the Holy of Holies. Bibi wanted to create a second opening so tourists could enter the tunnel in the Jewish Quarter, walk the full length of the tunnel, and exit again in the Muslim Quarter.

I was very familiar with the area because, knowing Jerusalem's apocalyptic potential, I made a habit of regularly touring the Omar Mosque, Al Aqsa Mosque, Solomon's Stables, and other holy sites. Like all Israelis of my generation, I read about the Temple Mount in Josephus, and when there I had the sensation of returning to the time of the Second Temple, or even further back to when Abraham prepared to sacrifice his son Isaac.

Sometimes I went on these tours with the Mufti of Jerusalem, a man who, like so many others, harbored some bizarre conspiracy theories. On a tour of the ruins under the Temple Mount, upon seeing a pillar mentioned in Josephus as a feature of the Second Temple, I turned to the mufti and said, "As a kid I read about this place." I really did feel like I was next to a piece of ancient Jewish history.

"You Jews are strange," he said. "You're always inventing history and then you start to believe in the invention." He truly thought we had conjured our historical connection to the Holy Land out of thin air.

Because the holy sites had a way of driving everyone mad, I cautioned the prime minister to cover his bases. There was nothing inherently objectionable about opening up the tunnel in the Muslim Quarter. Peres, like Rabin before him, had considered opening the tunnel before deciding against acting unilaterally, which would have jeopardized peace talks with the Palestinians. If Netanyahu was serious about opening the tunnel, I told him he would need to coordinate with our relevant partners: with the Jerusalem Islamic Waqf, the Muslim religious trust run by the mufti that manages the *Haram esh-Sharif* mosques; with Arafat; and with Jordan's King Hussein. If everyone was on board, why not? Archaeology didn't have to be political. So long what you do was coordinated and not unilateral, I repeated for emphasis, what was the problem?

Netanyahu seemed satisfied with my counsel, and I didn't give the issue any more thought until September 24, the day after Yom Kippur, when my top man in Jerusalem rang me up with the surprising news that, under heavy guard, the extension to the tunnel would be opened later that day. I couldn't believe my ears.

Netanyahu was in Germany meeting with the chancellor. I phoned up his deputy prime minister and figured out quickly that he could do nothing about it. In another telephone call, the minister of defense told me that Jerusalem wasn't the responsibility of the Ministry of Defense. His hands were tied.

Within an hour of the opening, the people at the waqf heard

the thumping of the hammers in the Muslim Quarter. Rumors spread like wildfire that we were digging a tunnel under the Mosque of Omar, to attack Islam and, with it, Palestinian national aspirations.

The next morning Netanyahu, still in Germany on an official visit, issued a statement calling the tunnel "the bedrock of our existence." Arafat, as surprised by the opening as the waqf officials, seized upon the incident as a desecration of *Haram esh-Sharif* and called upon Palestinians to respond. "We cannot accept the Judaization of Jerusalem. East Jerusalem is our capital!" The slogans unfurled by both leaders incited more violence and undermined the kind of coordination I had recommended to the prime minister.

Arafat, who had been waiting for months to receive more territory, used the tunnel opening as his chance to remind Israelis of his powers of disruption. His office issued a statement calling on Palestinians "to express their anger before the continuing aggression on the Al Aqsa Mosque and the desecration of the holy places." He ordered his men to orchestrate violent protests that caught our army flat-footed.

Rioting spread across the West Bank, Gaza, and East Jerusalem, overwhelming the IDF soldiers stationed there, who per our security arrangement with the PA were supposed to be conducting joint patrols with Palestinian security. A general strike was called, and Jibril and his men enforced it.

In Bethlehem and Ramallah mobs attacked our soldiers, and after they fired rubber bullets to drive back the protesters, Arafat's police opened fire on us. Palestinians were killed in the firefight, prompting more incendiary statements from Arafat.

Behind the scenes, the Shin Bet in the West Bank and Gaza worked with Jibril, Dahlan, and their people to try to bring about a cease-fire. Eleven soldiers, six Israeli civilians, and a hundred Palestinians died in what amounted to open warfare between two sides supposed to be building trust and signing agreements. My every instinct wanted to push aside reason and make the Palestinians pay dearly. But it was Netanyahu, I had to remind myself, who had opened the tunnel and triggered the chaos.

The most dangerous result of the fighting, beyond the lives lost, was the rapid divergence of the narratives our peoples were telling themselves. For an increasing number of Israelis, including former supporters of Oslo, scenes of Palestinian police using weapons we had given them to kill our men were all the evidence they needed of Arafat's supposed two-faced scheme of talking peace while pursuing his long-standing dream of driving the Jews into the sea. If it hadn't been the tunnel, they said, he would have found some other excuse. The slogan "We gave the Arabs land, and they gave us terror" would have staying power.

The Palestinian narrative, meanwhile, was increasingly the Hamas line that Jews understood only force. Shooting, not talking, was what would prevent the takeover of their sacred sites.

When Netanyahu returned from his trip abroad, he summoned me to his office to discuss the violence. The two of us had such fundamental disagreements on the cause of the Western Wall tunnel riots, as the incident came to be known, that I considered handing in my resignation. And I would have, too, if not for my sense of duty — to the army of Shabak professionals wading through the sewer, and most of all to ordinary Israelis cautiously returning to their buses and cafés.

The prime minister was ashen-faced and smelled of sweat and cologne. His grip on power was contingent on his promise of security, and now the country was mourning the death of seventeen Israelis. Under intense pressure from all sides, he was about to head to Washington, where President Clinton would want to know how he was going to get the peace process back on track. He asked me for the Shabak's assessment.

I began by pointing out the chasm between my recommendations for opening the tunnel and what he had done. Bibi blinked a few times, and I continued. "Mr. Prime Minister," I began, "there was nothing premediated about Arafat's order for his men to fire on us. He's afraid of losing the support of his people. Hamas is robbing him of his title as revolutionary and fighter for Palestinian rights by making him out to be our stooge."

His trip to Washington, I went on, was his moment of truth. If he didn't believe in the Oslo process, as he said ad nauseum while he was in opposition, he should let Clinton know that the trust-building process that was at the heart of Oslo had failed. Instead of gradually withdrawing from territory, he could push for an agreement on the core issues, Jerusalem, settlements, security, and the right of return. Only after all these fundamental issues have been agreed would you be able to hand over land to the Palestinians.

"Would Arafat agree?" he asked.

I told him I didn't know. But maybe, I said, "if you offer him something *big*, he will have something he can use to convince his people that the peace process is working. Then he might go for it."

"Big? How big?"

"A complete settlement freeze. Such an announcement would weaken Hamas and give Arafat and his people the upper hand." He just looked at me like he had a fish bone caught in his throat.

What I didn't tell Netanyahu that day — since my brief was security and not politics — was what I was learning by spending so much time in Gaza and Judea and Samaria. I had begun to see that more bypass roads, military outposts, and settlements would eventually destroy any hope of a two-state solution. If we kept up the building, before too long the Palestinians would conclude we had no intention of ending the occupation and allowing a Palestinian state alongside Israel. This would inevitably lead to the loss of hope and the triumph of terror.

Bibi returned from Washington and, pushed by the Americans, announced the withdrawal from the Hebron neighborhood. The message he sent to the Palestinians was that violence works.

Four months later Bibi sent another message to the Palestinians by greenlighting a major new settlement, Har Homa, in occupied East Jerusalem.

17

THE AWADALLAH BROTHERS

From time to time I would meet Arafat in the middle of the night in the Muqataa, usually joined by Jibril. Outwardly Arafat continued with his stereotypical Arab hospitality, shoving food at me — *Eat! Eat! You're not hungry? What's wrong with you?!* He had a way of springing up from his chair like a jack-in-the-box, tilting his head to one side, and sizing up his quarry. I soon learned to see past his theatrics. He was no fool; through his follow-up questions on whatever security issues I raised, he proved masterfully attuned to the smallest details. Only when I touched a nerve did Arafat, a superb actor, slip on a mask and feign confusion.

Hamas's most dangerous terrorist would soon reveal to me what lay behind the propensity for theatrics that Netanyahu and Arafat shared.

On a spring afternoon in 1997 — March 21, Purim Eve — Musa Abd al-Qadir Ghanimat left the West Bank village of Surif carrying a bomb built by Adel Awadallah, the head of the Qassam Brigades, Hamas's military unit in the West Bank.[28] His target was Café Apropo, my regular haunt on Ben Gurion Boulevard. Minutes after Ghanimat entered the café, another operative detonated the bomb by remote control.

When I arrived at the scene, the stench of cordite hung in the air and the body parts of people I had failed to protect were scattered across walls and salad plates. The victims of the attack were three women in their early thirties; one, a mother, absorbed the blast with her body to save the life of her six-month-old child, dressed like a clown for Purim.

Three months later two men in dark suits carrying attaché cases, looking like traveling salesmen, exploded themselves in the middle of Mahane Yehuda, the open-air vegetable market in Jerusalem. Their briefcases contained more than thirty pounds of plastic explosives, screws, and nails. Sixteen people fell victim to their bombing, including one American, and 178 were injured.

In September, Adel Awadallah struck again. This time a suicide bomber killed five people and injured 181 at the Ben Yehuda pedestrian mall in Jerusalem.

Bibi called an emergency meeting of the security cabinet to discuss the renewed wave of bombings, and during the meeting some suggested that we assassinate Hamas's spiritual leader, Sheikh Yassin. Others wanted us to take out Yasser Arafat. A former general said matter-of-factly: "We should just erase Ramallah from the map with tanks."

Of course, attacking Arafat's stronghold would only encourage more Islamic terrorism. I did my best to rein in the crazed calls for vengeance, reminding Bibi yet again that unless Palestinians had a stake in the Oslo process, we could count on a lot more violence.

The prime minister and his cabinet looked at me with barely disguised hostility for opposing their pretext for hitting Arafat and his regime and abandoning the hated Oslo agreement. Most thought Arafat had duped not only Rabin and Peres but also the head of the Shin Bet.

Following yet another gruesome attack in the West Bank, Netanyahu convened a meeting of his security advisers. I said I needed a few days to figure out who was behind the attack and that I'd return when I had intelligence we could act on.

That wasn't the response Bibi wanted so he turned to Chief of Central Command Uzi Dayan for ideas on how to get revenge. Dayan, Moshe Dayan's nephew, suggested turning a West Bank military base into a new Jewish settlement. Most of those present congratulated him on coming up with such "an appropriate Zionist response" to terror.

"Mr. Prime Minister," I said, standing up and gathering together my papers. "I want to make something clear. If we are here to discuss beefed-up measures in Judea and Samaria — more military patrols, better lighting on the roads where settlers drive, and the like — it makes sense for me to be here. But if you're going to talk about expanding settlements, count me out. My job is to provide advice on security. Building settlements is a political decision, and I won't be party to discussing actions I know will only incite more violence."

In the history of the Shabak, saying no to the prime minister was never done. By this point, though, I had decided that my job required me to tell the truth regardless of what our leaders thought. Jaws dropped as I turned and exited the room.

With most top Hamas militants behind bars or dead, Awadallah, who was still on the loose, was the operative most likely to bring on Armageddon. In the meantime, after two years in the Service, I felt it was time to introduce a code of ethics. The aim was to get more effective intelligence, and it was increasingly clear to me that torture produced bad intelligence — someone on the rack would tell you whatever you wanted to hear. Torture also dehumanized the torturer and hurt the organization because it had a way of turning fine professionals into brutes.

Another reason for the code came to me over a late-night dinner at a different café — I had to find a new haunt when terrorists blew up Apropo. Over dinner, a friend — a lawyer and a philosopher —asked me about my experiences in the Shabak. He also reminded me of the story of a Shabak interrogator who lied under oath about his actions.

This got me thinking about all the other times in the past that our people lied to the government, press, and even the Supreme Court about our methods.

Our leaders are no fools — they knew they were being lied to, but they raised no objections because they were also lying to themselves. In pondering the reasons for the lies and self-deception, my mind turned to the laws for robots dreamed up by Isaac Asimov, the science-fiction writer I read as a kid. His Third Law says a robot must do everything in its power to protect its own survival.

I translated Asimov's laws for robots into an organization's laws of survival. First, an organization like the Shabak will do everything to fulfill its mission. A related law is that in this myopia for success, in our case to prevent terror, an organization will bulldoze all obstacles in its path, including the rule of law and human rights. This is all the more the case when a terrified public prefers security over rights, especially when the rights to be violated are someone else's.

The code of ethics we began drawing up sought to tame this drive for self-preservation with Asimov's robotic Laws One and Two: A robot may not injure a human being or, through inaction, allow a human being to come to harm; a robot must obey the orders given it by human beings except where such orders would conflict with the First Law. Translated in the work of the Shabak, physical or psychological means of extracting information are only justified as a means of protecting innocent lives. Because our work depended on getting at the truth — reliable information — lies had no place in our toolbox.

One way we tried to bring a new culture into the otherwise hermetically closed society of the Shabak was to invite in outsiders such as philosophers, poets, journalists, and members of the Supreme Court to address officers.

Another innovation we made was in technology. To penetrate Hamas's military organization and its cells, we needed precise and, if possible, real-time intelligence, technology to replace the aforementioned "files."

One solution we came up with was going digital. The term "Start Up Nation" hadn't yet been coined; nevertheless, high tech was booming, and I looked outside the Shin Bet, to universities and research institutes, for the technical talent we needed to penetrate terrorist networks and extract useful information from raw intelligence.

The technology had its limitations because terrorists at the top of our list to capture or eliminate quickly figured out that we monitored cell phone traffic. The only network they trusted was human, people they'd vetted as loyal to them and to the Islamist credo of an unceasing jihad against us. The suicide bomber who struck Café Apropo, Musa Abd al-Qadir Ghanimat, was recruited by Ibrahim Ghanimat, a relative in the village of Surif. Ghanimat left no electronic or written trail.

In September 1998, I was back in Kerem Maharal, and, as usual, I was pacing the living room frustrated that the Shabak's success at preventing terror had allowed Israeli leaders to slip back into the old habit of ignoring the source of the violence, our occupation. A few months earlier, on what Palestinians call the Nakba Day or the anniversary of their loss of much of Palestine in 1948, the poet Darwish prepared another speech for Arafat. In the address the man most Israelis continued to see as the incarnation of evil said, "We recognize the suffering of the Jewish people . . . We do not seek to be captives of history or victims of the past. The Palestinian people have launched a redemptive journey to the future. From the ashes of our sorrow and loss, we are resurrecting a nation celebrating life and hope." It was Arafat's most incisive defense of Oslo to date, and when I had it translated and distributed it to members of the cabinet, people around the table just rolled their eyes.

I was also nervous because I'd just read an opinion poll from Shikaki backing up reports from Jibril and our informants in Palestinian towns and villages of a population nearing the breaking point. There was growing suspicion, fueled by settlement construction, that the occupation would never end. Support for the peace process was waning.

I heard the phone ring in the kitchen. From the caller ID on the secure line, I knew it had to be important — Yuval Diskin never called me at home just to chat.

"Got something for you." The tone of Diskin's raspy voice told me that this "something" was what we call in the security business actionable intelligence.

"What's up?"

"Adel Awadallah."

In clipped words he told me we had his "pinpoint whereabouts."

My skin tingled as I absorbed the news that we'd tracked down the man who had been evading our dragnet for so long. From the pictures we had on file of Adel Awadallah, he didn't look like a stereotypical fanatic. In his severe steel glasses, the former math and technology student at Sari Nusseibeh's Al Quds University could have been a programmer for IBM. But his years on the run from us and his extreme charisma had turned the bomb maker and strategist behind Hamas's terror into a Palestinian folk hero.

Diskin told me how forty-eight-year-old Imad Awadallah, Adel's brother, had escaped from a Palestinian prison a month earlier, where he had been locked up on charges related to the murder of an American archaeologist.[29] Jibril had instructed his interrogators to put Imad on the rack to pry out information on the whereabouts of his brother, but to no avail. After Imad's escape from prison, our analysts tracked down the two brothers to a farmhouse in Khirbet al-Taybeh, a village close to Hebron that was a nest of Hamas support. For the first time we had both brothers within our reach.

I congratulated Diskin on his good work, then said, "Now come up with an operational plan." The line went dead.

In my kitchen I wondered how much time we had to capture the two brothers. How long would they stay in the farmhouse? A few hours? A day? We had no time to lose.

The following day my leadership team met to discuss how to proceed. Diskin presented a plan for eliminating the brothers from the air, a simple and deadly operation that posed little risk to our men. And since they were alone in the farmhouse, this approach wouldn't have harmed bystanders.

I told Diskin we were going to get the two terrorists alive. By this point in my tenure, I'd crafted a policy for targeted killings that brought a modicum of ethics into the dirty business.[30] We should kill only as the last resort. In the case of the brothers, a full-scale military attack from the air to eliminate them would give them a martyr's death, inspiring a new crop of suicide bombers. Much better to strap them to a chair and squeeze out information, I argued. A clandestine group such as Hamas feared nothing more than for one of its leaders to break during interrogation.

Once Diskin came up with a preliminary plan, I rang up Prime Minister Netanyahu's office. Given the stakes, I assumed permission to execute the operation would be just a formality.

Walking into Bibi's upstairs office that morning in September 1998, I scanned the room and, as usual, admired the framed photo of Theodor Herzl hanging on the wall. Netanyahu's *Terrorism: How the West Can Win* stared at me from the bookshelves.

The prime minister sat behind his desk wearing the half-moon reading glasses he used for paperwork. He looked up from his reading and motioned for me to sit.

"What do you have for me, Ami?" he asked, tilting his head down so he could look at me from above his glasses.

"Awadallah," I said. "We've tracked down both brothers." I laid out the facts, then paused for a moment to let the weight of the news sink in before requesting permission to carry out our plan. Netanyahu leaned forward in his chair. With his hands on his long wooden desk, he stood up, his silver watch visible from just under the cuff of his white button-down dress shirt.

He tilted his head back and stared abstractly into a corner, the moonlight glowing through the Bauhaus windows illuminating his solemn face. "No," he finally said, arching his eyebrows. "I can't allow that."

I swallowed hard. Had he been an ordinary politician, I wouldn't have blamed him for being dizzy with panic at the idea that hitting Awadallah might unleash a fresh wave of revenge attacks. But this was a man who on camera accused Arafat of not doing his part to round up terrorists, and now he was rejecting the best opportunity he'd have during his term to do his own part.

"Sir," I began, measuring my words carefully, "intelligence of this quality comes along once in a lifetime. I have no intention of turning the brothers into martyrs. We'll do our best to get them alive, and if Hamas retaliates, well, we'll just have to deal with it. But the information we'll get from them on Hamas's terror infrastructure — the bombers and bomb makers, the sleeper cells, the source of funding — could help us reduce the level of violence."

He turned and looked at me, but not in the eye this time. Instead he stared below my face at my throat. Glowering, he shook his head again. "No."

"Sir, we've got them cornered!"

"I told you my answer."

With the lives of innocent Israelis in my hands, I wasn't about to back down. I made it clear to him that there were moments when we had to walk into the minefield. We understood that capturing the brothers might inspire revenge killings and that Hamas might try to kidnap Israelis to force the brothers' release. But we knew how to cope. Our level of cooperation with the PA had improved, and intelligence penetration was infinitely better than it was over two years ago when the killing of the Engineer triggered bus bombings.

"Okay, so let Arafat take care of Awadallah," he retorted. It was an attitude I had seen often among our top leaders. *We won't risk Hamas reprisals*, went this line of reasoning, *but we'll force Arafat to do it, even if it endangers his regime. Why should we care about Arafat, anyway? Once a terrorist, always a terrorist.*

"Sir," I continued, shifting from deference to a more direct approach. "Arafat isn't going to do this for us. He doesn't work for us." Besides, I reminded him, the brothers were in a village under our security control. The IDF wasn't going to allow the Palestinians to carry out an operation in areas we patrolled.

Netanyahu just pursed his lips.

We went in circles for two hours. When repetition and brow-beating failed, I played the last card I had: "Mr. Prime Minister, no one understands the threat of revenge attacks more than I do, believe me, but the day we stop defending ourselves because we are afraid of the consequences is the day we raise the white flag. With all due respect, what you're telling me is that Hamas has won! If I can't take operational action against the commander of the Qassam Brigades, someone currently working overtime to murder as many Israeli civilians as possible, I can't continue doing my job. If you don't authorize the operation now, I will be unable to continue in my post."

The prime minister was quiet. He lit a cigar and, puffing away, began nodding while rubbing his forehead thoughtfully with one finger. I assumed he was calculating the political fallout from my resignation. "Okay," he finally said. "Just don't fuck up."

Having already decided we would try to capture them alive, our team met to discuss logistics with members of the police counterterrorism SWAT unit that would help us carry out the operation. Out came the maps of the area around Hebron, a region of craggy hills filled with legions of people sympathetic to Hamas. The operation would have to be carried out under the cover of darkness, and the element of surprise would be key. We would also need to get out of the village without a mob blocking our way.

It took several more days of intelligence-gathering and planning, and finally a little luck, before we were ready. We knew where the brothers were, when they left the farmhouse, and how to get into the building. During one of their absences, our people turned the place into a reality television studio; there wasn't a corner of the house not equipped with an infrared camera and microphone. For four days, we listened in on the brothers' conversations: discussions about producing Hezbollah-quality rockets, preparations to detonate five massive car bombs in Israeli cities, plans to deploy chemical weapons and poison Tel Aviv's water supply. Another scheme involved kidnapping General Raful Eitan and my two predecessors at the Service, Yaakov Peri and Carmi Gillon.[31]

We also learned through the hidden mikes that Hamas, for all its violence, had red lines. When Imad vowed to kill Jibril for having him tortured, Adel said no. "We don't target fellow Muslims."

Once we were ready, we sent in our commandos, waiting nearby in a convoy of eight trucks and vans, to storm the farmhouse.

A small unit of commandos, accompanied by attack dogs, scaled the wall surrounding the house and burst into the building. From inside Shin Bet command center, I watched on the live video feed as Adel reached for his weapon and shot the dog before our men killed him. His brother, now awake, also went for his gun and got cut down.

After killing the brothers, the commandos cased the house and found nine grenades, two automatic weapons, two pistols, bullets, and five wigs, one of them blond. I had wanted the brothers alive for the intelligence we might have extracted from them. But we found strapped to Adel's back a piece of intelligence perhaps more valuable than anything an interrogator could have pulled out of him: a massive sack containing several hundred documents that amounted to the brain and central nervous system of Hamas's intelligence-operational infrastructure in the West Bank. Not even in my wildest daydreams had I thought Adel, a veteran guerrilla fighter, would make such an elementary mistake. Ironically, he trusted no one other than himself with the materials, which he feared might end up in our hands. His fear, it turned out, was well founded.

Just before midnight, immediately after the operation concluded, I phoned Bibi and insisted on another face-to-face meeting to explain the circumstances surrounding the killings.

We met in his office half an hour later. As I spoke, he leaned forward in his chair, his elbows on the desk, looking straight at me, the bald spot on top of his head reflecting the lamplight. His house slippers peeked out from beneath his desk.

"What are you going to do?" he asked.

"We'll have to issue a statement to the press."

He stood up, stretched his arms and legs, and sighed heavily. The prime minister seemed suddenly vulnerable among the trappings of power — the Star of David flag behind the desk, the framed picture of Herzl hanging on the wall.

"The press. Yes, let's say it was another work accident." He suggested we announce that the brothers had blown themselves up while preparing for their next attack.

"Mr. Prime Minister," I responded, "everyone knows we were in the area. Rumors are probably already spreading through the Palestinian grapevine and among the settlers. You can bet journalists will catch wind of it soon. You are the prime minister and you can give the world whichever version you want. As for me, I'm not going to lie to the media. If we start lying, no one will believe anything we say. This is a matter of credibility for the State of Israel and the Shin Bet."

"Credibility is not your department," said Bibi. "You stick with security."

"Our capability depends on our credibility. Like I said, I am not going to lie to the media."

"You do not understand the media," said Bibi.

Netanyahu lifted a finger like a pupil in a classroom, then seemed to change his mind and set his hand back on the desk. I heard him say something under his breath that sounded like a curse. "Fine, Ami," he finally conceded. "What do you suggest we do?"

"In the morning we'll release a statement to the press. We'll also have to make it abundantly clear to Arafat what we expect. His reaction will be key to preventing Hamas from taking revenge."

"How are we going to do that?"

"I'll go see him right now."

He dropped his chin as if to wish me good luck.

Well after midnight, I rang up the head of Arafat's office and told him I was on my way to see his boss. I requested that Jibril and Dahlan attend.

I arrived at the presidential compound in Ramallah an hour later in an unmarked car. I paused before delivering myself to the armed men guarding the compound, who took me upstairs to the chairman.

Arafat motioned to a metal folding chair. Just after I sat down, a guy pushed through the door with a platter of tea and dessert. "Eat!" Arafat predictably commanded, pointing to the platter of knafeh, a sweet cheese pastry he knew I loved, which he'd had a driver rush down from Nablus an hour to the north. But the knot in the pit of my stomach had left me without an appetite.

It was by this point early in the morning, and he looked worried. In addition to his ever-present black-and-white keffiyeh, Arafat wore a cheap cotton button-down shirt and a neatly pressed olive-green field jacket, missing the top button and slightly too big for him despite his corpulence. The entire ensemble looked like it could have come from a garage sale. This, too, was part of his myth: selfless, scornful of luxury, a man given over wholly to the liberation of Palestine.

His hand trembled from incipient Parkinson's as he held up his glass of tea. He had changed markedly since our first encounter in 1996, when Peres was in power and Oslo was a viable process, flawed yet strong enough to end the conflict. He'd now endured two years of Bibi and it showed in his suspicious comportment.

I cut to the chase: "Mr. Chairman, we killed Adel and Imad Awadallah this evening. In the name of the State of Israel, we ask that you do everything in your power to prevent Hamas from retaliating. They are your enemies just as they are ours."

Arafat sat up straight in his chair and stared at me, his bloodshot eyes moist. His response would determine whether the peace process would live to see another day.

I took a deep breath and continued with the statement I had rehearsed in the half-hour drive from Jerusalem. "Chairman Arafat, if Hamas or anyone else responds to this news by bombing us, you can forget about agreements and processes." There was no need to go into details. The potential consequences were crystal clear to Arafat. He paused and stirred more honey into his tea.

"I need two days to get set up," he finally said, sipping from the teacup, by which he meant sweeping up Hamas activists or warning them to lie low. He asked us to delay announcing the brothers' deaths until he was ready.

"Two days?" I repeated, looking over to Jibril and then back to Arafat. "More like four hours. We'll be releasing a statement to the press at six o'clock in the morning. We need to get ahead of the media, who are already sniffing out the story."

His eyelids fluttered, and he fidgeted with something on his desk, a tennis ball or maybe a pair of dice. He asked what I thought he should do first. I looked to Jibril, who met my gaze. "He'll know," I said.

Arafat turned to Jibril. I held my breath; I knew his reputation for screaming at lieutenants, cursing them, or banishing them from his inner circle for perceived offenses.

"What do you say?" he asked Jibril in Arabic I could easily follow.

Jibril nodded. "We know what to do, we just need your permission," he said.

"You have it."

In Gaza, Sheikh Yassin reacted to the news by telling his supporters: "This is the nature of war. Sometimes we win, sometimes we lose. Our response is coming soon, God willing."

Over the coming days, thousands of Hamas supporters jammed the streets of the West Bank demanding "revenge now." Rumors began circulating that the "martyrs" were victims of Jibril's cooperation with us, leading even some Fatah leaders to call for retaliation because, they said, violence was the only language the Israelis understood. Palestinians didn't know Jibril nearly as well as I did — that last thing he would ever do was hand over a Palestinian into our hands.

While Hamas rioted and vowed retribution, we pored over the information that had fallen into our hands: From the hundreds of documents duct-taped to Awadallah's back, we could map out the entire structure of Hamas in the West Bank. We got names of activists and their locations and a chart of Hamas's various terror cells. The treasure trove enabled us, through meticulous analysis and dozens of intelligence operations, to smash holes in Hamas's terror infrastructure. Dozens of operations by the army and Shabak, often in coordination with the Palestinians, stopped terrorism through 1999 and into 2000.

Had our politicians acted wisely we might have permanently crippled the organization.

18

THE TICKING TIME BOMB

According to the Oslo agreement, by the end of 1998 the Palestinians should have received most of the Occupied Territories, and the two sides should have entered into negotiations over final borders, security, Jerusalem, settlements, water, and refugees. But Palestinian and Jewish terror combined with the continued expansion of settlements to destroy Oslo. By October of that year, Arafat had received only a fraction of what he felt had been promised, and he was running out of patience because he couldn't show his people that negotiating with the Israelis had brought them any closer to ending the occupation.

The Americans shared his frustration; Clinton began pressuring Bibi to complete the transfer of territory. In parallel, he instructed the CIA to boost the Palestinian security apparatus's anti-terrorism efforts.

Netanyahu finally agreed to take part in a summit hosted by President Clinton at the Wye River Plantation in Maryland where Bibi and Arafat would finally negotiate face-to-face. On the table was Clinton's proposal that Israel withdraw from an additional 13 percent of the West Bank.

On the eve of the Clinton-Netanyahu-Arafat summit, Bibi's government announced plans to build twelve hundred homes near the Alei Zahav settlement, three miles inside the West Bank.

Amazingly, Jibril and his forces continued working with us. In one case we got information about an attack in the center of Israel being planned in the Nablus area by a Hamas operative close to Sheikh Yassin. A courier was on his way to Gaza to meet with Yassin in order to receive the final green light when we captured him at the Erez checkpoint.

Through various means, we already knew about the bomb maker in Nablus, and we knew the attack was planned for the following day. What we didn't know was the exact house where we could track down the terrorists before they could act. We had a classic ticking bomb on our hands, and I expected the interrogators to pull out all the stops to extract the bomb's location from the prisoner.

When the head of interrogation called me in my office, I told him to proceed with the interrogation as if dealing with a "ticking bomb." Picturing a car exploding in front of a kindergarten somewhere, I would have pulled the guy's fingernails out with my teeth if that's what it took to keep the bomb from going off. Nothing quite so barbaric was necessary.

Within half an hour, and without prompting — the interrogator never laid a finger on him — the man confessed everything: the precise location of the explosives and the operational outline of the attack.

At once, I called Jibril and told him what we knew. We agreed that one of our people would join his team in making the arrests, and he'd then hand over the terrorists to us.

Things went as planned. But once he had the terrorists in his grips, Jibril reneged on our agreement. "I just can't hand over Palestinians to the Israelis," he said. "You would not have given me a Jew who had planned an attack on us."

I was about to lay into him for going back on our agreement when he added a line that shut me up. "Ami, with us Palestinians, there is no *Saison*" — a French expression meaning "hunting season." Jibril, translator of Menachem Begin, was referring to a roundup of right-wing Jewish underground fighters, duly handed over to the British, which Ben-Gurion ordered in 1944.

While he spoke, I imagined a sly grin on his face. He was right, of course. I understood and released him from the promise. He then gave us all the information he had uncovered from the terrorists and offered for our interrogators to join his in extracting more. I refused the offer — his men undertook interrogation without our legal system, our Supreme Court, and our watchdog human rights organizations such as the Public Committee Against Torture.

I also knew we couldn't count on this cooperation forever. Jibril made it clear he was only working with me because he believed it would lead to the end of occupation. What would happen, I asked myself a thousand times, if the ranks of Palestinian police, and the two million Palestinians in cities and refugee camps, lost hope that we would ever clear out of Judea and Samaria? Would our partners turn to violence out of the fear that, if they didn't, their outraged countrymen would flock to Hamas? Might they even join the jihad?

In May 1999, I pushed such fears from my mind as I paced nervously behind the stage set up in Tel Aviv's public gathering place formerly known as Kings of Israel Square, renamed Rabin Square in 1995 after he was assassinated in the adjacent parking lot. On the stage stood Ehud Barak, the new prime minister whose life I was sworn to protect. My old colleague and former chief of the General Staff had just defeated Bibi in the national elections. To a throng of supporters at the rally he declared the "dawn of a new day." Unlike Netanyahu, who saw Oslo as a disaster for the Jewish people, Barak said he believed in two states for two peoples. His election slogan, repeated a thousand times, was *Anachnu po, hem sham* — We are here, and they are there.

I was too busy keeping an eye out for possible Yigal Amir copycats to pay much attention to the speeches and revelry, to the people holding up champagne bottles with Ehud's face on the label.

The crowds that evening, like the Palestinians, had faith that Barak, Israel's most decorated soldier and a genius famously able to build a clock out of a mousetrap, would pick up where his former Labor colleague Rabin had left off. And though Netanyahu had only implemented a fraction of what he promised at the Wye River summit, Arafat, too, was confident that Barak would hand him the rest and move the political process toward a solution. Another reason to be cautiously optimistic in those days, incredibly, was

Hamas. Their military wing was a mere shadow of its former self. In Gaza the Hamas spiritual leader Sheikh Yassin, recently released from prison,[32] said to an Israeli journalist, "We have to be realistic. We are talking about a homeland that was stolen a long time ago in 1948 and again in 1967. Let's declare a temporary cease-fire. Let's leave the bigger issue for future generations to decide." In those days, he understood that that was what the "Palestinian street" wanted.

A few days after his swearing-in, I returned to the second-floor office on Balfour Street. Ehud was the third prime minister I'd served in three years and a man I'd known for years. I was accustomed to his mannerisms. Like most leaders, he enters the room chin first.

Bibi's books on terrorism were gone, but otherwise the office looked more or less the same. I didn't see a gift I had given Ehud four years earlier when he retired from the military and went into politics.[33] It was a sextant, a model of an eighteenth-century navigational gadget that allowed captains simultaneously to see the horizon of the sea while measuring the angle of celestial objects, stars, and the sun. The device enables the captain to navigate through cascading waves while charting a course toward the final destination.

Though we had a lot to discuss, I began by asking him why he didn't have the sextant hanging on the wall or sitting on his desk. He shrugged. I reminded Ehud what I had said when I first gave him the gift. If the marshal's baton symbolizes military power and authority, the sextant illustrates a key aspect of wise political leadership. My point to Ehud was he would have to manage the day-to-day affairs of our country without losing sight of the "stars" — the long-term vision of the future.

I caught a flash of what might have been a smile.

Next, I presented my assessment of the security situation. Thanks to the security cooperation with the Palestinians and the Hamas archive we pulled from Awadallah's back, we had cracked the Hamas terror network in the West Bank. A year had passed since the last Israeli civilian died in a terrorist attack; two since a mass suicide bombing. Terrorists were as motivated as ever to murder Israeli civilians, they just couldn't get through our defenses. They were also hobbled by the drop in public support among Palestinians for terror, partly as a result in their belief in American leadership, which at Wye had succeeded in bringing the Israelis back to the negotiation table.

The new prime minister looked satisfied, and I thought back to what I had once said to Jibril: that our job was to lower the levels of violence so politicians could get on with the job of concluding a peace deal.

"There remain very serious dangers," I continued.

"Dangers?"

"Our intelligence tells us that if Arafat and the PA can't deliver on their promises, people on the Palestinian street will reject diplomacy and turn to violence. They'll come to see PA security apparatus as collaborators with the occupation." Security depended on a political horizon of hope, I explained, which Bibi never provided. Most Palestinians thought we used Oslo as a pretext to expand settlements. From Arafat's perspective, too, he got nothing in return for all of the political capital he had spent locking up our enemies.

Ehud shifted in his chair.

"You'll have to make it clear to the Palestinians that we're serious this time. Quickly. Lasting security depends on establishing a relationship of trust with Arafat."

Barak cleared his throat. "Ami," he finally said, "you don't understand these things" — by which I think he meant politics. He thought I was wasting my time talking about the importance of trust, of seeing our conflict through Arafat's eyes, and paying attention to opinion polls.

Having known Barak for so long, I permitted myself to speak frankly. "Ehud, I don't think you understand Arafat." I described to him the Palestinian leader's psyche as I knew it from my meetings with him, intelligence reports, journalism, and books, and I also told him what I thought would be necessary to forge a deal with him. After being burned by Bibi, he needed to see something concrete.

Barak pretended to listen, and even jotted down a few notes on a yellow office pad. "How do you suggest I build trust with Arafat?" he asked. But he sounded like he was already thinking about his next appointment.

My suggestion was a face-to-face meeting with Arafat followed by rapidly withdrawing from the territory Netanyahu had promised him at Wye.

"Something to think about," he said. Slamming his palm on his desk, he bolted up and accompanied me to the door.

I left the office fearing that Ehud might be too fixated on the stars, blind to the rogue waves coming right at him and at Israel.

For the next seven weeks, Ehud focused on forming his government, which included a number of pro-settlement cabinet ministers. That he found no time to meet with Arafat was noticed by the Palestinians, as were things he was saying in the Hebrew press. Ehud would prefer, he said, to leapfrog over the withdrawal Bibi promised Arafat and head directly to final status negotiations. To keep his coalition together, he also bragged to the Hebrew media how his government was going to build more settlements than Bibi, more than any other prime minister before him. He began rehashing an old speech about Israel being a "modern and prosperous villa in the middle of the jungle where there was no hope for those who cannot defend themselves and no mercy for the weak."[34]

"Hold on a second," Jibril said to me. "Something doesn't add up. Mr. Barak tells us we're heading toward a diplomatic agreement, and then he turns around and says something else in Hebrew? Is the person standing opposite us really a Rabin, may he rest in peace, or is he just another Netanyahu?" His fear was that Barak spoke only in the language of power and didn't believe in diplomacy.

During each meeting with Barak, I repeated the Shabak assessment that a one-on-one meeting with Arafat would dispel the mounting suspicions about Barak's intentions. Ehud and Arafat finally arranged to meet at the Erez checkpoint in the northern Gaza Strip.

As we were finalizing the security arrangements, I asked someone from the Prime Minister's Office what kind of gift Ehud would be bringing.

"Gift?" The man looked blindsided.

"Yes." I reminded the man that we lived in the Middle East, where gifts are signs of respect.

"We don't have anything to give him."

"You'll need to come up with something."

It was clear that they wouldn't. For Ehud to show up empty-handed to their first encounter, with the world's press there to document the niggardly snub, would be like a slap in Arafat's face. We raced helter-skelter around the Shabak office soliciting ideas, then got money from a rainy-day fund and bought a silver-plated Koran and Torah, in Arabic and Hebrew.

At Erez, Barak shook Arafat's hand and handed him the box — he probably didn't know what was inside. From where I was standing, I saw what looked like tears welling up in Arafat's eyes.

Two weeks later I met Arafat in Ramallah and the tears were still there. With sincerity I couldn't help but admire, the former terrorist praised Ehud for coming up with the right gesture: The Koran and the Torah touched the most sensitive nerves of both peoples, and the gift was a sign Barak understood this. I nodded respectfully while fearing that my old friend in fact hadn't a clue.

The meeting at Erez was important but couldn't replace policies and actions in the field. It was during this encounter that Barak sprung a new plan on Arafat. "Let's stop everything and conclude a framework agreement while discussing the core issues" — borders, settlements, right of return, security. Concretely, he wanted to push off the Wye withdrawals for six months and launch into final status talks.

"Think about it," he said.

"My mind is made up. I don't want this. Implement Wye right away! Netanyahu already agreed."

"Just give it some thought," Barak countered.

Ehud headed to Washington to win Clinton over to his plan. He also pulled in Egyptian president Mubarak. With all these maneuvers, Arafat's belief that Barak was Rabin reincarnate was fading fast. In Gaza, Dahlan threatened to quit if Arafat agreed to talks before getting the lands promised at Wye. Jibril, too, was becoming suspicious. "Ami," he must have said a dozen times, "we are not your collaborators. We don't put Hamas members in prison for you. We're only doing it because our public believes that at the end of the day, we'll have a state alongside the State of Israel. The minute we stop believing that, you can forget about cooperation." They were risking a civil war with Hamas to hold up their end of the bargain, and Barak wouldn't even give them the pittance Bibi had promised.

I had no response. Anyway, I reminded myself, my job wasn't to do politics. My brief was to stop the bombings, to prevent the territories from erupting into flames, and to provide objective information and advice to the prime minister — to be a gatekeeper.

To do this I had to know the mood among the Palestinians, and reading Shikaki's polls I sensed we were about to veer into an abyss. With the drone of cement mixers in the Occupied Territories in the background, more than ever Hamas's refrain — that Oslo was a trick and that Zionists only respond to power and force — was getting through. My sensors Matti Steinberg and Amira Hass in her dispatches in *Haaretz* told me that if a second Intifada broke out, it would be a spontaneous eruption from the street, fueled by bitter disappointment at the corruption average people saw in their leaders, most of whom came with Arafat from Tunis and hadn't faced the IDF and Shabak during the Intifada. The main reason would be loss of hope in a process that had only produced more settlements, roadblocks, and humiliation.

Behind the scenes, Barak turned his attention to getting a peace deal with Syria's President Assad, relegating the Palestinians to the back burner. Our Shabak assessment was that this was a disastrous move. A possible peace deal with Syria would take time, whereas time was a commodity we didn't have with the Palestinians. All the heads of the intelligence services — the Mossad and the IDF's military intelligence — agreed with us. We met with Ehud to clarify our position, but he didn't budge from his decision. I turned to the Americans to see if they could reason with him, but they ended up backing what would be a futile exercise. Talks with Assad went nowhere. Meanwhile Arafat felt betrayed.

It took all their finesse, coddling, and a bit of strong-arming for the Americans to reassure Arafat that Barak remained a committed partner. Eventually, with the help of Egyptian diplomats, the Americans persuaded Arafat to forgo the transfer of territories and proceed directly to a discussion of core issues. In my talks with Ehud, I kept pressing for establishing greater trust, especially after the Syria debacle. The flaws of Oslo were legion, and there was nothing sacred about the approach taken by negotiators five years earlier. There was only one problem with Barak's approach: "If Arafat doesn't trust you, he won't budge from his position." Negotiations would lead nowhere, and a new round of violence could break out.

Once again, he drummed his fingers on his desk and dismissed me.

In early September a French Jewish billionaire offered up his villa in the Israeli town of Savyon for a private dinner between Barak and Arafat. Maybe, just maybe, the two leaders, both paranoids, would warm up to each other away from the media and teams of diplomats. Maybe they'd even talk about a better future for both peoples. Maybe they'd establish a modicum of trust. Barak came with his wife, Nava. I was there with Barak's chief of staff and a former general. Abu Mazen, Arafat's number two, joined us around the table. Yasser Abed Rabbo, once a member of a Marxist-Leninist-Maoist group and a frequent target of Flotilla 13 commandos, was there, too. No one else even knew the dinner was happening; members of the Israeli cabinet learned about it afterward.

Over Moroccan couscous and tagine, the idea was for the initial small talk to lead to a comfortable atmosphere for the two leaders to talk. Barak began by telling a joke, but Arafat just stared into space. The atmosphere was frigid — the lack of trust between the two men was palpable.

But once the food came, the light banter gave way to a frostier atmosphere. Ehud loved to eat and dove into the couscous. Arafat just picked at his food and said nothing. The only bit of warmth came at the end when Arafat planted a kiss on Nava Barak's forehead.[35] The dinner was a disaster.

The Americans intervened to at least create the appearance of movement. Arafat eventually caved to American pressure and agreed to discuss Barak's alternative approach with the Israelis. Barak told him he was sending his chief negotiator to present some ideas. Arafat quickly put a negotiation team together headed by two ministers. Barak, though, ran into hurdles. It was a question of trust: There was no one in his government coalition or his cabinet that enjoyed his full confidence.

Struggling, Barak suggested that I head up his team. I refused at once because of the conflict of interest between my position at the Shabak and leading political negotiations. There was another reason I didn't consider the offer, however, which was my experience with Ehud. I knew him well enough to know that he would maintain multiple channels of communication, and that he would be the only one who saw all the cards. Transparency and trust were not part of his lexicon, and not only in his dealings with the Palestinians.

Polls in Israel and Palestine continued showing hemorrhaging support for both Arafat and Barak. Arafat had nothing left to offer Palestinian society to convince them that they would eventually reach an agreement with Israel. The Shabak was receiving more reports of gun smuggling, and in September, Hamas carried out bombings inside Israel. Only the bombers were killed, but it showed that Hamas was rebuilding its network, and Israelis were scared.

The moment I realized that everything was over, and we were already counting down to a new outbreak of violence, came in November. Following months of delay while Ehud put together his negotiation team, Arafat's team of senior ministers turned up for a meeting to hear from Barak's appointed chief negotiator, a former ambassador to Jordan. On the Palestinian side, the expectations were high because, at long last, they would hear the prime minister's ideas for racing ahead to final status negotiations.

For status-conscious Palestinians, sitting in a room with a diplomat and not a fellow minister was already a slap in the face. Even worse were the man's opening remarks: "Gentlemen, I don't have the authority to discuss the core topics." He added that he had a mandate to discuss only a few relatively minor issues — nothing touching borders, Jerusalem, and the refugees.

"Then why are we here?" the Palestinians turned and whispered to one another. "To talk about soccer?" Based on information I received, when Arafat got a report of the meeting, he was fuming. He felt he was being played, once again.

When the American negotiating team, sensing a new crisis, asked me for my position, I held nothing back. Clinton's envoys Dennis Ross and Martin Indyk wanted to meet every time they arrived in Israel in the context of peace talks. "Look," I told them when we sat down in my office, "if there is no change of direction in the process in the next six months, we're careening in the direction of a violent popular uprising, probably led by disappointed youngsters waving Palestinian flags. My best guess is that it will erupt around the settlements or the Temple Mount / Al Aqsa Mosque area in Jerusalem."[36]

Ross and Indyk looked at me as if the pressures of the job had gotten to me. "No way! Arafat just promised us that he had no intention of turning to violence. The prime minister also assured us that he and Arafat can make a deal."

"Gentlemen, my information says otherwise. Palestinian newspapers and public opinion polls tell us that Arafat no longer represents the aspirations of the Palestinian people. Try to find me a Palestinian who still sees Arafat as a leader. He's not the guy to talk to. The explosion is going to come from the street. We think it'll come by the end of 2000. Why? Because average Palestinians have lost confidence in Arafat just as my prime minister has lost the support of the Knesset and of his own ministers."

"Sure, Ami."

I looked around at these two well-meaning men working for a well-meaning president. I appreciated the Americans and knew that it was only because of their support and pressure that the peace process had survived Bibi. But I was also a sewage worker in the Middle East, and I knew from my dealings with the CIA and FBI that these people, with all their fine intentions, were lost in the complexity of the region. I didn't take their assessments seriously because they didn't understand we were sitting on a fault line. Some earthquakes are tremors that rattle the chandeliers; others can bring down an entire civilization.

19

BREAKING MY SILENCE

There are a thousand hacking at the branches of evil to one who is striking at the root.

— Henry David Thoreau

When I came up with a list of people to interview for my memoirs, I included a man who had been a senior officer under my command. We met at an Irish pub on the ground floor of a Tel Aviv skyscraper housing tech companies and lawyers' offices. Antlers hung from the walls, and a big green carnation decorated the side of the bar. With our voices barely audible above the din of people talking, clanging plates, and blaring pop music, it was a good place for a conversation about secrecy and intrigue. We ordered burgers and two pints of microbrewed pale ale.

"So how have you been, Ami?" the man started.

"Personally, things have never been better. Family's fine. Just finished remodeling the upstairs. Lots of time to read. Doing laps every day in the pool in the backyard keeps me fit. Politically, though, I'm more depressed than ever."

"I know the feeling," he said, raising his pint in commiseration. The old colleague nodded along at most of what I said about how the diverging national narratives had triggered the Second Intifada. He raised no objections to my analysis that most Israelis continued to believe we had wanted security and got terror, while Palestinians, who wanted independence, felt they had only gotten more settlements, more military occupation, and more humiliation at checkpoints. That we'd screwed them.

It was good to catch up, but I left the pub frustrated, mostly with myself. If Shikaki had done an impromptu poll of those in the pub, members of Israel's business and entrepreneurial elite,

I'm sure that most would have agreed with our grim assessment — and then returned to their offices to cut the next big deal. Ideology isn't the problem with career-oriented, taxpaying, liberal, open-minded Israelis such as the ex-agent and me. Our problem is that we never get angry enough to rock the boat. Maybe life is too good. We'll march in the Pride parade or get worked up over animal rights, say, but we can't be bothered with the plight of Palestinians on the other side of the Separation Wall. Perhaps we're also afraid. Though our democracy may seem to outsiders as solid as a Merkava tank, in reality it is fragile and could easily tip into fratricide. And though we'll moan about politics, we are too much a part of a system that serves us well to take risks that might damage our reputations. Lines I read somewhere from Henry David Thoreau remind me of what we Israeli liberals almost never do: "If the machine of government is such a nature that it requires you to be the agent of injustice to another, then I say, break the law. Let your life be a counter-friction to stop the machine."

The only reason I can look myself in the mirror is that, in my better moments, since leaving the Shabak I've aimed a few wrenches at the machine.

From the pub I drove to pick up Biba at her sister's in the Tel Aviv suburb of Givatayim, then headed to Habima, Israel's premier stage, for a benefit production of the play *Shakespeare in Love* for AKIM, a national nongovernmental organization for people with intellectual disabilities and their families that I chair.

During the performance, my mind turned to the convoluted path that led me from fighting terror to watching men in tights cavort on stage. My niece Zohara has special needs, and during my time at the Shin Bet, she lived at an AKIM-run group home. During our visits to Zohara, Biba made sure that I learned about the organization's good work. One thing led to another, and now twenty years later I'm its volunteer chairman. The benefit performance that evening was particularly poignant because, from the stage, AKIM honored an extraordinary Arab Israeli woman whose bravery in the face of life's challenges goes beyond anything I ever did on the battlefield. If we Israelis want to preserve and strengthen our democracy, we'll have to harness the values of inclusion, justice, and humanism that AKIM embodies. To quote Rabbi Jonathan Sacks, a man I greatly admire, we "honor God by honoring His image" in people frequently ignored or shunned.

Supporting AKIM isn't about throwing a wrench in the machine. Where Biba and I headed the following evening is. We drove to Jaffa for a party to welcome the new director of Breaking the Silence, an organization, much reviled in most quarters, that was founded by combat soldiers distressed by what they'd seen and done while serving in the West Bank and Gaza.[37] Their public testimony creates counter-friction by revealing to Israeli society the crimes being committed in their name.

It took us half an hour of driving through Jaffa's dark side streets to find the building. A guy with a tattoo on his arm, maybe a former commando, was checking bags outside the entrance. We took the stairs because the elevator was out of order, dodging feral cats and stepping over broken car seats and dead car batteries. On the sixth floor, like in old gangster movies, someone peered through a crack in the door to make sure we belonged. At last we entered a room filled with revelers shouting over throbbing Israeli pop music.

People set down their drinks to hug us as we made our introductory round through the room. I then navigated through the throng, shaking a dozen or more hands, to reach the bar, grabbing a couple of Maccabee beers before heading back to find Biba standing in a corner deep in conversation with old friends, who for all their criticisms are patriots and Zionists who believe in a democratic Jewish state alongside the State of Palestine. The way I see it, Breaking the Silence follows in the Israeli tradition of biting rhetorical attacks on injustice: During the Knesset debate about Minister Bennett's proposal to ban Breaking the Silence from schools, a member of the Knesset and supporter of Breaking the Silence read aloud Nathan Alterman's poem "Al Zot," the same poem my father had read to me at the age of three.

I began following the organization's work after the disastrous 2009 war in Gaza. Though it pained me to hear hard-nosed soldiers describe witnessing the pointless destruction of hundreds of houses and mosques, and soldiers shooting at civilians used by Hamas as human shields, I also knew they weren't flower-tossing pacifists. Their testimonies should be front-page news. Shortly before the party, the organization had made waves — more "counter-friction" — by taking a group of American writers on a tour of Judea and Samaria. One of the writers, the Jewish novelist Michael Chabon, said afterward: "Security is an invention of humanity's jailers. Anywhere you look, it is and has always been a hand of power drawing the boundaries, putting up the separation barriers and propagandizing hatred and fear of the people on the other side of the wall. Security for some means imprisonment for all."

Chabon is right. We never struck a balance between identifying security dangers and identifying the opportunities for peace.

Not long ago, during an interview, an Argentinian journalist suggested to me that *The Gatekeepers*, the documentary I collaborated on, was the Shabak version of Breaking the Silence. I raised no objection to the comparison to Israel's most hated NGO.

In the past I've publicly defended the organization. When our government threatened to shutter a gallery in Jerusalem for hosting one of their events, for instance, I told journalists that we in Israel are experiencing "incremental tyranny." I took the expression from my friend Brian Jenkins, an adviser to the president of the RAND Corporation and a former officer with the US Army 5th Special Forces. In the realities of a never-ending war, security trumps civil rights, minority protections, and pluralism, and with court approval we hollow out civil society and slip on our own shackles. One day we'll wake up and remember that once upon a time we lived in democracy.

In early 2000, Barak asked me to stay on at the Shabak until the end of the year even though my tenure was up in May. Since he would soon be signing a new framework agreement with Arafat, he assured me radiating confidence, he wanted me to help guide the agency into the new era. I countered that I would be leaving as planned, and that he should begin looking for my replacement immediately because my successor would have to be prepared for the explosion of violence we in the Shabak saw coming.

Ehud didn't know what I was talking about, because he had lost contact with reality. He didn't feel the rising temperatures, the waves forming whitecaps, the black cirrus clouds — the telltale signs of a hurricane coming our way.

In May, I turned in my badge and magnetic card, and Barak appointed my deputy director Avi Dichter to replace me. I was fifty-five and had to figure out what to do with myself. Professionally, you might say I had reached the mountaintop. Private-sector job offers came pouring in, but I was still too much a son of the kibbutz to join other ex-IDF, Shabak, and Mossad experts in peddling arms or advising companies, politicians, and rogue regimes in the dark arts of security. So what was I to do with myself?

Eventually I took a job as chairman of Netafim, the drip irrigation company launched by a kibbutz in the Negev. It was a way to get back to my kibbutz roots while making a contribution well beyond Israel's borders: Drip technology Netafim invented helps feed hundreds of millions of people worldwide.

I also got to be a full-time husband and father for the first time in my life. Hacking away at weeds and pruning dead branches, sweat coursing down my face in the company of my best friend in life, Biba, reminded me of the honest physical labor I was raised to adore. As a kid I carried loads of bananas on my back. Now I was working a scythe. I even took a scuba diving vacation on the Cocos Islands in the Indian Ocean, swam with sharks, and started reading novels again.

But my mind would not let go of what was happening to my country. The peace talks in July played out just as I had feared. Sure enough, Barak got Clinton to strong-arm Arafat into discussing the core issues at Camp David in the woods of Maryland, and when Ehud presented Arafat with a deal, Arafat walked away.

Ehud called me from his cabin and asked me to fly out and join him because he would need support once the international media caught wind of the debacle. What he really needed was a coconspirator in rewriting history. He wanted me to stand by his side nodding as he told the world: "I am hereby revealing Arafat's true face. Arafat is no partner — the Palestinians aren't partners."

I declined his request. *Who knows if Arafat is a partner?* I was thinking as I hung up the phone. Partnerships evolve out of a process of building mutual trust. Since Rabin's death and Peres's electoral defeat, neither Netanyahu nor Barak had lifted a finger to build such a partnership.

Barak flew back to Israel and, with the American administration behind him, blamed the failure of the summit on Arafat alone. The "no partner" line proved the single most catastrophic PR stunt in Israeli political history. I spoke freely to him. "It's up to us to decide which story we tell ourselves. Arafat in my experience doesn't have a single face, he's got a thousand. You can pick out the 'no partner' face just as easily as you can a partner face, and the particular face you've been selling to the public says more about you than it does Arafat. Let me tell you something, as someone who has accompanied you from the day you became prime minister. Which of Arafat's faces you choose to present to the world now is the most important issue you have, and you owe it to the citizens of Israel to make the right choice."

Through the month of August, I felt like a ship captain tracking an oncoming storm. In September I told the magazine *Nekuda*, a monthly put out by the settler movement, the bitter, inexorable truth: We had lost the First Intifada, just as we'd lose the new intifada heading our way. The journalist gasped, unaccustomed to a military man playing the role of Nostradamus.

A couple of weeks after the interview came out in *Nekuda*, Ariel Sharon, the Likud opposition leader, strode up to the Temple Mount, the very site I felt in my gut would trigger the apocalypse. By this point Barak was too weak politically to prevent it. Surrounded by dozens of armed policemen, Sharon announced he was there to assert Jewish claims. Israeli police responded to rioting Palestinians by firing rubber bullets and tear gas. From Sharon's perspective, the visit was no doubt a masterstroke, simultaneously harnessing settler support while dealing a body blow to Barak. The move also crippled Arafat because the masses, including many of his supporters, lost hope in the negotiation table.

Violence at Al Aqsa spread like a virus to Israeli Arab villages in the north, then to Gaza and the West Bank. The Shabak's position was that loss of hope had led to the uprising. The IDF claimed the whole thing was a premeditated act of war, as if Arafat had decided to stir up mayhem after having failed to achieve his goals at Camp David. They accused his regime of coordinating with Arabs in Israel and directing the armed uprising to destroy Israel.[38]

Barak accepted the army's baseless narrative, and the IDF thought they were fighting fire with fire — except that at this stage the rioting mobs were armed mostly with knives, Molotov cocktails, burning tires, and rocks.[39] Over the next few days the IDF fired 1.3 million bullets.

At first Arafat had an interest in calming things down, but as the funeral processions multiplied, his instinctual need to survive got him talking about jihad. On Israel radio I compared Arafat to a man riding on the back of a wild tiger pretending to steer the beast; in fact he had no control whatsoever.

On October 13, I got a call from the producer of a Channel Two news program asking me to be interviewed by Shelly Yachimovich, a top Israeli journalist and news host. The interview, set for that afternoon, was at the main Channel Two studio on the road from Tel Aviv to Jerusalem. I hesitated; my entire career in the security business had been behind the scenes. If I stood in front of the camera, which I did only infrequently and with great reluctance, it was to present facts as I saw them as a professional working for our military or government.

I thought about what my friend the politician had told me. "My job is to lie, and your job is to tell the truth."

It was time for me to break my silence. I agreed.

A few hours later I sat solemnly in front of the blinding lights and beeping cameras. A screen behind me played, over and over, footage from a lynching. A day earlier, Corporal Yossi Avrahami and Sergeant Vadim Nurzhitz took a wrong turn while driving to their base in Beth-El, a West Bank settlement, and ended up surrounded by a seething mob in a squalid neighborhood in Ramallah. Arafat's cops dragged Nurzhitz and Avrahami, a newlywed, to the second floor of an old stone police station in el-Bireh, a short distance from Arafat's presidential headquarters, where a bloodthirsty mob lunged at our soldiers with metal bars and knives.

On the screen behind me looped images of Aziz Salha, an unemployed nineteen-year-old Palestinian, pitching Nurzhitz, whose wife was three months' pregnant, out of the window into the mob that responded like a school of piranhas in a feeding frenzy. Afterward, Salha threw his bloody hands in the air as if he'd scored a winning goal. A member of Arafat's security forces stood by and did nothing, his finger on the trigger of a Kalashnikov, while the mob battered Nurzhitz's lifeless body with sticks.

Yachimovich, her eyes shifting between the images of the lynching and me, asked if we Israelis were headed for the shoals. Was our national boat about to capsize? Had the time come to break out the life rafts? *Were we doomed?*

On the high seas, I responded, a skilled captain and a good crew can manage most tempests, no matter how ferocious. It is only when nature pummels a ship from three sides — the perfect storm — that prayers are in order. That was what was happening to our country. "The storm is fierce," I said, continuing with the seafaring simile. "And there's no question that in the Middle East there's always the risk that our ship could capsize."

Yachimovich, lowering her voice a few octaves, repeated what everyone in Israel was saying, that human beings are not capable of such barbarity and therefore, by implication, the Palestinians must be some breed of wild beast. Clearly, she hoped that, given my experiences, I might offer privileged insight into the murderous pathologies of our enemies. We offered peace to Arafat and his gang of hooligans and look what we got in return! The cudgel and the whip, not peace treaties, are what such animals understand. "Are Palestinians even capable of being partners in peace?" she wanted to know.

I recall sitting upright in my chair, my pulse quickening, and with a pen in my hand staring directly into the camera. It was as good a time as any to shatter cherished Israeli legends.

For more than four years, I said with eyes locked on Yachimovich, I worked closely with many Palestinians, from Arafat on down, to prevent attacks and apprehend terrorists. I explained in as measured a tone as I could muster that when Palestinians felt that preventing terrorism would lead to the end of our occupation and the establishment of their own state, they cooperated with us. What most Palestinians sought, more than anything, wasn't our blood — they just wanted to trust that the Israeli government would end the occupation and allow them to be free. "And we've given them little reason to trust us." What I was thinking but couldn't yet bring myself to say publicly was that our pursuit of peace was a sham. We were still caught in the Zionism of my parents' generation that saw the entire Land of Israel as our birthright. Since we refused to admit that Palestinians have rights and roots in Judea and Samaria, too, we were always looking for ways to renege on our promises. What we wanted was security, and if we could get it without handing over any more of the Land of Israel, we'd do it.

"But . . ."

I cut her off. Our instinctive resort to disproportionate force, I barreled on, has created the opposite of what we want to achieve. We jeopardize our own security each time, in the name of security, our soldiers gun down Palestinian stone-throwers, and our actions fuel calls for revenge. Yachimovich finally intervened with the question on everyone's mind. "So what about these rioters?" she wanted to know, returning the conversation to the lynching. "Who are they?"

"I'll tell you who they are." Flashing in my mind was something I had read in one of Dr. Shikaki's reports: The people behind the Second Intifada were disillusioned supporters of the peace process. "They're not fanatics. I may not know them personally, but I've met lots of people like them, once ardent backers of Oslo."

I was thinking of the men I'd met who worked for Jibril, guys who risked their necks pursuing Hamas terrorists. If some of these men were now dancing in our blood, it wasn't because they were beasts, it was because they'd lost hope.

At the end of the interview I used the same sextant metaphor I had tried out on Ehud Barak with so little success. True leadership keeps one eye trained on the realities of the ground, I explained, with the other fixed on where and who we want to be in the future.

Yachimovich must have been impressed because she asked if I would consider politics. "No, never," I declared calmly, looking straight into the camera.

"Do you really mean that?" she prodded. Ex-generals, after all, fill Israel's governing ranks.

"I have absolutely no interest in politics," I breezily assured her. The irony is that in early 2006, four years later, Shelly and I would both be elected to the Knesset.

20

"HOPE IS A POWERFUL WEAPON"

You use a tank even if [a kid] is holding a BB gun . . . Why?
Because you're a state. A state makes use of stately tools.

— Avi Dichter, in *The Gatekeepers*

Most of the people who rang me up after the Channel Two interview thought I had come down with an acute case of Stockholm syndrome, an affliction named for the people taken hostage during a bank robbery in Stockholm in 1973, who, when rescued, refused to testify against their former captor. It was easier for people to assume I'd lost my mind than to admit my assessment might be right.

Hamas capitalized on the despondent political climate and bounced back quickly from the blows we had dealt its terror infrastructure. The rocks and Molotov cocktails of a popular uprising quickly turned into a wave of suicide attacks. Six Israeli civilians died in a series of bombings, a nasty portent of what was to come.

The targeted killings we conducted during my four years at the Shin Bet were tightly focused, done with the greatest possible discretion, and usually masqueraded as "work accidents." These quiet hits delivered a message: We targeted only ticking bombs, imminent threats to our civilians. This was something I had learned in the commandos operating inside refugee camps in Lebanon: If you want to send a message up the chain of command, it's a lot more effective to fire one bullet between the eyes of the person in the act of laying the bomb than to carpet-bomb an entire camp. Precision bears the stamp of intelligence.[40]

We were not adhering to this approach in 2000. With renewed attacks by Hamas, my government radically ramped up the number of extrajudicial killings, and publicly bragged about actions whose effectiveness had, at least during my tenure, depended on plausible deniability. "The liquidation of wanted persons is proving itself useful," said Chief of Staff Shaul Mofaz. "It paralyzes and frightens entire villages." Barak's deputy defense minister chipped in, "If the game is a guerrilla war, we are the champions of the world."[41]

No one, it seemed to me, was asking the question, *Who is a legitimate target?* Beyond the "ticking bombs," can we legitimately target people behind the scenes: the planner, the weapons supplier, the bomb maker, the assistants, the driver who takes the suicide bomber to the target, or even the religious and political leadership of the movement who indoctrinates the terrorist?

Turning a policy of going after a ticking bomb into one of going after a "ticking infrastructure" is akin to turning a tactic into a strategy. Terror spread. At the end of December the militant settler Noam Livnat, who had insisted on meeting me before I took over the Shabak, rang me up to ask for help. "Terrorists just killed Binyamin Kahane and his wife," he said, "and now his children are in danger." Binyamin, a proponent of his father Meir Kahane's idea of expelling Arabs from the entire Land of Israel, had been traveling in the West Bank when Hamas militants sprayed his van with bullets. "Their grandfather was murdered," Noam continued, referring to Meir's assassination by an Egyptian American in New York City in 1990. "Their parents have been murdered, and now I need you to help me save them." It was dark, and gunmen could be anywhere.

I turned to the commander of IDF Central Command and asked him to send an armored vehicle to protect Kahane's children.

Three hours after the Kahane killings, Dr. Thabet Ahmad Thabet, a member of Physicians for Human Rights, and for years one of the top PLO officials identified with Peace Now, was backing out of his driveway to get to work. The dentist was a lecturer on public health at Al Quds University, director general of the Palestinian Ministry of Health, and secretary general of Fatah in Tulkarem. He was also a leader of Fatah's militant group the Tanzim, someone who had returned to the old PLO mantra that violence was the only language the occupiers understood.

Just as the doctor reached the end of his driveway, a team of snipers the IDF borrowed from my old Flotilla 13 commando unit shot him dead.[42]

Fatah people, hitherto hesitant to join in the Hamas murder campaign, interpreted the assassination as Israel's answer to the Hamas killing, and vowed revenge. In January 2001, Dr. Thabet's nephew, Raed Karmi, a member of Jibril's Palestinian Security Service, set out to avenge his uncle's death. In the name of the "Thabet Thabet Battalion," he planned the abduction and murder of two left-wing cousins who ran a trendy café called Yuppies on Shenkin Street in Tel Aviv. The attack took place while the cousins were eating hummus with a Palestinian friend in an Arab village outside Tulkarem.

Jibril ordered Karmi's arrest but, under pressure from street demonstrations, let him go.

Attacks multiplied. On January 1 a Hamas bombing injured sixty in the Israeli town of Netanya. Secular Israelis were most shocked by an attack at the beachfront nightclub Dolphinarium in Tel Aviv carried out by the twenty-two-year-old Islamist Saeed Hotari, in which twenty-one Israelis were killed. After the massacre, Hotari's neighbors in Qalqilya arranged flowers in the shapes of a heart and suicide vest in his honor; children vowed to follow him to the martyrs' paradise. An Israeli mob responded by attacking a mosque in Tel Aviv.

The murder of the two restaurateurs and then the kids at the discotheque got even the bohemians on Shenkin Street repeating Barak's "no partner" slogan. Barak, paralyzed by the fighting, resigned, and in February, Ariel Sharon won an election to become prime minister. He emerged from the political rubble as the King of Israel because he promised to use our military might to crush the uprising.

With Sharon in charge, we began terminating people "with extreme prejudice," to adopt CIA lingo, and then bragging about it as if we'd put heads on pikes. The defense minister's office published a list of wanted men — including Dr. Thabet's nephew Raed Karmi — that was more or less a liquidation list.

In May the air force used F-16 fighter planes to bomb a Nablus prison run by Jibril's security service. The target, Mahmoud Abu Hanoud, the planner behind the Dolphinarium attack, escaped lightly injured, but eleven of his jailers died. In June one of the men on the Israeli list, Osama Fatih al-Jawabra, died when he picked up a booby-trapped public telephone in the old city of Nablus. The blast blew his head off.

Later that month an American-brokered cease-fire went into effect, and the number of attacks dropped.

Knowing what I did about Arafat and the Palestinian Authority — that Arafat had only encouraged the attacks because otherwise Palestinians would have turned their rage on him — I thought the cease-fire had a chance. And then after seven weeks of relative quiet, on August 1 an IDF helicopter fired missiles through the windows of a Hamas office in the middle of Nablus. The target, Jamal Mansour, was a member of the political arm of Hamas, a university student leader in Nablus, and head of the Palestinian Center for Studies and Media. Mansour, two journalists, and two young brothers, one seven years old and the other five, died in the explosion.

I thought I was losing my mind. Not only was Jamal Mansour not a terrorist, he was a prominent media figure who belonged to Hamas's political wing and had also publicly backed Arafat's decision to enforce the cease-fire.

Killing Mansour was a classic example of producing terrorism in the name of fighting it. Betraying just how little we cared about returning to the negotiating table, we violated an already tenuous cease-fire to assassinate a supporter of a political approach to conflict resolution. Our missiles eliminated the seeds of pragmatism within Hamas and provided a boost to the hardcore militants.

I called up my successor Avi Dichter and vented my frustrations. "Just two weeks ago Mansour came out with a statement saying the peace process should be given a chance!"

"Never heard about it," Avi said. "Anyway, what difference does it make?"

"Are you kidding me?" I said, my voice calm even though I felt like shouting. "Mansour was a religious leader. In the media he published his call on believers to provide an opportunity for a political process! The whole goddamned world knew! How could you possibly have been in the dark?"

Palestinians wasted no time in avenging Mansour's death: Gunmen wounded five Israelis in drive-by shootings just days later. Our government vowed to stay the course. "Such attacks as the one on [Mansour] must continue, and more intensively," declared Sharon's public security minister Uzi Landau.

On September 6 the air force shot a missile at Raed Karmi, the man who had planned the abduction and killing of the two Israeli restaurateurs. The missile barely wounded Karmi while killing two young activists from the Al-Shams refugee camp.

After the 9/11 attacks in New York, I thought my government and Arafat might just get out from the corner into which they had painted themselves. Colin Powell announced he was coming to Israel, and Arafat instructed the leader of the Tanzim, Marwan Barghouti, and people under him such as Raed Karmi, to stop all attacks. The Shabak told Sharon that Arafat was serious this time.

And for a few weeks terror stopped. That is, until January 2002. Through informants, the Shin Bet learned that Karmi visited his mistress most afternoons. He traveled via a narrow footpath next to the old Nablus cemetery, apparently sure that an armed Israeli Apache helicopter couldn't see him if he kept close to the wall and under an overhang. There were other precautions he didn't take, though. A booby-trapped section of the wall killed him during his afternoon walk.

The plan was to make it appear as if Karmi was carrying a bomb that went off accidentally, which no one believed.[43] I still can't say with certainty what lay behind Sharon's foolish decision to knock off Karmi. Most Palestinians thought the aim of the killing was to eliminate any chance of resuming the political process with Colin Powell's arrival in the region. Whatever pragmatism was left among Fatah activists disappeared.

For the first time, Fatah leaders began organizing their own suicide attacks. In Tel Aviv two terrorists, one from Islamic Jihad the other from Fatah, jointly carried out a suicide bombing at on outdoor mall.

Just after the Karmi operation, Avi Dichter invited me along with three other former directors, Avraham Shalom, Yaakov Peri, and Carmi Gillon, to Shin Bet headquarters in Tel Aviv to discuss the Karmi assassination. We were a roomful of aging, frustrated men, like retired experts on infectious diseases gathering after a renewed outbreak of the plague.

We pummeled Avi with criticism Israeli-style, with no regard for protocols or niceties. Too much was at stake for us to refrain from pointing out the problems with his strategy and proposing what could be done to prevent the next bloodbath.

I reminded him that in the twelve months leading up to the Second Intifada, only one Israeli died at the hands of terrorists. Why? Because at the time most Palestinians were opposed to terrorism, and Jibril and Arafat's security forces could therefore fight Hamas without being perceived as collaborators and traitors, this despite the fact that the number of settlers in the West Bank had more than doubled since Oslo, from 100,000 to 220,000. "And now?" I continued. "We're getting more terror because our way of fighting it has robbed the Palestinians of any hope that we are willing to give them their freedom."

"I don't do politics," Dichter said. "We had an opportunity to hit a terrorist, so we took it."

"But Avi, your job isn't to kill terrorists. It's to prevent terror, which isn't the same thing. Karmi had backed the cease-fire. Now we're going to get more terrorism, not less."

Yaakov Peri used more colorful language to critique the new policy: "The Service can't be a supplier of targets to satisfy the prime minister and fill up his belly, which is already swollen from schnitzels and other delicacies. We're killing Arabs morning, noon, and night."[44]

Avi shrugged off our warnings, and the killings continued.

I left the meeting so frustrated that I asked to meet with his boss, Sharon's minister of defense, Binyamin Ben-Eliezer. During our meeting, I asked him why in the hell he'd ordered Karmi's elimination.

"What do you want from me?" he said. "It's that crazy thinking over at the Shabak. I felt pressured."

"But you're the minister of defense. It's your call."

"Ami, why don't you just enjoy your retirement? You've earned it."

For more than four years we at the Shabak had worked our tails off to prevent the next attack. Now with time to reflect, I realized that the most valuable lesson I had learned — seeing Palestinians as people, not targets — had little long-term institutional effect on the Shabak, and none on the army.

My frustration led me to accept Professor Mary Kaldor's invitation to participate in the panel discussion in London where I met two like-minded men, Dr. Sarraj and Sari Nusseibeh. On the plane back from that gathering, I couldn't stop thinking about Dr. Sarraj's assertion that our tactical military successes were handing "victory" to the terrorists. Hamas was winning by luring us into gratuitous violence and bloodlust, thus undermining our moral foundation as a liberal democracy.

Back in Israel, part of me wanted nothing more than to take long walks with Biba, get to know our three boys better, and join in Netafim's vision to "paint the world in green" through a revolution in agriculture. I wanted to meet farmers in China, India, Australia, and Brazil. But I couldn't look at myself in the mirror if I didn't do something to translate my newfound knowledge about the role of hope into action. I returned to what I had jotted down on the napkin in my meeting in London with Sari.

I enlisted a small group to help me refine the ideas. Aryeh Rutenberg kept his promise and joined the brainstorming. So did my old friend Orni Petruschka, and Boaz Tamir, an economist and PhD from MIT who was also a colleague at Netafim. I'd brought him in as an advisor during my years at the Shabak.[45]

We spent several months going back and forth, mainly adding

lines about the 1948 Palestinian refugees, until I felt ready to present the ideas to Sari. I phoned him and asked if we could meet at his office in Jerusalem. "*Ahlan wa sahlan*," he said without hesitation: I was welcome to visit.

I parked the car in West Jerusalem and walked toward the Flowers Gate of the Old City. The Al Quds University administration building was in an old Arab villa across from the Rockefeller Museum.

Over those few blocks I found myself looking at the city with eyes alert to signs of ethnic warfare. When I was a boy, Imma used to tell me how as a schoolgirl she'd enter the Old City through the Dung Gate and wander the streets, a trip that sometimes took her out through Damascus Gate into the wealthy neighborhoods outside the old city walls where the Nusseibehs, Husseinis, and Nashashibis kept grand stone villas. The shabby streets I passed through that morning were lined with dozens of green-bereted Border Police keeping a watchful eye on the *shebab* — clutches of teenage Arab boys who roamed the neighborhood. The sour smell of tear gas hung in the air. The ubiquitous Shabak agents must have been scratching their heads at the sight of me striding through the streets, unarmed.

Sari was waiting for me in an office befitting the scion of one of Jerusalem's most illustrious families. A photo of his father Anwar, the Oxford-educated lawyer who was the Jordanian minister of defense before the 1967 war, hung on one of the walls. While my father was fighting the Syrians in the Jordan Valley and the Jordanians at the Gesher police station on the Jordan River in 1948, Anwar Nusseibeh lost a leg fighting our forces in Jerusalem. Another face on the wall that I recognized was that of Abu Jihad, the cofounder of Fatah and a man I helped assassinate.

I explained to Sari, who was rubbing a string of blue worry beads, that I wanted to share with him a refined version of the points he had agreed to in London.

"Go ahead," he said, setting down his worry beads and lighting up a cigarette. "No thanks," I responded when he offered me one.

"Tea or coffee, then?"

"Just water." I pulled from my bag a slip of paper with my proposal, but Sari asked me to put it down. "I don't want you to read. Just tell me what you came up with."

An assistant arrived with a bottle of water for me and a cup of tea for Sari. Rarely do I feel nervous, but that morning I sensed a quiver in my voice as I laid out the plan. By this point I agreed with Bibi and Ehud on one thing: The piecemeal approach wasn't going to work. Road maps and confidence-building measures only give power to spoilers. No matter how vigilant our defenses, someone was bound to get through. A lone wolf, perhaps, some disgruntled tractor driver swerving into a bus stop.

"Go on," Sari said, lighting a fresh cigarette from the embers of the old one.

I gave him the new version of my napkin proposal in London, including our proposed solution to the refugee question. When I finished talking, I raised my eyebrows as if to say, *What do you think?*

"Let's do it," he said, running the fingers of one hand through his mop of white hair. The other hand still gripped the worry beads.

21

OUR MOST DANGEROUS ENEMY

I've always been intrigued by philosophers because of something Biba's father, David, once told me: Philosophers and comedians have insights that escape the rest of us because they know how to step outside everyday reality and see themselves and society from the perspective of an outsider. This was true of Sari, but that doesn't begin to explain how he could have so quickly joined forces with me. I might have been putting my reputation on the line for our joint venture, but no one was going to gun me down. Sari, on the other hand, by teaming up with the former director of the same enemy organization that was busy terrorizing Palestinian society, willingly stepped into a minefield. Being labeled a collaborator with Israel was for his community the worst crime in the book. In Hebron, Jibril's cousin Musa Rajoub had been accused of this offense. A mob shot him, beat him, and strung his body by his left foot from an electricity pylon.

Soon after we started working together, I invited Sari to my house. Might as well get things out in the open so there would be no surprises. Imagine if one of Sari's enemies found out before he did that his Israeli partner lived in a former Arab home.

I had also researched Sari's family. That his father had been a judge and former Jordanian minister of defense was common knowledge, but learning his mother Nuzha's story deepened my admiration for Sari's moral bravery in working with me.

In 1948, when my father was defending our kibbutz on the Sea of Galilee against the constant shooting and shelling coming from the Syrian army, Nuzha, born into a family of landed aristocrats, was in the town of Ramle. In June the Israeli army showed up. On Prime Minister Ben-Gurion's tacit order, Yitzhak Rabin, commander of the Palmach, expelled her and the rest of the

Arabs.[46] Sari's mother, pregnant with him at the time, walked across enemy lines by foot. She raised Sari to believe that the Palestinians had been, in her words, "robbed by people who were just evil, people who came from nowhere, from Mars."

During his visit to our home, Biba and I took Sari on the dirt path out back to show him the empty stone farmhouses once inhabited by the residents of Ijzim. In our garden I handed Sari a fig from a tree planted by the dispossessed family that had once lived in our house. Without speaking, Sari ate it and picked another. Taking that bite, like the one in mythic Eden, must have been excruciating for a man raised by a mother who never transcended the traumas of the past.

After dinner I told Sari that I thought it was unlikely we would ever develop the kind of warm rapport, with banter and ribbing, I had with Jibril.[47] Staring off into space, a cigarette in his mouth like Albert Camus, he agreed with a nod. He said he had always been allergic to violence in all its forms, in particular when it came from men wearing uniforms. "I usually don't like army types," he said, looking at me pointedly. Ironically, I thought to myself, *Nor do I.*

We had in common, however, the fact that both of us, Sari as a Palestinian patriot and I as a proud Zionist, sought a way out of our regional catastrophe. We would work on a series of simple principles we could present to people as a pragmatic, commonsensical approach to ending the conflict, once and for all. Our hope was that during several meetings, mainly at his university office in Jerusalem or the New Imperial Hotel inside Jaffa Gate, we could quickly — within weeks — take my draft and further refine our common positions on the thorny issues of borders, security, Jerusalem, the holy sites, Jewish settlements, and refugees. Sari's main additions were that Israel express regret for the suffering caused the refugees and participate in an international fund to offer financial compensation and resettlement in the State of Palestine.

We found ourselves laughing at our audacity, thinking we could pull off what Clinton, Barak, and Arafat had failed to do at Camp David.

It was a good plan, but as with most plans in our part of the world, reality intervened. Weeks turned into months; I had to work for a living, and so did Sari, who both ran Jerusalem for Arafat and was president of a university under an IDF siege.

I spent a great deal of time following a debate in the High Court of Justice. In January 2002, Siham Thabet, the widow of Dr. Thabet, backed by the Arab Jewish ex-communist Hadash Party and the Public Committee Against Torture, petitioned the Court to stop the government from "executions without trial" of Palestinians. In a country with no capital punishment, Mrs. Thabet and her lawyers argued, the courts had a responsibility to put an end to the death squads.

The government's argument was prepared by the IDF's Legal Division and rested on logic my friend Brian Jenkins would have characterized as an example of incremental tyranny. Their position had long been that Palestinian violence against the State of Israel was orchestrated by the Palestinian Authority. Since Israel had the right to self-defense, and given the fact that our enemies often cannot be arrested and taken into our custody, the state had the right to use lethal means to protect its civilians. What our government didn't ask was if the intifada was a popular uprising independent of the machination of leaders, and whether our actions, instead of stopping the violence, only added more fuel to the flames.

Now I knew for sure that the terrorists were winning. Hamas had seduced all of Israeli society, starting with its democratically elected leaders, into taking actions no free society should permit. What was once a legitimate fight against terror organizations had degenerated into a war against the Palestinian people. Our democracy was, bit by bit, devolving into tyranny, and it was only a matter of time before we devolved into George Orwell's *1984*.

We Israelis were so distracted by our all-out assault on terrorists, as well on a good number of nonviolent pro-Palestinian activists, that we missed opportunities to silence the true ticking bombs.

At around 5 PM on March 27, 2002, just as millions of Israelis like me were racing around their homes preparing for Passover,

Abdel-Basset Odeh posed before a camera clutching an AK-47 assault rifle in the West Bank city of Tulkarem.

The photo, subsequently uploaded onto a Hamas website, betrays no wild-eyed fanaticism. From his expression, he could have been posing for his driver's license. The twenty-five-year-old had failed to get a work visa to America to escape his dead-end life working at his father's vegetable stand. Salvation came when Hamas's underground outfit, the Qassam Brigades, promised him a fast track to paradise. With nothing to lose, Odeh accepted his mission: to avenge our assassination of Raed Karmi.

After recording the video, Odeh removed the green bandanna from around his forehead, shaved off his stubble, and slipped on a dress and a shoulder-length brunette wig.

Just after 5:00 PM my family and I left Kerem Maharal and drove to Biba's sister's house for the Passover Seder, a feast I was raised on the kibbutz to identify with the liberation from tyranny. On our drive we passed the city of Netanya on the Mediterranean coast. The dusk hid from view the glistening glass and metal office buildings housing the high-tech firms that line the highway.

I was in an uncommonly good mood, over the moon about auspicious news coming from the Arab League summit in Beirut. King Abdullah, at the time the crown prince of Saudi Arabia, had just that day presented a plan that offered Israel the right "to live in peace within secure and recognized boundaries."

"You know what this means, Biba? This is victory! The entire Arab world, starting with the Saudis, just declared us the winner of a hundred-year war." I felt like rolling down the window and shouting at the people next to us in the traffic jam, *We won!* Finally, we had something to celebrate.

I was already rehearsing my response to the traditional Passover question, *Ma nishtana ha lyla ha zeh mikkol hallaylot?* Why is this night different from all other nights? *Because we won*, I was prepared to say.

Still on the road, I gave Matti Steinberg a ring. "What do you think about . . . ?"

"The Saudi initiative?" he said, finishing my sentence. "It's an earthquake, Ami. The Saudis are ready to bury the hatchet and have normal relations with us on the basis of a withdrawal from the Occupied Territories. The fact they announced it on Passover says something."

"A gift to the Jews, you mean."

"You might say that. Let's just see if we Jews will understand the historical significance of the offer." The Arab Peace Initiative formally put an end to fantasies such as returning to the 1947 Partition Plan, or the standard post-1967 mantra of "no negotiation with the Zionist entity." Arafat himself had called it a "very strong platform," though he couldn't be in Beirut in person, as our government had barred him from traveling to Lebanon.

"We won't have a choice," I declared optimistically. "I mean, how could we reject an offer signed off by the Arab League, and backed by the Saudis?"

Matti said he admired my optimism but then came out with his version of Abba Eban's oft-quoted line, that the "Arabs never miss an opportunity to miss an opportunity." In Matti's rendering of the cliché, it was our turn to play the fool.

By about this time Odeh was standing on King David Street in front of the Park Hotel in Netanya in his wig-and-dress disguise. The security guard noticed nothing unusual about the medium-sized woman rolling her suitcase through the lobby and into the dining hall. Hundreds of Israeli Jews, including a number of Holocaust survivors, as well as guests from Europe and America, were waiting for the Passover readings to begin. They never got to that ancient Aramaic dirge "Ha Laḥma Anya," "This is the bread of affliction."

At approximately seven forty we were in the middle of the Seder at Biba's sister's when the news came over the radio. The explosives in Odeh's suitcase transformed ball bearings and metal shards into projectiles powerful enough to bring down the ceiling. The electricity in the hotel went out and water pipes burst. Thirty people died in the attack and more than a hundred were wounded. One eighty-nine-year-old woman had survived Auschwitz only to be killed by Odeh's bomb.

Our grief turned into indignation once Israelis learned about Palestinian reactions to the carnage. Journalists visiting his village the next day heard locals praising Odeh's grisly crimes. "We do to them what they do to us," his father Muhammad announced. "If they kill us, we kill them the day after. It will never stop." The town's criminal court judge, a pillar of the community who, with his suit and tie, embodied respectability, described the crime as "wonderful." "Every time there is an action there's a reaction," he opined. A member of Fatah and a legislator in Palestinian parliament spun the suicide attack as an act of self-defense. "We have nothing else with which to fight this huge machine of Israel's. They have everything; they have all the power. We have nothing but our bodies."

The Arab Peace Initiative, needless to say, wasn't on anyone's agenda; even Shimon Peres, Sharon's foreign minister and the man behind Oslo, sounded like a military hawk in his response to it. He dubbed it a "diktat," accusing the Saudis of pushing us into a corner, and conditioned a positive Israeli response on an "end to terror," a classic case of putting the cart before the horse.

That night Sharon declared a state of emergency, called up twenty thousand reservists, and launched Operation Defensive Shield. It was the largest military operation in the West Bank since 1967. In the violence of the operation, we followed the path paved by militants on both sides: for the Palestinians, Hamas and the suicide bombers; for us, Yigal Amir, Baruch Goldstein, and the radical right.

Our youngest son, Roy, a paratrooper, got called up. Never in all my years in the commandos had Biba been so nervous; my doubts about the operation affected both of us. He ended up joining the reconquest of Nablus.

Arafat, whose rival Hamas had committed the bombing, was nevertheless Sharon's first target. My government's propagandists spun the attack as another example of Arafat's war against us, the hotel bombing only the latest strike in a nationalist offensive stretching back to the Mufti of Jerusalem in the 1930s.

The IDF's massive assault dismantled the Palestinian Authority's governmental systems. In a predawn attack Israeli tanks, armor, and troops invaded Ramallah, placed the whole city under a curfew, and encircled Arafat's compound, the Muqataa.

The absurdity of the mismatch between the Middle East's premier military power and the head of the Palestinian Authority with no authority left strangely strengthened Arafat, who was back in his role as symbol of Palestinian suffering and resistance. He appeared on Abu Dhabi television, where from behind rubble he stuttered, "Don't you know me by now? I am a martyr in the making." Three times he repeated, "May Allah honor me with martyrdom."

Mahmoud Darwish, still one of my key sensors, offered a different form of defiance, one infinitely less tragicomic. "State of Siege," the poem he penned in those days, is addressed to a "killer":

If you reflected upon the face
of the victim you slew, you would have remembered
your mother in the room
full of gas. You would have freed yourself
of the bullet's wisdom,
and changed your mind: "I will never find myself thus."

Amira Hass, as always a reliable truth-teller, renamed Operation Defensive Shield "Operation Destroy the Data" because "this was not a mission to search and destroy the terrorist infrastructure . . . There was a decision made to vandalize the civic, administrative, cultural infrastructure developed by Palestinian society." Operation Defensive Shield produced scorched earth and left only an empty pit into which what was left of the Palestinian Authority simply disappeared. Nobody asked the simple question: After we killed the terrorists, who would be left to talk about building a better future?

Stopping terror required sophisticated intelligence, and so when the Shabak attacked the PA's computer systems, Jibril could no longer contain Hamas. Maybe that was the point. Anyway, Jibril was soon out of a job: Arafat fired him after a verbal brawl, with Jibril imploring Arafat to crack down on the "Martyrs Brigade of Al Aqsa," and Arafat countering that Rajoub had allowed a Palestinian mob to free sixty Hamas terrorists from a Hebron jail. In the end mercurial Arafat pulled out a pistol and called Jibril an "Israeli spy" and "CIA agent."

I was starting to worry about Sari. Since our first meeting in his office, my admiration for the man grew in direct proportion to my insight into his connection with Palestinian civil society. Al Quds University, which he ran, catered to a poorer population than other universities in the West Bank, with a higher percentage of students from refugee camps. In the science and technology faculties, many of the most talented, ambitious students supported Hamas if only because they had benefited from the organization's charitable work. Among the geeks, Adel Awadallah, a former student there, was considered a hero.

Sari, I discovered, was expert at navigating these divergent student factions. He could get Hamas students in chemistry labs, for instance, to refrain from building bombs, channeling their sense of humiliation and rage into more constructive pursuits like getting a degree and finding a job.

His skillful moderation made him an Israeli target. *The Guardian* ran a story about how "Israeli intelligence officials began hunting members of Mr. Arafat's administration, including Sari Nusseibeh." The Israeli daily *Yedioth Ahronoth* ran a similar story quoting a top security source as saying, "Because of his sophistication, Nusseibeh is much more dangerous, as far as we are concerned, than many other figures in the Palestinian leadership." Another article in *Yedioth* was titled "Dr. Sari Nusseibeh: Beware of Deadly Coral Snakes Posing as Harmless Skipjack Snakes."

On the evening of April 2, IDF soldiers invaded Sari's television station outside of Ramallah. This was where Sari produced the Palestinian version of *Sesame Street*.[48]

At gunpoint, soldiers locked employees in the basement before ransacking the rest of the four-story building. They slipped in porno to replace the cartoons and sprayed graffiti on the walls such as PALESTINE, NEVER and DEATH TO ARABS! They then smashed equipment, carted off computers, and tossed the television cameras out the top-floor window.

Though I would have understood if he wanted to lay low for a while, Sari just shrugged off the attack. We continued to focus on drafting our joint paper, though we had to drop our plan to meet on an island in the Aegean Sea, at the invitation of the Greek government, to finalize the work because he couldn't get a permit to leave besieged East Jerusalem.

What we finally came up with was a set of six principles that bracketed out history and religious dogmas, not because they were unimportant but because of their latent power. Our respective "absolute rights" — the historical right of the Jews to their ancestral homeland, and the Palestinians' right to their ancestral lands in what is now Israel — were in such basic conflict there was no point discussing them. I assumed other Israelis were like me: Through the Bible and my parents' stories, I felt connected to the Cave of the Patriarchs, Rachel's Tomb in Bethlehem, and the Temple Mount. But to continue to build the State of Israel in the spirit of the Declaration of Independence, we had to separate dreams from reality. As such, I never brought up to Sari rights I still clung to, and he never pulled out a key from his mother's villa on land that is now a part of the Israeli town Ness Ziona, the "Miracle of Zion." Peace was more important than absolute historical justice.

It was important to us to boil down our agreement to a single page, with no annexes or footnotes, none of Henry Kissinger's "constructive ambiguity," no fine print, and no tricks. What could be realistically achieved given our region's political and security realities? The narrative we chose centered on the self-interest of Israelis who wanted to sit through lunch without a suicide bomber killing them and of Palestinians who wanted to leave their villages without facing a uniformed teenager barking out orders.

Our one-pager laid out our plan: two states for two nations based on the June 4, 1967, borders, with selective acre-to-acre land swaps to benefit both peoples. Palestinian refugees would mainly return to the demilitarized state of Palestine, while Jewish settlements that remained in Palestinian territory after an agreement on borders would be evacuated. We agreed that Israel would explicitly acknowledge its role in the suffering of the Palestinians and vow to participate in an international fund to compensate Palestinian refugees for their 1948 losses. Once a peace agreement was signed, both sides would unambiguously renounce all claims.

Jerusalem would be an open capital of both states, with the Arab neighborhoods under Palestinian control and the Jewish neighborhoods under Israeli control. We agreed that the standard concept of national sovereignty wasn't applicable to the holy places in Jerusalem. Palestine would be designated Guardian of *Haram esh-Sharif* for the benefit of Muslims; Israel, the Guardian of the Western Wall for the benefit of the Jews. With the holy sites, we weren't saying anything new. All of these points, with the exception of the Temple Mount, had been agreed upon during the peace talks between 1993 and 2000; hidden by the "constructive ambiguity" of our leaders, this wasn't known to the public, and we wanted to spell it out in plain language.

Once the Jerusalem siege was partly lifted and Sari could travel, Greek foreign minister George Papandreou once again invited him and me, along with a group of academics, Nobel Prize laureates, and (for one of the meetings) former American president Bill Clinton, to a Greek island for a discussion on the directions Europe and the Middle East were heading.

On our way to Greece, we got a reminder of why our agreement was so necessary. In my jeans and sandals I sailed through security at Ben-Gurion Airport; in his professorial blazer and necktie Sari got pulled aside and grilled by a twenty-something security officer who had probably just finished his army service. I wanted to intervene and point my finger in the kid's face, but I knew Sari wouldn't have approved of the "protection." He wanted me to witness for myself the daily humiliation Palestinians endure. So I stayed until the examination was over. The security people stared at me wide-eyed: What was the former Shabak boss doing with a Palestinian philosopher?

On the Greek island, Bill Clinton, who had squandered so

much of his political capital with the failed Camp David summit, stood next to Papandreou and listened to our presentation. Clinton seemed impressed with the simplicity of the approach to a hundred-year war that had generated billions of words and a library of proposals.

After our presentation, Sari whispered to me that he half expected Clinton, who had nodded along to our pitch, to say something along the lines of Pericles' Funeral Oration: "Therefore, having judged that to be happy means to be free, and to be free means to be brave, do not shy away from the risks of peace." Clinton indeed marveled at the simplicity and clarity of the document. "How did you manage to summarize in one page the essence of the plan that I tried to promote during my eight years in office?"

While we were huddled together on the island, back in Jerusalem public security minister Uzi Landau, a great fan of targeted assassinations, ordered dozens of police and Shin Bet agents to seize Sari's university office. In the nighttime raid a locksmith opened the front door, and police vans were loaded with files and computers. The entire building was then sealed off with heavy steel shutters over the doors and windows.[49]

The assault prompted an international outcry; even US ambassador Dan Kurtzer chided Sharon and Landau for cracking down on a moderate man who was overseas pushing for peace. I was just as puzzled, so I phoned Landau to ask him why he did it. "He openly calls for an end to the killing of Israeli civilians, and he's been attacked for it by his own people. Just tell me. Why the hell did you go after him? If anyone represents hope for the Palestinians, it's him."

"Why?" Landau seemed genuinely surprised by my question, as if the answer to the puzzle was obvious. "Because this professor of yours is our most dangerous enemy." Elsewhere Minister Landau dubbed Sari "the pretty face of terrorism."

With such talk from Landau, a systems analyst by profession who had a PhD from MIT, I had proof that Israel was not just slipping into tyranny. We were also rapidly going insane.

22

TRAVELS WITH SARI

What is hateful to you do not do to your neighbor.
This is the whole Torah; all the rest is commentary.

— Rabbi Hillel

At the end of July 2002, Sari and I signed our agreement in a modest ribbon-cutting at a hotel in front of our core supporters. In the navy we like reciting the Roman writer Seneca, who said that no wind will help a sailor who does not know where he wants to sail. With his destination chosen, the same sailor can use any wind to get there. Our paper, which we called "a destination map," aimed to set such a goal.

But a philosopher and a retired-admiral-turned-drip-irrigation-executive needed a lot more than a roomful of well-wishers to draw attention to our plan. Months earlier President Bush, with a stirring quote from the Book of Deuteronomy — "I have set before you life and death; therefore, choose life" — began promoting his Road Map to Peace. Bush got the Europeans and Russians, along with Sharon and Arafat, to sign off on a path both Sari and I knew would lead nowhere. First, it demanded absolute security from the Palestinians, which given their shattered institutions they couldn't provide even if they wanted to. It was also unworkable because of the wild success of Barak's "no partner" slogan coupled with Sharon's strategy of destroying Palestinian institutions. The Palestinians will never be partners, he was saying, therefore we must act strictly from our self-interest, with no regard for Palestinian aspirations.

The new Palestinian government, installed through international pressure, brought no change in my government's underlying position, even though Prime Minister Mahmoud Abbas, a pragmatist and longtime opponent of political violence, had the courage to tell his people that terror and violence would bring only destruction and death. With his second in command, Finance Minister Salam Fayyad, a graduate of the University of Texas who was equally opposed to an armed uprising, Abbas presided over institutions in ruins.

Our war continued. Within days of our ceremony in the hotel lobby, an air force F-16 dropped a one-ton bomb on the home of Salah Shehade, who after being released from Israeli prison in 2001 had taken over as commander of Hamas's Qassam Brigades in Gaza. Fifteen people died in the blast, including Shehade, his wife, and his fourteen-year-old daughter. Dozens of bystanders were injured.

This attack, praised by Sharon as "one of our greatest successes," led to international condemnation and widespread dissent within the Israeli air force: a group of thirty Black Hawk helicopter and F-16 fighter pilots signed a letter refusing to fly bombing raids on Palestinian cities. "You hear it in the streets of Israel; people want revenge," said one pilot. "But we should not behave like that. We are not a mafia."

It was in this context that, over the coming weeks, Sari showed himself to me as much more than an ivory tower philosopher. Having known him for nearly twenty years, I can say about Sari that he has an endlessly curious mind coupled with a steely determination to defeat our occupation using words and arguments and grassroots activism. During the First Intifada, Sari ran afoul of the Shin Bet, and wound up behind bars, because he smuggled messages from Abu Jihad to activists. He has also shown an independence and willingness, always in short supply in our part of the world, to break nationalistic taboos. Shortly after the Six-Day War, he volunteered on a kibbutz just to get to know Israelis.[50]

Sari and I usually met on Fridays at hotels, in cafés, or in his office. Our conversations helped me understand and interpret events in the West Bank. From him I learned how areas hitherto governed by Arafat had degenerated into fiefdoms ruled by warlords; boys with peach fuzz for whiskers lugged around machine guns and barked out orders. Instead of soccer stars, kids worshipped the *shahid batal*, the martyr hero. "Thousands of young men and women are ready to be blown up," Sari told me, quoting a local leader. "This is a new phenomenon. You have no idea how big it is."

Sari thought much of the mayhem in Palestine arose directly out of Sharon's diabolical brain. The prime minister's ultimate aim, he argued, quoting the Israeli political scientist Baruch Kimmerling, was "politicide" — to destroy the Palestinians' will for self-determination and sovereignty over what they considered their homeland. Sari cited approvingly from Kimmerling's book *Fighting the Demons: Israel's Killer General and His Legacy*: "The aim . . . is to make life so unbearable that the greatest possible majority of the rival population, especially its elite and middle classes, will leave the area 'voluntarily.' Typically, all such actions are taken in the name of law and order; a key aim is to achieve the power to define one's own side as the law enforcers, and the other as criminals and terrorists."

Sari knew Palestinian history a lot better than I did, and he rattled off a long list of Sharon's attempts to kill Arafat and destroy the PLO. Sharon's current plot, Sari said, was to produce Somalia-like chaos in the West Bank and Gaza, thus delegitimizing Palestinian nationalism and justifying our continued occupation.

Like a lawyer in a courtroom, Sari presented as evidence the constant raids on his university as well as the way IDF troops had ransacked the PA's Central Bureau of Statistics and shut down the Arab Chamber of Commerce offices and the nascent stock exchange in Nablus. "A war on terror is one thing. But why go after the stock market?"

I couldn't argue against Sari's politicide thesis. Some of my colleagues in the military liked to say about Sharon that he was all tactics, no strategy. This assessment badly underestimated a man who, even when he was dead wrong, always thought in political-strategic terms. While no one can say if Sharon realized he was handing Palestine over to Hamas by dismantling Arafat's regime, he certainly knew what he was doing when he crushed the hopes that the Palestinians could be partners.[51]

Our strategy since our first meeting had been to change the narrative of the conflict by taking diplomacy out of the smoky back rooms and into the streets. The question now was how to get the public to take notice of our proposal. Aryeh Rutenberg, who had issued the original challenge that led me to approach Sari, opened the conversation by suggesting we launch a PR campaign, replete with billboards and radio ads. But we knew we'd have to do more to get the number of signatures we were hoping for.

One day in December 2002, not long after Arafat, ever the unpredictable despot, fired him as the PLO representative in Jerusalem, Sari and I sat in a café and discussed a central paradox of our conflict.

As the cycle of killings and revenge attacks quickened, we noticed a strange paradox. Shikaki's polls continued showing that average Israelis and Palestinians were ready for peace more or less along the lines of our paper.[52] Seventy percent on both sides wanted a two-state solution, the highest numbers in recorded history. Yet these same people were calling for blood. In the face of an immediate threat, it seems, people lose sight of why we are killing and being killed and turn to a strongman who promises security. But the same people, when asked about the future, say they want peace and prosperity for their children within the framework of a two-state solution and claim they will do almost anything to secure it.

The reason for the schizophrenia, we hypothesized, was that almost no one trusted the leadership on the other side. We thought if we showed Israelis and Palestinians that we all wanted a better future more or less along the same lines, we could translate the optimistic opinion polls into a mass movement. Individuals would be asked to express their opposition to the status quo and their support for our proposed solution through the simple act of signing off, with their names, on our document.

While we had no idea how many signatures we would collect, our quest on the Israeli side was to gather enough to create public opinion pressure on Knesset members and ministers to adopt our platform.

We set the official launch for June 2003, giving us six months to create two organizations, one Israeli and one Palestinian, to gather the signatures.

Sari called his organization Hashd, an Arabic acronym for the "People's Campaign for Peace and Democracy," and presented a platform with the message that to liberate Palestine, Palestinians had to end the armed uprising, stop terrorism, and show skeptical Israelis that they have a partner. The tacit threat was that if the Israeli government continued to refuse the terms of peace, the masses could form a nonviolent civil disobedience campaign along the lines of South Africa's African National Congress.

Drawing on his experiences as a leader during the First Intifada, Sari recruited ex-prisoners, people with credibility on the streets, as his local leaders. One of his recruits had been wounded in a gun battle with a settler and spent nine years in prison. Sari's man in Nablus had been Abu Jihad's assistant; another deputy had developed an expertise in making Molotov cocktails during the First Intifada. His point person in Hebron had worked for Jibril after serving a ten-year prison sentence.

Our Israeli organization, the People's Voice, had a board of directors whose twenty-four members hailed from nearly every sector, including the leader of a feminist organization, a former Israeli chief of police, an ex-senior-official in the Mossad, a professor of Jewish studies, and the owner of a talent agency — no ex-cons, though.

For our headquarters we rented two rooms in a building next to the stock exchange in Ramat Gan. We recruited dozens of volunteers who took time out from their regular jobs to help. To gather signatures, hundreds of students were slated to knock on doors, stop people on the street, and approach shoppers in malls.

At the end of June, at a press conference in Tel Aviv, Sari and I launched the campaign. I had always operated discreetly — under the surface of the sea and in the dark. Now I had to rouse support in assembly halls, schools, and social clubs, shaking hands and talking to people from all backgrounds, including Russians, Ethiopians, traditionally right-wing religious Jews, and Israeli Arabs. Putting myself in the spotlight was for me like leaving water and crawling onto land.

In my stump speeches I avoided meandering political theories or reflections on Clausewitz; my talks omitted flashbacks to the Jewish humanism of our Declaration of Independence. I boiled down our message to its hard-hitting core: We needed a two-state solution not because we like Palestinians or we think Arafat deserves a state, but because if we don't withdraw from Palestinian territory and acknowledge their right to have their own state, Israel cannot survive as a Jewish democracy. Continued occupation would inevitably lead to a single state and end Zionism as we know it.

At first, my message encountered plenty of skepticism. "Yes, yes, Sari's a great fellow," I heard a hundred times. "But we're not making peace with *him*, but with *them*" — the violent, murderous inhabitants of the jungle. Soon, though, the signatures began to flow in, and in greater numbers than I had expected. By October ninety thousand Israelis had signed the statement, and each month we got twenty thousand more; following Orni's idea, we got signatures from three former Shabak directors, Avraham Shalom, Yaakov Peri, and Carmi Gillon. Needless to say, my parents, as well as most of the members of Kibbutz Ma'agan, signed onto the plan, even though the water level of the Sea of Galilee or the size of the banana harvest were probably more important to them than peace with the Palestinians.

An Israeli journalist described Sari's campaign this way: "As compared to the financiers, managers and advertising experts who are working with Ami Ayalon, Nusseibeh gives the impression of trying to navigate around a blocked dirt road in the territories with a beat-up old car."[53] Since telephone and internet lines rarely worked in bombed-out Palestine, signatures needed to be collected one by one, face-to-face. Sari and his band of former jailbirds walked, rode donkeys, hitched rides on farmers' tractors, whatever it took to reach villages, refugee camps, and cities under curfew.

Sometimes Sari's activists were harassed by Hamas who saw them as enemies and collaborators with the Israelis, and sometimes IDF soldiers arrested them at checkpoints because they had spent time in Israeli prisons. Some of Sari's team in Jenin were hauled in by Shabak agents who tried to win them over as informants. When they refused, the agents retorted, "But you are already collaborators. Look, you are working for Sari, and he is working with Ami, and Ami was once the head of the Shin Bet." Sari's critics blasted him for partnering with the "man who has attacked us, tortured us, and assassinated our leaders." They predicted that his would be the only signature he collected. Sari's mother Nuzha, for instance, refused to sign.

"Ami used to be an enemy, I'll give you that," Sari responded to his critics. "But you don't make peace with peaceniks, and besides, we have mutual interests. He knows that what's best for Israel is for us to have a state of our own."

A combination of Sari's tenacity, sincerity, and reasoning power succeeded in bringing in the signatures. In the Arroub refugee camp near Hebron, eleven hundred out of nine thousand residents joined. In Jenin, Sari won over three thousand supporters and seventy local Fatah leaders. Thousands more signatures came from Gaza, where Hamas had its stronghold. One woman told Sari she signed because she had lost her son in the first week of the Intifada. She supported the campaign because "I don't want to lose more children."

We also attracted a lot of support internationally. The European Parliament endorsed our project. In a *New York Times* op-ed, Robert McNamara, who had been secretary of defense during the Vietnam War, joined Zbigniew Brzezinski, Jimmy Carter's national security adviser, Frank Carlucci, Reagan's secretary of defense, and Warren Christopher, Clinton's secretary of state, in a statement of support. Separately, Bush's secretary of state Colin Powell indicated his approval in public statements by his spokespeople.

In October 2003, Sari and I took the show on the road. We spent an hour with Deputy Secretary of Defense Paul Wolfowitz, a neocon security hawk, in his Pentagon office overlooking the

Potomac. He found our plan so convincing that he praised it in a public speech at Georgetown University. With someone so influential inside the US administration endorsing the plan, Israeli policy makers suddenly sat up and noticed. "Everyone in Israel is reading [Wolfowitz's speech] very carefully," an Israeli official said. "If it comes from him, it's serious."[54]

Back in Israel we received an invitation, in late December, to present our plan at the Herzliya Conference, an annual gathering of Israel's and the Jewish world's financial, political, and academic elite. The conference has evolved into a forum for introducing new thinking on strategic issues facing Israel and is where the prime minister typically delivers the Israeli version of the State of the Union address.

Sari called it a beauty contest because ours and various other peace plans were to be discussed. He was also dubious because, a year earlier, Sharon had used the conference to unveil his plan to erect a wall cutting Israel off from much of the West Bank and Gaza. It ran straight through the Al Quds University campus in East Jerusalem.[55]

I assured him that attending the conference would be a good thing. It was a golden opportunity to tell the Israeli political and intellectual elite the truth.

Meanwhile Orni came up with a different way to get our message to the masses. His idea was to get *Yedioth Ahronoth*, with its circulation of six hundred thousand on a Friday, to do an interview with me and the three former Shabak directors who backed the People's Voice. *Yedioth* considered it a coup — never before had the mystery-shrouded heads of our secret police addressed the public.

Readers of the Friday interview were in for a shock. "The former Security Chiefs," went the article, "warn of an impending 'catastrophe' for Israel and urge the public to rally behind a document created which sets out the principles of a two-state solution for Israel and Palestine."

During the interview, Yaakov Peri, the director during the First Intifada, waved off any suggestion that he, or any of us, were "leftists."

"One of these days someone should study this sociological phenomenon. Why does everyone — heads of the Service, chiefs of staff, former security people — after a long security career become a standard-bearer of reconciliation with the Palestinians? Why? Because we've been there. We know the people, the landscape; we know both sides."

Carmi Gillon, my predecessor, translated the message of People's Voice into terms average Israelis could understand: "I am very worried about our future. I look at my daughters, who are still young, and it's clear to me that we are heading toward disintegration."

I pitched in that if we continued along the present course, our victory over terror would "march us steadily toward a place in which the State of Israel will not be a democracy and a Jewish national home."

In retrospect my most fateful words, as I would learn at the upcoming Herzliya Conference, were these: "In these terrible circumstances, when citizens are slaughtered in restaurants and on buses, I don't think there's any other path but to take independent steps. If the State of Israel would get up tomorrow morning and get out of Gaza, and seriously begin dismantling illegal settlements as we promised the American president, then I believe, from my years of familiarity with our future partners, that the Palestinians would come to the table."[56]

Handing Gaza to the PA would prove that we were serious about negotiations, force them to step up, and rebuild a working relationship that had stopped Hamas terrorism once and could do so again.

23

THE WRONG WAY OUT

The Herzliya Conference opened on December 18. Various groups, including the People's Voice, were asked to present plans to resolve the Israeli-Palestinian conflict. Conference participants would then vote on the various proposals before breaking for lunch.

The first people on the stage, the Israeli Yossi Beilin and the Palestinian Yasser Abed Rabbo, presented their Geneva Accord, a plan similar to ours, though without the grassroots component. The next presenter was Avigdor Lieberman, a former director of Netanyahu's Prime Minister's Office, founder of the right-wing Yisrael Beiteinu Party, and eventually the Israeli minister of defense from 2016 to 2018. His scheme was what you'd expect from someone who once proposed drowning Palestinian political prisoners in the Dead Sea:[57] Lieberman called for the annexation of all the empty land in the West Bank while dealing with the demographic time bomb inside Israel in a straightforward apartheid arrangement. Areas within our pre-1967 borders with a large Arab population were to be handed over to Arafat, while Arabs remaining in Israel would have to take a loyalty oath to the "Jewish-Zionist country"; otherwise, they'd be expelled. Simple.

Sari and I presented last. When the organizers tallied up the votes, we got 65 percent; the Geneva Accord 25 percent; and Lieberman's annexation scheme, 10 percent. The results didn't get Sari and me patting each other on the back, because the people in the room were from the elite, not the grassroots. But the vote still had value, especially given what was about to happen in the afternoon session.

No one outside his inner circle knew when Prime Minister Ariel Sharon lumbered up to the stage after lunch that a week earlier a group of American Jewish leaders had visited Sharon in his office brandishing a copy of "The Spooks Speak: Former Shin Bet Chiefs Talk of Peace," a translation in *The Jewish Forward* of the *Yedioth* article. "After this interview," they told Sharon, "we will find it harder to defend you on the Hill." Together with the growing international support for Beilin and Rabbo's Geneva plan, along with a group of conscientious objectors, officers and pilots refusing to serve in the occupied territories, the meeting convinced Sharon to take drastic action to keep American Jews on his side in his war against the Palestinian government.[58]

For the prime minister, dressed in a dark suit and bright-red tie, the Herzliya speech was the political equivalent of crossing the Suez and encircling the Egyptian Third Army during the Yom Kippur War. He began with a discussion of Israel's role in the world, how we needed an open society if we were to compete in the new global economy, how Israeli security depended on our relationship with Western democracies, and how we needed to be an attractive destination for American and European Jews accustomed to living in free societies governed by laws. I could have written and delivered that part of the speech myself.

In a confident, steady voice, Sharon next detailed a vision for the future that also could have come from a People's Voice pamphlet. Israel, he said, desired to coexist with a "democratic Palestinian state with territorial contiguity in Judea and Samaria and economic viability." No one had ever heard such dovish language from the general.

Sari, wearing earphones for the instant translation, turned to me with eyes wide open.

"Just wait." I motioned with my hand. I knew Sharon far too well to be taken in by him. Something smelled fishy.

Sure enough, in a flash the human bulldozer was back. "Only security will lead to peace," Sharon declared, "and in that sequence." As Shabak director I had told three prime ministers unequivocally that peace and security were intertwined. Security cooperation with the Palestinians was key to combating terror, and this cooperation was only possible in the context of genuine hope among the Palestinian public that our occupation would end. Sharon's message headed in the opposite direction, with a dig at those of us who "deceive the public" and create "false hope":

> Without the achievement of full security within the framework of which terror organizations will be dismantled it will not be possible to achieve genuine peace . . . The opposite perception, according to which the very signing of a peace agreement will produce security out of thin air, has already been tried in the past and failed miserably. And such will be the fate of any other plan which promotes this concept. These plans deceive the public and create false hope. There will be no peace before the eradication of terror.

It was an impossible standard — "full security" and the complete "eradication of terror" — that, given ongoing settler and army violence, no government, not ours and certainly not the badly crippled Palestinian Authority, could achieve.

Then Sharon dropped his bomb: He proposed evacuating settlements "which will not be included in the territory of the State of Israel in the framework of any possible future permanent agreement" while "strengthening our control over those same areas in the Land of Israel which will constitute an inseparable part of the State of Israel in any future agreement." Presumably, only the settlements on our side of the security fence that our government was building with such gusto would remain under Israeli sovereignty.

Sharon was a strategist, his steps carefully calculated. What was he up to? The general public perception was that the prime minister proposed swinging a wrecking ball at his life's work by taking Israel's first ever concrete step toward ending the occupation by removing settlements. I wasn't so sure.

It was only weeks after the conference, once the details of what came to be called the Sharon government's "disengagement plan" were made public — a full withdrawal from Gaza and from four small West Bank settlements, leaving the vast majority of settlements in Judea and Samaria in place — that I started to grasp some of the nuances of Sharon's proposal. The Strip, with its teeming refugee camps, had always been a headache for Israel. From Sharon's point of view, the disengagement was an opportunity to wash his hands of this liability while collecting credit for moving the peace process forward. Was Gaza to be a trial run followed by the evacuations of major West Bank settlements, or by leaving Gaza was Sharon sacrificing a pawn to save the queen, Judea and Samaria?

I polled my friends to get their opinions. Pinchas Wallerstein surprised me with his mixture of pragmatism and opposition. Many settlers, he told me, were resigned to leaving Gaza — for them, too, it had become a nightmare. Still, Pinchas believed Sharon had "sold his soul to the devil." In earlier political speeches Sharon had attacked Labor for any hint of pulling out of Gaza. The settlements, he said, were as much a part of Israel as Tel Aviv. And now with no discussion and barely a nod to the democratic process, he intended to pull out the settlers, by the ankles if necessary. "Sharon is dangerous," he said, "because we thought we were getting one thing and now it seems we have something else." Pinchas had a point.

Matti Steinberg's assessment was just as scathing. Sharon's "crass unilateral format," he said, ran a Sherman tank over secular, moderate Palestinians like Sari and Mahmoud Abbas with whom we could reach a settlement to end the conflict once and for all. By crushing hope and elevating suspicion and fear into core strategic principles, Sharon tipped the balance of power toward Hamas in Gaza, thus fomenting the kind of chaos that could justify additional unilateral steps. Instead of a single Palestinian state alongside Israel, there would be at least two, possibly more, "Palestines" filled to the brim with angry, despondent people.

Sari echoed Matti. Sharon's plan was an elaborate ruse to crush moderates and boost the very fanatics committing most of the terrorist attacks. The idea, said Sari, was to "contain the animals"

— Palestinians like himself — "on the other side of walls." It was specifically designed to prevent coexistence campaigns like ours.[59]

But whatever Sharon's intentions were, his plan became for most people, including the American administration, the only game in town.

Sari and I redoubled our efforts to counter Sharon's politics of fear; signature by signature, we demonstrated that our peoples could be partners in peace. By early 2004, 350,000 Israelis and Palestinians had joined our campaign. Sari got the head of Fatah in Gaza to come around. The governor of Nablus, whose two sons were killed by the Israelis, also signed. Erratic Arafat refrained from sending goons to drag Sari off to prison, as we had feared, and actually tacitly backed him. When Sari came to a meeting of the Fatah leadership and presented our main points, they shouted that he was a traitor because our plan renounced the right of return. Arafat, ever a master of ambiguity, said nothing, which Sari interpreted as approval.[60]

The mass killings continued. In January and February, Hamas and the Al Aqsa Brigades, an amalgam of secular armed groups, many affiliated with Fatah, dispatched suicide bombers to murder more Israelis. Sharon decided it was time to take out Sheikh Ahmed Yassin, the quadriplegic founder and spiritual head of Hamas. On March 22, as bodyguards wheeled him into a mosque for morning prayers, an Apache helicopter gunship killed him, his bodyguards, and nine bystanders with an American Hellfire missile.

After a previous assassination attempt against him, the sheikh had said with chilling prescience: "Days will prove that the assassination policy will not finish Hamas. Hamas leaders wish to be martyrs and are not scared of death. Jihad will continue and the resistance will continue until we have victory, or we will be martyrs."

By killing Yassin, Sharon handed Hamas a martyr of the highest profile, guaranteeing that the terrorist disease Sharon was supposedly trying to contain would spread. Two hundred thousand people attended the sheikh's funeral, and for the first time

Shikaki's PCPSR opinion polls among Palestinians in the West Bank and Gaza showed a majority backing Hamas.

The next phase of Sharon's disengagement plan swung the pendulum yet further toward Hamas and away from secular and pragmatic Fatah. In his April 14 letter to President George W. Bush, Sharon declared, "There exists no Palestinian partner with whom to advance peacefully toward a settlement." Nor was Sharon going to coordinate the Gaza withdrawal with Palestinian prime minister Abu Mazen's government in Ramallah; the IDF would just pull out and permit the most violent force in Gaza, Hamas, to come out on top.

While I supported leaving Gaza, and not a day too soon, with Sharon's unilateralism I wanted to put my head between my knees. Hamas, even before we took down our flags and cleared out the IDF bases and settlements in Gaza, was savoring its victory. Capitalizing on the widespread narrative among Palestinians that peace negotiations with Israel had brought only doom, yet more power shifted to Hamas.

Hamas had begun its campaign of slaughter in reaction to Oslo. Its murder of hundreds of Israelis had helped derail the peace process, and our government was about to reward them by handing them Gaza, free of charge. In an op-ed I dashed off to *The Jerusalem Post*, titled "The Wrong Way Out," I wrote, "By being willing to sweep out entire Israeli communities with nothing in return and no final objective defined, Sharon has seemingly fulfilled radical Arab dreams of ejecting us — by force and bit by bit."[61]

In May the Labor Party organized what was forecast to be the biggest rally by Israel's peace camp since Rabin's death, marching in support of Sharon's Gaza policy. Peace Now, the same organization that had protested the Sabra and Shatila massacre twenty years earlier, joined the planning. The organizers, who equated disengagement with security, asked me to open the event, speaking just before Shimon Peres.

I agreed because it was clear we couldn't leave Gaza a day too soon. In the week leading to the rally, Islamists in Gaza, to commemorate Nakba Day, targeted Israeli army vehicles, killing thirteen soldiers. In retribution the IDF hit Gaza hard. Thirty-two Palestinians died in the attacks, and more than three hundred were wounded.

There was another reason I agreed to do the opening act. My Shabak years had turned me into a student of national narratives. For years I'd been warning Israelis about the danger of unilaterally handing Hamas a victory and bolstering their narrative that the Zionists understand only force. Now I saw another deeply worrying narrative taking root.

Disengagement polarized Israel, drawing a line between the majority, who wanted to get out of Gaza fast, and the religious settlers. But if the left hadn't been stuck in a fog, they would have seen that settlers, the vanguard of frontier Zionism, were a latter-day version of the kibbutzniks, like my parents, who forged Israel's settlement and security ethos. What secular Israelis failed to see was that we all shared a fierce love of the Land of Israel and had no doubt it was our right to "redeem" it. Since 1967 religious settlers had been pouring their sweat and blood into Judea, Samaria, and Gaza, and their efforts got the Arab world to come to terms with us. Rather than ostracize settlers as aggressive weeds to be plucked by the roots from our carefully manicured secular gardens, we secular nationalists should be carrying them on our shoulders as national heroes returning home.

I finished writing the speech a few minutes before Biba and I jumped in the car and drove to Tel Aviv.

More than 150,000 Israelis packed into Rabin Square on that Saturday evening, May 15. The stage behind me was festooned with a banner that read: EXIT FROM GAZA, BEGIN TALKING, even though "talking" had no role in the prime minister's chess game.

The secular left-wing crowd was in a festive mood, celebrating what they saw as disengagement from the Palestinians and, no less so, from Jewish "fanatics" in their yeshivas and settlements — the bane of "our" Israel. The timing of the rally, just after Shabbat, incidentally excluded observant Jews; they simply couldn't get there in time.

When I took the stage and looked down on the Peace Now banners, the balloons, the hooting and hollering, and the festive mood, snatches of conversation with rabbis and settlers came back to me — how right they were to point out the hypocrisies of the leftists living guilt-free on former Arab lands while they pointed accusing fingers at West Bank settlers.

At a certain point in the speech, after supporting disengagement, I asked, "Where are our brothers the religious settlers of Judea, Samaria, and Gaza?" Silence spread over the crowd. The lights were blinding, and I could barely recognize my own voice, as it was amplified a thousand times to fill the square. "Are they not here because we didn't want them to be?

"We never created a real dialogue with the settlers," I continued, "because we never really wanted to. We turned settlers into enemies. We arrogantly turned them out. We monopolized the quest for peace. That is why the majority did not come here today, although I know that today of all days they wanted to come . . . The majority wants to leave Gaza as much as we do. But they want to do so after lowering the national flag to half-mast, observing a minute's silence, and wiping a tear at the shattering of their Zionist dream. The majority will feel connected to us only when the pain of those slated to be evacuated drowns out the rejoicing of those who will do the evacuating."

My partnership with Sari had already cost me friends on the right, and with the speech in Tel Aviv that night I now lost friends on the left. "Whose side are you on?" people asked. I wasn't sure how to answer. I still thought I was merely defending the Zionism on which I was raised.

24

THE SEXTANT

Where there is no vision, the people perish.

— King Solomon

We will never know what Sharon really intended with the disengagement. Was he really sacrificing Gaza, the pawn, to defend the queen — Judea and Samaria? Dov Weisglass, director general of the Prime Minister's Office, interpreted the disengagement as a means to prevent a political solution. Abandoning Gaza "supplies the amount of formaldehyde that's necessary so that there will not be a political process with the Palestinians. When you freeze that process, you prevent the establishment of a Palestinian state, and you prevent a discussion on the refugees, the borders and Jerusalem. Effectively, this whole package called the Palestinian state, with all that it entails, has been removed indefinitely from our agenda . . . until the Palestinians turn into Finns."

Sari, no fan of formaldehyde, decamped to Harvard's Radcliffe Institute in the fall of 2004 to write his memoirs, around the same time that Arafat passed away suddenly in Paris. Along with most Palestinians, Sari was convinced that Sharon had put his nemesis in the grave. Because Harvard no longer permitted smoking inside buildings, Sari wrote out his memories onto notepads while sitting or pacing in Harvard Square.

He began his memoir with an account of his father Anwar, the Oxford-educated judge, and his struggles against my father's generation of Zionists. When I was a boy, the sea, the sky, and the deserts seemed limitless until I looked just to the east of our banana plantations. There the barbed wire, land mines, and Syrian guns on the Golan formed an impenetrable barrier. The Arab world was for me a vast no-man's-land.

Sari's no-man's-land began behind his family villa. As a boy he liked sitting in his upstairs bedroom and staring off at a UN observation and border-crossing station, the signs warning of land mines, and a grapevine that had managed to survive all the fighting. He'd also peer over the back wall and wonder about the Jews on the other side. The fact that he couldn't pass through Mandelbaum Gate, the Checkpoint Charlie between East and West Jerusalem, didn't produce in him a sense of claustrophobia because, before 1967, Palestinians could easily travel to the rest of the Middle East. Sari's one-legged father, wounded by one of our snipers while defending the Old City of Jerusalem in 1948, could freely steer his Oldsmobile to Damascus, Beirut, or Bagdad.

Sari's book ends with a description of his contemporary Palestinian life in an East Jerusalem neighborhood abutting Sharon's Separation Wall:

> My wife Lucy and I once liked to sit on the balcony just before dusk and look out at the church towers on the Mount of Olives, the golden sheen coming off the Dome of the Rock, the weaving contours of Suleiman the Great's walls wrapping their way around the city. We both were intoxicated by the unique fusion of earth and the sunlight basking the entire pastoral surroundings. Today, if I somehow managed to climb onto the balcony of the apartment — it has been abandoned — I would see a 20-foot high, fortified steel barrier crowned with razor wire, complete with watchtowers . . . ribboning its way through Jerusalem like a malevolent landscape sculpture.

The book's other bleak images include those of IDF "soldiers parading through the streets of Jerusalem"; the "bigotry and sanctimoniousness of Israeli officialdom"; the "continuing onslaught against the city my family has lived in for 1,300 years"; and the specter of a "gruesome bi-national reality of apartheid."

By the end of 2004 my joint project with Sari had led me to reassess the vow I'd made to Shelly Yachimovich four years earlier in the television interview, and I had begun to consider entering politics. I was also moved by the disengagement, and our response to it. Most Israelis accepted that we had to leave Gaza if we were ever going to make peace with the Palestinians. My problem with Sharon was with *how* he yanked out the settlers. His unilateral actions reinforced the Hamas line that we understand only power.

If despite all my decades of experience it had taken Dr. Sarraj to open my eyes to Hamas's "victory" over us, I couldn't blame average Israelis for mistaking brute force for strength. Israelis needed a sextant to help them see where their leaders were taking them. They also needed leaders whose actions inspired hope in a better future, for us and for the Palestinians. I felt I had no choice but to try to throw a wrench into our malfunctioning political system.

In December, I walked to the Labor Party headquarters in Tel Aviv and tossed my hat into the ring for the next parliamentary election. Asked by a reporter outside the building about my intentions, I held nothing back: "I am not entering politics to be another Knesset member. If I enter the political arena, I want to be prime minister. Period." Stating my ambition so bluntly was the first of many mistakes I would make in politics.

On my first day of political life I made some formidable enemies. Israel's political system is run by party machines and power cliques, which makes it next to impossible for outsiders like me to rise to the top. Biba, who never questioned my prowess in fighting naval battles and terrorists, confessed she didn't think I was cut out for politics. "You're way too honest," she said to me one day in the grocery store. Referring to my cocky self-confidence outside party headquarters, she reminded me that "even on a wonderful spring day when the sun is shining, you're still five foot four."

"Biba, I'm entering politics *because* I'm honest," I responded. Pointing at the other shoppers, I added, "All I need to do is reignite people's hope in a better future."

Biba, drawing on her decades of experience as a social worker and family therapist, tried to talk some sense into me. "Look," she said as she pulled items from the shelves and dropped them into the cart I was pushing. "I love you, but let me tell you something. If an abandoned child gets adopted, he has hope. But if the same child gets abandoned a second time, his fear of abandonment is so extreme you'll never reignite that initial flicker of hope. Fear is a safer option. You are dreaming if you think you can get Israelis, who've been betrayed so often, to hope."

Though I suspected she was right, her message conflicted with my upbringing. To be sure, centuries of persecution and being surrounded by enemies have taught Jews to be fearful. But my parents' generation buried the painful past and focused on building a better future. If they could do this after losing family members in the Holocaust, why couldn't we? I figured we just needed a different kind of leader, someone orienting us toward the possibilities of the future and not the traumas and failures of the past.

It turned out my entry into politics would have to wait a year. The disengagement Sharon initiated was in full swing, and during this period, for the first time in our marriage, Biba and I joined forces politically to push for a better Israel. We both empathized with the settlers. How would my father feel if the IDF sent in bulldozers to uproot our plantations and knock down everything we'd built? Biba became a founding member of Shuvi, Hebrew for "come back," a civil society organization to support the settlers who'd lost their homes, synagogues, and cemeteries. Just as I had said in the speech in front of the Tel Aviv crowd at Rabin Square, Shuvi's message was that settlers were neither weeds nor enemies; they were instrumental in forcing the Arab world to come to terms with us, and as such supporters of peace should carry them on our shoulders as returning heroes.[62]

Amid the turmoil surrounding the disengagement, Imma died, leaving Abba alone in the hut they'd shared for more than half a century. Aunt Hava, too, was sick with cancer, and I dropped by the kibbutz whenever I could. With a journalist for the Hebrew daily *Yedioth Ahronoth*, who wanted to know more about my early influences, I returned to the Sea of Galilee and the Kinneret Cemetery. But I didn't bring her to the kibbutz to meet Abba. Why not? she asked. I told her that Abba, ever the idealist and dreamer, had little respect for politicians these days — myself included. "He's happy to talk about equality, solidarity, the prophets of the Bible, or our Declaration of Independence. But our conversations steer clear of contemporary politics."

"And what is his dream now?"

"That a person's life span be shorter than the expiration date on his dreams."

When I said this, I didn't think the journalist was taking notes. To my surprise, when the article came out it included the lines about Abba's shattered dreams. I immediately phoned him up and apologized.

"No need," he said. "The article wasn't so bad. You just told the truth."

Abba began to lose weight and, for the first time in his life, stooped and shuffled and wheezed when he breathed. He suspected he had cancer, but doctors found nothing wrong. Though I never dared raise the subject with him, I suspected he suffered from the death of a dream. Israel had become bourgeois, and many of the kibbutzim were privatizing; even Degania Alef, the mother of kibbutzim — which houses a museum to the utopian visionary A. D. Gordon — was being privatized. An additional reason for his melancholy was that the kibbutz revolution, the determination to win back the Land of Israel acre by acre, was most alive in the thriving religious settlements in Judea and Samaria. He saw with perfect clarity how the ideals he had pursued in his youth had metastasized into a messianic religious vision leading to the oppression of the Palestinian people.

Each time we left the cramped hut and headed to the lake, we had more or less the same conversation. I'd ask him about his heart condition, and he'd change the subject by pointing to a cluster of exposed rocks close to shore.

"Island's still there."

"Yes, it is."

"Damned drought. You remember how high the lake used to be when you were a boy?"

"I do."

"It would take quite a storm to cover those rocks," he'd say with a frown. "Do you think it'll happen?"

"We've had big storms in the past, Abba."

"But what if the storms don't come?"

"Abba, the storms will return." And even if we run low on water, I added, we were leading the world in desalination technology and drip irrigation.

After one of these visits, in the car driving back home, it finally dawned on me that Abba hadn't really wiped the slate of history clean as I had claimed to Sari and the people at Macalester College in Minnesota. The past maintained its grip on him, even if he wasn't aware of it. I began to suspect, for example, that he'd kept me in the dark for years about leaving his parents in Romania not because they didn't matter but because he felt guilty that he left them behind to face the Holocaust.

The more time I spent with him, the more contradictions I noticed. He abandoned religion in his youth and replaced God with human solidarity, yet he never touched pork. "I have the stomach of a religious Jew," he told me. On Shabbat he listened to cantorial concerts on the radio.

I also realized that I'd inherited some of Abba's contradictions. During a discussion on the Gaza disengagement, Rabbi Yoel Bin-Nun, a towering figure in the religious settler community who was one of the paratroopers in 1967 who conquered the Temple Mount, asked me if I felt like a foreigner in Hebron.

Hebron? I told him I hated the place. During my time as head of the Shabak, the only reason I'd ever go there was because an Arab had murdered a Jew, or a Jew an Arab.

"Let me rephrase the question," he replied with an expression of concern as if speaking with a wayward soul. "At the Cave of the

Patriarchs in Hebron, do you feel that you are a stranger without any spiritual connection, like an Israeli tourist visiting the Lincoln Memorial?"

During the 1967 war, I recalled feeling elated when news came that we had seized the Western Wall, Rachel's Tomb, and the Tomb of the Patriarchs. We had liberated what had been stolen from the Jewish people two thousand years earlier. "No, Rabbi, I don't feel like a foreigner in Hebron," I finally replied. "As a Jew, the Cave of the Patriarchs is a part of me."

"Ami," said the rabbi rubbing his stringy white beard between his fingers, "you are someone I can talk to. I have nothing to say to a leftist who tells me that the Cave of the Patriarchs belongs to a sheikh. If we agree that Hebron is ours, then it is ours to keep or give away. We'll get it back when the Messiah comes, God willing. What is important is that everyone knows it belongs to us."

It would be years before I would finally give up the toxic belief that we could make peace with the Palestinians without calling into question whether we Jews were the only ones who had historic rights to the Land of Israel.

In August 2005, Pinchas and the religious leaders of the settlement movement helped prevent a violent reaction when our government returned eight thousand settlers in Gaza and one thousand in North Samaria to the State of Israel. Secular young commanders involved in the evacuation of Homesh, a settlement near Rabbi Shapira's Yitzhar, told me how hard it was for them to evacuate religious Jews, people with whom they thought they had almost nothing in common.

Predictably, Hamas took credit for ousting us from Gaza. I feared before long we'd have a full-blown religious war on our hands. This fast-moving disaster revived my intention to shake up Israeli politics.

Palestinian elections slated for late January 2006 further bolstered my resolve. Palestinians went to the polls to choose their own government, and Jibril, who headed the Fatah list in the Hebron district, was slated to be a powerful figure. Maybe, I found myself thinking, the two of us could dispense with Barak's myth of "no partner" and finish what our dead leaders, Rabin and Arafat, had started.

The United States poured millions of dollars into supporting Fatah by building schools, cleaning streets, providing computers to community centers, and staging a soccer tournament. Almost no one I talked to thought Hamas had a chance because its platform seemed so far-fetched. Hamas had declared that "not one inch of the historic soil of Palestine will be ceded" and called for the liberation of all of pre-1948 Palestine, including Tel Aviv and Haifa.

Two weeks before the election, Fatah seemed poised for a landslide victory when Ariel Sharon, that great destroyer of Palestinian dreams, suffered a massive stroke at his ranch in the Negev. The former mayor of Jerusalem, Ehud Olmert, took over and immediately called for a snap election at the end of March. To brandish its security credentials, the new head of the Labor Party, Amir Peretz, offered me a top place on its list of candidates, and I took him up on his offer.

Heading into the Palestinian election, Khalil and other pollsters were sanguine. Voters, exhausted by four years of conflict, having buried over three thousand people and with the economy in tatters, would surely give secular Fatah the victory.

But Hamas didn't run on a platform of sharia law and Qassam rockets. Rebranding itself as the Party of Change and Reform, the terrorist group promised to sweep away years of Fatah nepotism, kleptocracy, and slime.

When the results came in, Hamas, a charity with an underground terrorist network, crushed mighty Fatah, an organization hitherto synonymous with the Palestinian struggle for independence.

I didn't dare phone Jibril to get his assessment because rumors were that voters had rejected him in part because he had once "collaborated" with Israel to repress the Islamists. His brother Naif, the Hamas leader, won.

To make sense of Hamas's victory, I turned to my sensor Matti Steinberg. For years Matti had been telling Shabak directors, prime ministers, cabinet ministers, and IDF brass that Hamas was a lot more popular than people thought. Matti agreed with what Dr. Sarraj had told me in London: Blow by blow, our military overreach strengthened a movement that fed off hopelessness and feelings of victimhood. His warnings having gone unheeded, Matti described his state of mind to me by likening himself to the Chinese dissident who wanted to engrave on his tombstone, HERE LIES ONE WHO DID A FEW THINGS THAT NEEDED TO BE DONE AND SAID A FEW THINGS THAT NEEDED TO BE SAID.

Matti foresaw two Palestines, one in Gaza, a festering sore run by a triumphant terror organization, and the other in the West Bank dependent on Israel to keep its government in power. "I am thinking about the immense burden we are imposing on the coming generations," Matti said about Israel's self-defeating strategy.

In March, I entered the Knesset. The Labor Party was a junior member of a governing coalition with the Kadima Party's Olmert as prime minister. Labor's Amir Peretz, who'd fought in the Yom Kippur War but had no experience as a military commander, took over the Ministry of Defense. Bibi, as if risen from the dead, led the opposition.

The predictable Palestinian civil war broke out within months. Even though President Bush had been talking about democracy in the Middle East for years, he threw his support behind Olmert and his decision to boycott and arrest the democratically elected Hamas leaders in the hope of keeping Abu Mazen in power. According to Matti, these machinations only strengthened Hamas, which now branded itself as a national party acting on behalf of the Palestinian people, against Israel and a Palestinian government cooperating with the occupier. The Israeli government's actions also lent credence to Hamas's argument that violence, not diplomacy, was the most effective weapon against the occupation.

After the election Hamas seized total control of Gaza. Hamas fighters, faster and smarter than the Fatah forces, fired mortar shells at the headquarters of the security forces in Gaza, a complex of buildings I knew well from my meetings there in the 1990s. Hamas executed some of the Fatah security men with shots to the back of the head; others they tossed from the rooftops of high-rises.

On July 12, Hamas's ideological brothers in Lebanon, the Hezbollah, killed three IDF soldiers in armored Humvees on our side of the border, and abducted two other soldiers; five more soldiers died in an attempt to rescue their kidnapped comrades.

The next morning I woke up to my pager beeping. It was Minister of Defense Amir Peretz. He called a few minutes later with an update on the Hezbollah attack and asked me for advice.

"My recommendation is that together with Olmert you call a press conference and, in front of the world's media, give Hezbollah and the Lebanese government a twenty-four-hour ultimatum to return the abducted soldiers."

"Do you think they will accept our demand?"

"No. But it will buy you a day. Neither Olmert nor you has commanded wars. You need time to lay out your strategy. Never start a war if you don't know how you're going to end it."

In the end Prime Minister Olmert and Minister of Defense Amir Peretz ignored my advice and conducted one of the most unnecessary wars in the history of the State of Israel. For thirty-four days I watched an underground movement with a few thousand fighters fend off the strongest army in the Middle East. Barbara Tuchman would have called the war a March of Folly.

As with Hamas, the more often we decapitated the Hezbollah Hydra, the greater its support from the Palestinian masses and Islamic governments. The Saudis, Iranians, and other potential adversaries took notice of our failure.

By the time the fighting finally stopped and the military funerals slowed to a trickle, I was convinced Peretz, as head of the Labor Party, shouldn't be our candidate in the next general election. As a member of the Knesset's Foreign Affairs and Security Intelligence Subcommittee, I had seen up close the egregious arrogance of the leaders who got us into the war. I told Peretz I was challenging him earlier than I had planned. If I won, I'd also take over the Ministry of Defense in a country reeling from the latest Lebanese debacle.

Just as the election for head of Labor heated up, Ehud Barak returned from retirement to challenge me. I enjoyed the theatrics of campaigning against him. I must have spoken in town halls or high school gyms in every community in Israel, Jewish and Arab. Battles come in many forms: For some you have to put on a wet suit and swim across enemy lines; others require a wiretap and a black hood. For this one my weapons were stump speeches, handshakes, and debates with Ehud about Israel's greatest threats and opportunities. My model was Tony Blair, and my mantra was "New Labor." I even enlisted my friends from Flotilla 13 to appear with me on a talk show. There is nothing commandos detest more than politics and public relations, but for me my former comrades-in-arms sat in a television studio and told the Israeli public they were ready to go into battle with me to defend the values and ideas we shared.

I told voters that Barak hadn't learned the lessons of the 1990s. We needed to foster trust, a concept lacking in his lexicon, if we were to bridge the wide rifts within Israel among secular and religious. To defeat Hamas's terrorist wing, we would also need to regain the trust of our Palestinian partners by taking concrete steps toward Palestinian independence. Helping Palestinians build their own state would make Israel both safer and more just.

While I talked about trust and hope, Ehud based his platform on fear. We were living in a jungle, he said. With Hezbollah to the north and Hamas to the south, did voters really want an untested politician like this "extremely left-wing" Ami Ayalon calling the shots? No. Israel needed steely-eyed men with no illusions.

Just four days before the Labor Party election, my message of hope was ahead by 4 percent in the opinion polls. People were already slapping me on the back. Here's to the next minister of defense! Here's to the next prime minister!

Not so fast, more cynical friends cautioned. Ehud recruited all the Labor ministers and most Knesset members, and we were neck and neck among 120,000 members of the Labor Party. There was also our twisted psychology at work. "Ami," said one old friend who'd been in the game much longer than I had, "don't believe the polls. People might say they want hope, but the minute they get into the voting booth and the curtains are drawn, they'll vote with their gut. Don't underestimate the power of fear."

How right these pessimists were.

25

WAR AMONGST THE PEOPLE

Hope must be a mine field.

— Yehuda Amichai

Just as people had warned, from the privacy of the voting booth Labor party members chose Ehud.

Soon after the loss Prime Minister Olmert invited me to his upstairs office on Balfour Street, a place I was very familiar with by this point. "Ami," he said once I settled into my usual spot in front of the prime minister's desk. "I'd like you to join my cabinet." He wanted me to be what he designated "minister of the Prime Minister's Office," which meant that I'd be his point man on whatever he chose. I opened my mouth, ready to repeat what I had said to Rabin in 1995: No way. Olmert had long been associated with the hard right. For years he had repeated like a mantra that we should keep every square inch of the Land of Israel. He opposed the Camp David Accords that gave us peace with Egypt; as mayor of Jerusalem, he dispatched fleets of cement trucks to build settlements in East Jerusalem. Oslo he called a "dark cloud over the city."

I'd run for office because I wanted to shake things up, not sell my soul for a government-issue Volvo and a fat salary.

But before I could get the words out, Olmert barreled on. "Ami," he said, "I want you in my government because I believe your vision for a future agreement with the Palestinians is our best chance at peace." I blinked rapidly as if to stop myself from hallucinating.

With his eyes fixed on mine, Olmert assured me he wanted a fair deal with Abu Mazen along the lines of Sari's and my one-pager.

I was incredulous, but I believed him, because I knew him to be a man of his word.

"Where do I sign, Mr. Prime Minister?"

Olmert immediately pushed for a peace deal with Abu Mazen. At the Annapolis peace talks organized by President Bush, he promised "serious and in-depth negotiations, which will not avoid any issue or ignore any division that has clouded our relations with the Palestinian people for many years." His explanation for his urgency sounded like something straight from a People's Voice pamphlet: "If the day comes when the two-state solution collapses, and we face a South African–style struggle for equal voting rights (also for the Palestinians in the territories), then, as soon as that happens, the State of Israel is finished."

No prime minister had ever pursued a deal with as much conviction. Tragically for us all, a month after I entered the government, the attorney general ordered an investigation against Olmert for breach of trust and fraud. Less than a year later Olmert announced he would be standing down once his Kadima Party held its primaries. Naturally the peace talks were on ice. The cabinet devolved into a sort of Borgia-like court, split into factions jockeying for power, and the government ceased to function.

In parallel with his earnest pursuit of a peace deal, Olmert made a mess of Gaza. Following Hamas's takeover, Israel teamed up with Egypt to impose a hermetic blockade on Gaza, entrapping a million and a half people with barbed wire and our navy's ships. The idea was that if we ratcheted up the level of despair, Gaza's population would rebel against Hamas. Just as in our misguided assault on Hezbollah in Lebanon, we embarked upon a strategy with no evidence to support it. Inside the cabinet my protests fell on deaf ears; my fellow ministers lacked the will to examine the situation or engage in an honest discussion. We were like drunken sailors on a ship headed for the shoals.

On Tuesday, November 4, at 6:00 AM I scooped up the morning edition of *Haaretz* from the front yard and read that polls projected

Barack Obama to win that day's US presidential election. The mightiest nation on the planet, a unipolar mega power whose War on Terror had brought mayhem to my corner of the world, was about to elect a young idealist. Even if most of my colleagues in the military and government wrote off Obama as a dreamer who would probably sidle up to the Palestinians, I let myself hope that Obama might steer America toward a more cooperative foreign policy and leave behind the heedless wars that only advance the causes of terrorists.

Two hours later my driver pulled up behind the house to take me to the airport. I was traveling to Madrid and Paris to speak at memorial services for Rabin. Over breakfast a couple of days earlier, my son Guy had joked: "Abba," he said looking up from a bowl of cornflakes, "if they arrest you, all of us" — he meant he and his brothers — "will do a commando action to rescue you." I laughed and told him I'd be fine. In Holland lawyers for a Palestinian named Al-Shami sought my arrest and extradition for torturing him during my Shabak days.[63] I assured him the French had promised not to stick me in shackles and extradite me to the Dutch.

Our two dogs, hoping for a scratch behind the ear, followed me outside. The high white fence swung open, and I climbed in the back of the Volvo. Once on the road I continued reading *The Utility of Force* by Sir Rupert Smith, the British general who had headed up the United Nations Protection Force in Bosnia. General Smith captured in words what I had experienced in my raids on PLO guerrilla camps in the 1970s: "War no longer exists as battle in a field between men and machinery" or "as a massive deciding event in a dispute in international affairs." In Smith's historical analysis, the last large-scale industrialized conflict between states was the Yom Kippur War. Wars since that time have tended "to be timeless, even unending," and are "fought amongst the people, not on the battlefield."

So that's the reason we win battle after battle while losing the wars. "Just" wars involve the use of proportional force and discrimination between combatants and noncombatants, and should only be fought as a last resort. *The Gaza blockade met none of those conditions.* "A just war against terror must employ appropriate weapons," I wrote in the margins of Smith's book, "and today those weapons must include hope for the 'enemy' population." In Gaza our war produced only despair.

Following my address in Paris, I shook hands with local dignitaries before politely declining a dinner invitation. I walked out of the hall in the direction of the Eiffel Tower to join the crowds awaiting election results from the US. The French threw the biggest election victory party east of Chicago. Red, white, and blue balloons filled the sky, and that night the Eiffel Tower sparkled with a thousand flashing lights. In a sea of tens of thousands of people, no one knew or cared who I was. After two years in the spotlight, it was a relief to be just one of the crowd.

Then, just as a chill November morning broke, as we all watched the live news on an outdoor video screen as large as the side of a semi-trailer truck, the crowd called out the countdown in a mixture of French and English: *Dix, Neuf, Eight, Seven* . . . I may have been the only person shouting the numbers in Hebrew. As I shouted *ahad!* — one! — CNN announced that Barack Hussein Obama was the next president of the United States. The crowd's roar was more deafening than cannons on a battleship. The moment felt like an inflection point in history, Yigal Amir's bullets in reverse. Two women in hijabs, both wearing matching Obama T-shirts with HOPE written in block letters, stood next to me, and in front of us were two tattooed men holding hands. An old man in a beret held up a sign: OUI, NOUS POUVONS. Yes, we can. In my mind, I heard Herzl's famous words: *Im tirtzu, ein zo agada.* If you will it, it is no fairy tale.

That's democracy, I said to myself. Taking in the intoxicating atmosphere with its whiff of rebellion, I silently recited the poet Yehuda Amichai's lines:

hope needs to be
like barbed wire to keep out despair;
hope must be a mine field.

As I wandered away from the crowds, I reflected on my decisions and actions over the previous months. Abba had died the previous January, and in a simple ceremony we buried him next to Imma, Yona, and Hava, four pioneers beneath a straight row of gravestones. In clearing out Abba's few belongings, I found notebooks filled with his scrawl. There was also a stack of photographs taken during his youthful days in the Zionist training camp in the Transylvanian mountains in 1935. I was struck by the optimism in his eyes. My parents' Zionist dream sprouted from the hopes of "self-determination" nations were claiming for themselves after the First World War, but just as much from the quest to build an equitable and just society. They could have gone to university and studied law but, fired up by *Im tirtzu, ein zo agada*, they chose to brave the British army and the infernal desert heat.

Thinking about the simplicity of my father's life on the kibbutz, I was struck by a sense of melancholy. Why couldn't the land of high-tech miracle workers select an Obama-like leader with a vision that represents the best of humanity? Why were the world experts at microprocessors and drip irrigation systems also so adept at building walls and producing despair?

I crossed the Seine on the Pont Neuf and stopped at a café close to Notre Dame. As I sipped a cappuccino I asked myself if it was time to quit the fight. I had no real influence within the present government, and all signs suggested the next one wasn't going to be nearly as aggressive as Olmert's in pushing for a peace deal.

When I returned from my trip, I headed directly from the airport to a Labor Party conference that combined the Rabin memorial with a discussion of the upcoming elections. After their horse-trading that afternoon, Party members confirmed that Barak, who was polling in the single digits, would be their candidate against the Likud's Bibi Netanyahu. There was for me no greater contrast imaginable than between commemorating Rabin and his legacy and back-room deal-cutting. I sat off to the side wishing I were pruning olive trees with Biba instead of witnessing the implosion of the party that had built Israel.

Just after the conference, which was broadcast live on TV, my son Nir called and told me that he could no longer vote for Labor in the next election. That sealed it. I immediately resigned from the cabinet.

I had already packed up my office by the time Gaza spiraled into an even bigger debacle than Lebanon. Hamas had been firing Qassam rockets into southern Israel for months before the Egyptians negotiated a six-month cease-fire. Once the cease-fire ended, in the middle of December, Hamas proposed to extend it for another six months, but only if Israel lifted the blockade around Gaza. Yuval Diskin, speaking on behalf of the Shabak, told the government that Hamas was "interested in continuing the truce, but wants to improve its terms . . . it wants us to lift the siege of Gaza, stop attacks, and extend the truce to include the West Bank."

Olmert rejected the terms, so Hamas fired even more Qassams. The two sides went back and forth until Olmert said he'd had enough. The rockets, said Olmert with Barak's backing, had made a "military decision" necessary. Somehow Olmert, so rational in his pursuit of peace, had a blind spot when it came to Gaza, and simply couldn't see that fighting fire with fire only bolstered Hamas's popularity in the Palestinian street. In the crazy, upside-down world of asymmetrical warfare — crude rocket versus F-16s — we strengthen the enemy by hammering them. Olmert kept his head in the sand and barreled on.

Operation Cast Lead was launched on December 27. General Smith's expression "war amongst people" describes well what happened in Gaza that winter. From the opening salvo, my government articulated no strategic goal, held out no hopes for peace talks once the hostilities were over, offered nothing to the Gazan people, and strove neither for diplomatic success nor for reconquering the territory and ousting Hamas. Journalists and much of the public toed the government line. On the third day of fighting French foreign minister Bernard Kouchner offered a cease-fire on humanitarian grounds, but the Israeli government refused.

For twenty-three days Hamas employed the strategy of leading the IDF into fighting in a crowded urban space. With cynical indifference for the people of Gaza, the terror organization invited mass destruction in an effort to portray Israel as a heartless occupier. We foolishly took the bait. Our bombardments killed fourteen hundred Palestinians and turned world public opinion against us.

In the sense of Dr. Sarraj, Hamas was the victor hands down. As kids on the kibbutz we played the game Rock, Paper, Scissors. Paper defeats rock because stone, even though it is stronger, lacks flexibility. Hamas was paper to the IDF's rock. They took a pounding militarily but won on the Palestinian street because they refused to surrender and vowed to continue the fight. They won because they understood the nature of modern warfare far better than we did.

26

GATEKEEPERS

Although Kadima won the most seats in the Knesset, Tzipi Livni, who took over party leadership from Olmert, failed to form a government. Netanyahu returned to power and predictably abandoned Olmert's bold move toward peace. In Gaza he compounded the prime minister's mistakes by refusing to cooperate with a team of international investigators led by South African judge Richard Goldstone into possible war crimes. Bibi would later blast the Goldstone Report as "a prize for terror."

In the spring of 2010 the London School of Economics invited me to participate in a panel discussion of the report. The British ambassador in Tel Aviv cautioned me against taking part. "I can't guarantee you won't be arrested," he warned, because of efforts by civil rights groups to "bring me to justice" for torturing Palestinians. I thanked the ambassador for the counsel but decided to go anyway. Biba gave me Amos Oz's *A Tale of Love and Darkness* to read on the plane, and perhaps behind bars. It's widely considered the companion piece to Sari's *Once Upon a Country*, and I was eager to read it.

Fortunately, I sailed through customs at Heathrow without incident. While in London I was struck by the narrative I heard from the British media: Israel was to blame for Palestinian suffering. Hamas's criminal use of noncombatants as human shields was of course a violation of the laws of war, but our propaganda machinery could do nothing to counter a viral three-minute video of a soldier illegally shooting an unarmed civilian holding a white flag. Instruments of modern war — tanks, snipers, helicopter gunships, politicians' television speeches — were useless against such images.

Back in Israel, I had a message for my patriotic countrymen foaming at the mouth at Judge Goldstone or the truth-telling of Breaking the Silence testimonies, or the fact that European human rights organizations threatened to arrest a former Shabak chief. In the age of cheap video cameras and the internet, I said repeatedly, the battle for international public opinion is just as important for our security as weapons systems. What matters most is the perception of justice.[64]

I felt like I was speaking to a wall. With the new right-wing government, so long as the cities were free of explosions and the economy prospered, no one seemed to care that we were digging our own graves. I asked myself how I could possibly cut through a fog so thick and entrenched. I'd tried and failed to convince people through politics. Attending academic conferences or writing essays on the nature of modern warfare, while useful, could never be a be a "counter-friction to stop the machine," to return to my motto from Thoreau.

My frustration reached a boiling point in May 2010. The Turkish ship *Mavi Marmara* left for Gaza on what the organizers said was a humanitarian mission to break the Israeli blockade, which had turned Gaza into the world's largest prison. With the ship steaming toward Gaza and the Israeli government vowing to stop it, I gave an interview in which I suggested we create our own flotilla of dozens of private yachts. We'd then meet the boats in broad daylight with massive banners saying WELCOME. And in the meantime, in Gaza we'll meet Gilad Shalit, the Israeli soldier Hamas kidnapped in 2006. We'll even bring Shalit's parents along so they could see their son for the first time in five years.

"Do you think Hamas would go along?"

I reminded the interviewer that my idea was a thought experiment and not an operational plan. The political leaders of Hamas probably didn't even know where Shalit was, I said, and had no control over the militants. My real point was that the Marmara was political theater. The organizers knew perfectly well that we would stop the ship, and especially if there were casualties, it would be yet another example of Israel playing the role of brutal Goliath against defenseless David.

Naturally, the government neither asked for nor listened to my advice. When members of my old sea commando unit, Flotilla 13, boarded the ship to prevent it from reaching Gaza, a small group of activists attacked them with bars and knives. The commandos' response left nine activists dead. Unsurprisingly, the international media blamed Israel — and Hamas won again.

In late 2010, I got another glimpse into the bleak future our leaders were leading us into. In December I noticed from our backyard in Kerem Maharal plumes of smoke rising like a mushroom cloud. My son Guy rang me up and told me his kibbutz, Beit Oren perched high on Mount Carmel, was ordered to evacuate because of a raging forest fire racing through hills parched by years of drought. The fire had spread so quickly that it trapped and killed a busload of experienced firefighters. Guy and a few friends ignored the orders and stayed put to save their houses on the kibbutz. Guy's wife and two kids came to stay with us.

Residents of the nearby Arab village of Ein Hawd also refused to leave their homes, but for very different reasons. Even when the rescue and fire services sent warnings that their lives were in danger, they insisted on staying. "We've already left once," they said, referring to the *Nakba*. In 1948, IDF forces had driven them from their original village of Ein Hod, where my friend Yehuda now lives.

As far as they were concerned, for the State of Israel to demand their evacuation was a continuation of the *Nakba*. Their irrational fear mirrored our own. The chief of police and minister of the interior at first asserted, without a scrap of evidence, that the fire had been set by Arab terrorists — even though we quickly learned that a Druze boy smoking a hookah had inadvertently started the blaze. In the Israeli Jewish paranoia, behind the smiling faces of Arabs building our homes or selling us tomatoes we suspect Islamists with jihad on their minds. Despite the fact that Arabs in Israel seek equality within the state of Israel and have proven their loyalty in their nonviolent struggle for equal rights as citizens, we believe that given the chance they'd drive us into the sea. The fact we have a booming economy and the fifth strongest military force on earth, vastly beyond anything our Arab enemies had at their disposal, does nothing to dull our basic insecurity whose source might be a history of deportations, pogroms, and the Holocaust but is whipped up by populist politicians to get elected.

Even if I didn't yet fully understand the deep — and to me irrational — source of our fears, I felt the need to counter the suspicion and pessimism eating away at Israeli society. Just as our start-ups were conquering the NASDAQ, we were collectively sinking into a suicidal depression, and nothing in the arsenal of civil society groups seemed capable of snapping us out of it.

Just as I began to suspect that, as in a madhouse, only shock therapy could lead us away from the ledge, one day out of the blue the documentary filmmaker Dror Moreh phoned me to discuss an idea that I thought might work.

"I want to make a film about the Shabak," he said. His idea at the time was to call the film *Shomrei HaSaf*, Guardians of the Threshold, as in the Book of Exodus.

"How do I fit in?" I asked.

Though a leftist, like so many people in our film industry, Dror had developed such a fascination with Sharon that he made a film about him. During his interviews with members of Sharon's inner circle of advisers, including Director General Weisglass, Dror learned that Sharon's decision to quit Gaza was prompted by the interview we retired Shabak heads had done in the Hebrew newspaper *Yedioth* in 2003. Had we been leftist peaceniks, Sharon would have ignored our message. The fact that we were security professionals Sharon admired and knew personally, and whose support unlike Bibi he was unwilling to lose, triggered in him a fundamental reassessment of his strategy.

"If we could make a documentary about Israel and Palestine," he said to himself, "it would be extraordinary."

What flashed in my mind as I formulated a response were images from *Fog of War*, Errol Morris's Oscar-winning documentary about Robert McNamara, a Harvard Business School whiz kid who served as defense secretary to Presidents Kennedy and Johnson and was the architect of the catastrophic Vietnam War. One scene in particular stood out in my memory: decades after the war McNamara wags his finger at the camera, a kind of Dr. Frankenstein confronting his own monster, and admits that already at the beginning of the war, he felt intuitively the Americans couldn't win. Vietnam wasn't industrialized Germany, and its ragtag peasant army couldn't be bombed into submission. Well over a million people died because McNamara didn't translate his gut feelings into different policies. I have no moral right, he was saying, not to tell the truth — that his government had sent young men into needless combat, and many of them returned home in boxes.

Maybe a film on our conflict would be one way to tell the Israelis the same thing — we cannot win our fight to keep Palestinians under our boots. Maybe a film could be the shock therapy I knew we needed.

My one proviso to Dror was that I wanted all the other former directors to participate. I made the rounds and helped Dror get everyone to agree to be interviewed on camera.

In making the film Dror was repeatedly astonished by, as he put it, the "dynamite on my hands." One telling example: Interviewing Yuval Diskin, Dror quoted the Israeli philosopher Yeshayahu Leibowitz's famous lines from a year after the Six-Day War that made the Shabak out to be a malignant presence: "A country that controls a hostile population of a million foreigners will necessarily be a Shin Bet state, with everything that requires, with implications on education, freedom of speech and thought and on democratic governance. The corruption characterizing every colonial regime will also infect the State of Israel. The administration will on one hand have to deal with suppressing Arab rebel movements and on the other cultivate quislings, Arab traitors."

Without so much as flinching, Diskin, his eyes trained on Dror, said, "I agree with every word." In fact, all of us former Shin Bet directors did.

Diskin also described the experience of having to partner with former PLO terrorists to stop Hamas. "How could I suddenly sit down with terrorists I'd spent my career chasing? I realized that we were, in a way, equals. As the saying goes: One man's terrorist is another man's freedom fighter."

Avraham Shalom, the gatekeeper during the First Intifada who had to resign because he ordered terrorists executed junta-style to deliver the message that no terrorist will survive an attack against us, went so far as to call the IDF "a brutal occupying army" that he compared to the Germans in their treatment of non-Jews in occupied Western Europe. Shalom grew up in Nazi Austria and experienced firsthand what it meant to be a pariah in a racist regime. "We're slowly becoming professional conquerors," he added, "and from that stems very dangerous behavior among ourselves. It's behavior that ultimately becomes a part of your character. And that's what scares me. You're standing in a road-block, and if one Arab gets tired of standing in line, and he has an outburst, then you hit him with the butt of your gun. That's not an unusual thing. It becomes a norm for you."

"Yes," chimed in Carmi Gillon, my predecessor. "We cause millions of people's lives to become impossible."

I chipped in the stories about the old fisherman in Gaza and Dr. Sarraj's line: "Victory is to see you suffer." I emphasized how our various counterterrorism tactics — building walls, entrapping Palestinians in their cities and towns subject to our raids without notice, cutting off electricity and water, and blockading Gaza — produce more terror and hence reinforce our own fear.

I also talked about empathy: how fighting terror requires seeing our actions through the enemy's eyes and how violent repression escalates the cycle of violence.

All of my colleagues agreed with me when I tried steering the film in a positive direction by quoting Clausewitz: "Victory is simply creating a better political reality." The brighter future we must aim for, I said, is Israel as a democratic state with a Jewish majority and with progressive education and welfare systems in the spirit of our Declaration of Independence. Had the two Intifadas, or Defensive Shield and Cast Lead for that matter, brought us any closer to that future? No. In this regard, Israel had been winning battles and losing the war against terror for a generation.

I didn't leave it at that. I told Dror about going to Balfour Street in Jerusalem after the Yom Kippur War and not finding a wise old man at the end of a long corridor keeping us all safe, an anecdote I hoped would represent the film's central message:

> For most people it is a very, very sad moment when you suddenly realize . . . nobody was behind the door. For me it was like I suddenly saw the light. I realized the simple concept of democracy. It is me who needs to take the responsibility. I am responsible. Democracy says that each of us has the right to influence. And in the case of crisis we not only have the right, but the responsibility to influence. This is my advice to every Israeli youngster. You have the right and the responsibility to influence. Even if you are in a minority. Don't assume that a leader cares about doing the right thing; their decisions are often motivated by staying in power and not what is best for Israel. It's up to you.

That's what Herzl meant when he said, "If you will it, it is no fairy tale."

We six ex-gatekeepers sat in the front row for the documentary's premiere at the Jerusalem Film Festival, the first time I saw the production in its final form. The opening scene thrust me back into the brutal reality of working in the sewer: A military aircraft follows a white van through the warrens of a refugee camp. The voiceover explains the dilemma of having a top terrorist in clear sight, and yet not knowing if innocent people are with him in the van. What do you do? There is no judge next to you, no cabinet minister or prime minister. It's your call. The van explodes in a puff of gray smoke.

During the film's final segment, titled "The Old Man at the End of the Corridor," I waited in vain for what I imagined would be the redemptive moment in this otherwise relentlessly bleak film.

What the hell? I thought to myself, slouched in my seat. Dror had cut my message of democracy and freedom, ending his documentary on a dark note. "If you need reassurance or grounds for optimism about the Middle East," wrote the film critic for *The New York Times*, "you will not find it here."[65]

And that was, for me, a big problem. I rang up Dror and asked him why he had edited out my message of hope. He replied that it was an artistic decision.

"You're the artist, Dror, and it's your film. But there's more than art at stake here. This is our future we're talking about!"

"What can I do? I see no way out."

"But I told you during our interviews how I thought you should end the film. The strength of Zionism is that our fate is in our hands. Not God's. Not some historical forces beyond our control. We can still decide to change direction and avert disaster. Our future is in our hands. I even quoted Herzl's motto, 'If you will it, it is no fairy tale.'"

Dror thought the line from Herzl was a slogan.

"It's not!"

"Then make your own movie," he said with a chuckle.

The film was nominated for an Oscar but didn't get American Jewish leaders banging on Bibi's office door, as they had in response to our comments in the original *Yedioth* interview. Perhaps the film's bleak outlook spread our national depression to the Americans. Though it was a big hit on Israeli television, *The Gatekeepers* failed to rouse the mass of viewers from their passivity.

I soldiered on, repeating what people like Dror considered my quixotic message of "If you will it, it is no fairy tale" to the ever-dwindling circle of people willing to listen. Being accused of war crimes, as well as my dealings with the Goldstone Report, motivated me to pursue a master's degree in law at Bar-Ilan University. I wanted to get a better grasp on international law. At sixty-two I was the oldest guy in a classroom full of students who, as schoolkids, had lit a million candles after Rabin was assassinated. My classmates were prime examples of Israel's dilemma, spectacularly optimistic about their private lives and darkly pessimistic that we'd ever find a peaceful solution to our impasse with the Palestinians.

Dror and I stayed in touch. One day he called to ask if I had heard President Obama's speech at a Jerusalem convention center packed with university students. "No," I replied. "I had been invited to attend, but I'm sick of speeches that lead nowhere."

"It's a pity you missed it," he said, because the president had pushed, essentially word for word, for what I had been advocating. "No wall is high enough . . . to stop every enemy that is intent on doing so from inflicting harm," Obama told the students gathered there. If you want security, he said, start by "putting yourself in the shoes" of the Palestinians: "Look at the world through their eyes. It is not fair that a Palestinian child cannot grow up in a state of their own. Living their entire lives with the presence of a foreign army that controls the movements not just of those young people but their parents, their grandparents, every single day."

It was in fact a fine address, and the students reacted to his speech with a roar of applause. But I knew from personal experience that, just as Israeli voters did not respond to the message of *The Gatekeepers*, the students who cheered Obama would grow up incapable of acting upon his injunction. A speech by a well-meaning American president was no substitute for an Israeli leader giving our people a realistic plan to secure our survival as a democracy.

With terrorism and security on everyone's mind, I remained a popular speaker at symposia and conferences and think tanks. But I was preaching to the choir. I could have paraded a hundred former Mossad and Shabak directors, retired IDF generals, and other security experts in front of the press, all saying the same thing: If we continue to dish out humiliation and despair, the popularity of Hamas will grow. And if we manage to push Hamas from power, we'll get al-Qaeda. And after al-Qaeda, ISIS, and after ISIS, God only knows. The majority of voters, as if gripped by a collective death wish, would continue to back a right-wing government hell-bent on betraying the humanistic values upon which Israel was founded.[66]

I began turning down radio and TV interview requests because nothing I said seemed to make much of a difference. It was bad enough to be failing at the most important mission of my life. More distressing, I didn't know why Israel tends to overreact to the smallest of threats, why we prefer bullets over words, why we refuse to explore opportunities for peaceful conflict resolution, and why we so easily swallow political demagoguery. As Ari Shavit had put it in his book *My Promised Land*, we act as if we are in "deep shit," and I didn't know why.

Until the spring of 2013, that is. I was on the second leg of a grueling twenty-three-hour trip to Sydney — a Jewish organization there had invited me to talk about *The Gatekeepers*. On the flight I flipped open the book by the Tel Aviv philosopher Chaim Gans, *A Political Theory for the Jewish People*. Two more stone tablets falling from the sky wouldn't have struck me harder.

27

THE PHILOSOPHER'S STONE

Who controls the past controls the future.
Who controls the present controls the past.

— George Orwell, *1984*

On a torrid July day in 2017, perspiration running down my face, I dodged kids racing on in-line skates as I stepped into Professor Gans's favorite Tel Aviv café. Once inside, I was met by a blast of cold air, the smell of freshly ground coffee, and the sound of Biba's favorite Arik Einstein song playing in the background:

Please, don't bid me farewell
Just say, "See you soon"
Because war is a dream,
Soaked with blood and tears.

Though we'd communicated by email to arrange our meeting, I'd never met the professor in person. I scanned the tables, which were all taken, before spotting a large man in a leg cast, round wire-rimmed glasses, three-day white stubble, and a safari-style khaki shirt waving me in his direction.

He stood to greet me, and I shook his left hand because he was using his right one to hold on to a crutch. "Good to finally meet," I began.

"Likewise." His voice was remarkably soft for such a big man.

While Chaim hobbled off like a wounded soldier to the men's room, I ordered an orange juice and croissant. I glanced at the headlines in the copy of *Yedioth* that was lying on the table. There was something about Hamas digging more tunnels and another article about Prime Minister Netanyahu's bribery and kickback scandals. *Nothing new under the sun*, I mused.

Chaim returned, but before sitting down, like a man wanting to get something off his chest, he complimented me on something I recently said to a journalist from *The Guardian* about Israel being in the grip of an "incremental tyranny," and about how our "ongoing war" against the Palestinians ensured "there's always an enemy just like Orwell's *1984*."

Nodding, I said to him, "One sunny morning we'll wake up and poof, we'll look back and realize we long ago forfeited our freedom. And we won't know how to get it back."

After Chaim sat down, I jumped right into asking him about his personal story. The noise of the café, and his almost velvety voice, forced me to lean over the table to hear him. He told me how his parents had arrived in Palestine in 1934 from Transylvania, just on the other side of the Carpathian Mountains from where my parents grew up. The similarities stopped there. His father, strictly Orthodox, kept the European family name and raised Chaim in a middle-class Tel Aviv home.

In high school Chaim, born three years after me, skipped from one youth movement to the next. Already a rebel before the age of sixteen, he lasted just two days in Bnei Akiva, the religious youth group, which gave him the boot for some infraction.

"Religion just wasn't my bag," he said.

"How did your father react?"

"He didn't have to say a word. His silence said it all."

Two years later, not yet eighteen, Chaim heard from a schoolmate a history of Israel that contradicted the standard textbook pieties: Arabs in 1948 hadn't left their villages and cities out of the belief that triumphant Arab armies would push the Jews into the sea; they had been mostly expelled.

"It was a shock for me to learn what really happened," he said, "because I thought we were the righteous ones, the 'light unto the nations.'"

I told him how on the kibbutz we, too, were raised to think we liberated the Land of Israel. "No one ever talked about the Arabs of 1948. Arabs existed only as terrorist gangs beyond the borders; as for the Arab citizens of Israel in the villages and towns in and around Haifa and Lod, they were invisible so long as they didn't take up arms against us. They just weren't a part of the reality in which we grew up."

"Most Israelis still believe this," he said.

"Which is why I asked to meet you."

After graduating from high school, with time to kill before doing his military service, he moved in with a friend in a Jerusalem neighborhood close to the Hebrew University. A few months later Chaim began his military service in a unit that would go on to help seize the West Bank during the Six-Day War. His friend would lose his life in the war.

At one point Chaim's unit entered the Dheisheh refugee camp. "I couldn't believe my eyes: the poverty, the misery of the Palestinian refugees. How could I square the squalor of Dheisheh with my comfortable life back in Jerusalem?"

Chaim's next story explained how he got a fifteen-year head start on me in glimpsing the cruelty of our occupation. In the early 1970s, while I was conducting commando raids around the Mediterranean, a call-up for reserves in Gaza interrupted Chaim's study of law and Greek philosophy at the Hebrew University. Arafat's fedayeen fighters were launching attacks from across the Egyptian border, and to stop them Ariel Sharon concocted a brutal counterinsurgency strategy involving soldiers firing live bullets into crowds of demonstrators. What Chaim witnessed in Gaza turned him into a fierce critic of the occupation.

He then left Israel for a few years, which helped him gain enough distance to see Israeli society and history more objectively. His first book, which he wrote in English and was based on his dissertation at Oxford, was on philosophical anarchism and political disobedience, themes that made me think of my favorite Thoreau quote about being the "counter-friction to stop the machine."

I told Chaim how transformational his book, *A Political Theory for the Jewish People*, had been for me. "You've probably earned a few royalties from all the copies I've passed out to my friends."

"Breakfast is on me," he said with a smile, before pressing me to share exactly what aspects of his book had made such an impact.

"For the longest time," I explained to Chaim, "I suspected our national pessimism might have something to do with the Holocaust, even if my aunt Hava, who otherwise said almost nothing about her youth, talked more about the German soldier who saved her life than the horrors of Auschwitz. It wasn't until I read your theory of narratives that, in a flash, our collective fear, as well as so many other things, made sense."

Gans's book had forced me to turn my tools of interrogation inward. At long last I began to understand myself — and to understand the country I had served all of my life. Our problem isn't really with the Palestinians. It's among us Israeli Jews. We haven't yet decided what kind of nation we want to be in the Land of Israel. Furthermore, the stories we tell ourselves about ourselves are fatally flawed. "What Orwell said . . ."

Chaim cut me off and finished my thought: "He who wants to control the future, has to control the past?"

"Exactly. And 'whoever controls the present, controls the past.'"

I told him why his theory of narratives got the scales to fall from my eyes. Like most people, I had always assumed history was a set of immutable facts. From Chaim, I learned that our perception of the past is a blend of facts and fables we tell ourselves — we selectively assemble facts to reinforce the past as we've chosen to understand it. My parents' generation of socialists, for instance, constructed a narrative about our returning to land that had been stolen from us, plundered, and occupied by others.[67] In this rendering they erased two thousand years of Jewish history in the diaspora and returned to the heroic age of the Israelite kingdoms and to our wars against the Greeks and Romans. Their most recent Jewish relatives were the fighters during the Bar Kokhba revolt. Then, as now, the fight was about liberating what was exclusively ours. Chaim calls this confection "proprietary Zionism."

European Jews who then found themselves in conflict with native Arabs used plows and guns, watchtowers, and commando raids to actualize our narrative of being the sole owners of the Land of Israel. Our historical construct turned Palestinians into "plunderers" or "holders of stolen property." This ideology justified the War of Independence and all the acts committed during the war. Once we "liberated" Judea and Samaria in 1967, we rushed out of our kibbutzim to build new settlements. I quoted back to him one of his lines: how Israel introduced in the West Bank a regime of "entrenched dominance of Jews over Palestinians" and, even worse, a "structural commitment to state violence." In a word, if the occupied territories are our property, then all of our actions — the settlements we build on ruins of towns we destroyed in the war, the exploitation of resources, the walls and system of control — are justified.

"Look," I reminded Chaim, "I'm a security guy, not an academic. I'm not a leftist or a rightest. About the only thing I care about, besides my family and a few friends, is the security of the State of Israel. If someone had asked me in 1969 why I was heading off into an us-or-them battle with the Egyptians, I would have responded with the standard arguments about settlement and security. My job was to fight our enemies so my fellow countrymen, including many of my friends, could settle our newly liberated lands.

"Later, in the 1980s and into the '90s, I was again motivated by thoughts of security when I concluded that, even if we were the true owners of the Land of Israel, we needed to make a strategic retreat from most of Judea and Samaria and cede control to the Palestinians in order to maintain the liberal democratic order that gives all Israelis, including Israeli Arabs, equality and a sense of belonging. I lived in the present. Never once did it occur to me to question how the stories all Israelis were raised on determine the way we act and how we view the future."

Chaim nodded, more like a psychiatrist than a philosopher, as I recounted how, on the flight to Sydney, his arguments explained so many things. For instance, how someone like Abba, a man who never set out to oppress another people, also never objected to bulldozers destroying the village of Samakh so its former inhabitants would have no place to return to. If you are trapped inside a narrative, everything you come upon tends to reinforce it. Each act of terror reinforces the belief that Palestinians are interlopers, free-loading squatters on land that rightfully belongs to us.

I reminded Chaim about how he called out the hypocrisy of a quote from the settler-bashing leftist playwright Shmuel Hasfari, artistic director of one of Israel's top avant-garde theaters. Hasfari once said, "We are here because the Bible is our deed to our beloved Land of Israel." How can someone believe this and, in good faith, blast settlers for building colonies in Judea and Samaria?

For a long time I thought just like Hasfari. Even after my experience in the refugee camp in 1988, I couldn't answer the elementary question of why the kibbutzim my parents' generation built were any different from West Bank settlements. If Zionism is only an ancestral land grab, there's no moral difference between what my parents did and what Pinchas and his pals have been up to since 1967.

I looked around the café again. Most people were speaking Hebrew, but a nearby couple was conversing in Russian, and some English words hung in the air as well. Through the window, I noticed a line of sweating patrons outside the door waiting for tables. How many of these people, I found myself asking, had even heard of Chaim's book? None, probably. I couldn't blame any of them for not studying a difficult work of theory. How many decades had it taken before I was ready to read such a tome and absorb its lessons?

"There was something else your book explained for me."

"Tell me." Chaim leaned forward in his chair.

"It was how to reinvent the past." I repeated back to him, with as much fidelity and clarity as I could, his alternative to proprietary Zionism he develops in his new book *Just Zionism*, what he calls a "Zionism of egalitarianism and self-determination," which I believe provides the only remaining legitimate foundation for our national existence as a state in the Land of Israel.[68] Chaim didn't need me to recount his own theory, of course, but I wanted to make sure I was a faithful disciple.

I gave him the same elevator pitch I give to anyone willing to listen: For a century, the international community has recognized a people's right to self-determination within a nation-state in which they can live in accordance with their culture, language, calendar, and leaders. To define themselves as they please.

And that's what my parents' generation came to do. The United Nations Partition Plan of 1947 provided a legal foundation for this natural right: Jews, the world agreed, especially after the Holocaust, had the right to build our nation-state and exercise our self-determination in the Land of Israel because our sense of nationhood, our historical memory, and our culture were rooted in this land. Our Declaration of Independence speaks of Israel's natural right "to be master of its own fate, like all other nations," a right accepted by the international community in November 1947 and, together with our historical connections to the Land of Israel, is one of the two foundations upon which the State of Israel was founded.

Making self-determination and not an ancient land deed the cornerstone of our claims made so much sense to me because it explained what I'd been doing most of my life. I've fought, killed, and buried friends because in 1948 the Arabs rejected our right to self-determination in the Land of Israel. They attacked us, and for decades after our War of Independence the attacks kept coming. Until 1967 the wars we fought and the actions we took were justified because we were defending a right endorsed by most of the world. Even since 1967, we remained on a war footing against enemies seeking to deny us our right to exist as a nation on this land. In this regard, for thirty years I killed and buried friends in the context of a just war.

But if our wars have been just, why our national pessimism — the feeling of being mired forever in "deep shit"?

"And this is where your theory is such a powerful analytic tool for me," I said. More than ever, Israelis seem to believe the Land of Israel is all ours, and since most of my countrymen also believe the other side feels the same way about historic Palestine, they conclude that to make any territorial compromises is to be a sucker. Settlers brandishing a divine property deed are reinforced with the conviction that no matter what we do, the Palestinians will continue attacking us. Talking is useless, diplomacy is for fools, bullets are the only language Arabs understand.

Over a second shot of espresso I summarized my thesis that we Israelis are at war with ourselves, and not with the Palestinians. "We've already created an apartheid situation in Judea and Samaria where we control Palestinians by force, denying them self-determination. Eventually they will give up on the dream of a state, and they and most the world will demand a single state where Jews will lose our majority and we can kiss our self-determination good-bye. From a security point of view, at that point we'll stop fighting just wars and become world experts on unjust ones."

Chaim nodded pensively before looking down at his watch. The line of sweating people outside the café had grown, and I knew we needed to wrap things up. He paid for the coffee and croissant, just as he'd promised, and before he heaved himself back on his feet he asked me, in a wistful tone, how many Israelis I thought "agree with us."

"In their heart of hearts, not many. I can count them on my nine and a half fingers." I chuckled and showed him that one of my fingers was missing a knuckle. "But I'm not here to blame anyone. Reinventing the past isn't easy. Usually it only happens after a catastrophe occurs."

CONCLUSION

REINVENTING THE PAST

Kerem Maharal, July 2018

On the drive to Jerusalem to meet Sari at his home in East Jerusalem, I planned on running through the questions I wanted to ask him, but I couldn't tear my mind from what was happening in Gaza. Last week one of our snipers shot in the neck a Palestinian volunteer medic, a twenty-three-year-old woman wearing a white uniform. She was one of more than a hundred unarmed participants gunned down by the IDF in what Palestinian activists are calling the Great March of Return. The YouTube video of the nurse's killing had gone viral. My longtime sensor Amira Hass was on target when she wrote, "What is cowardice if not the decision to kill masses of unarmed detainees who are demonstrating against their prolonged imprisonment?"

When Sari and I come together it feels like we are veterans swapping war stories. He quit his position as president of Al Quds University in 2014 after hooded Hamas activists stormed the campus waving green banners and carrying papier-mâché Qassam rockets and pictures of suicide bombers. I've also endured my share of agitated protesters. A couple of years back a group of pro-Palestinian activists at King's College London disrupted my talk on ending the occupation by hurling chairs, smashing windows, and chanting something about "Ayalon's crimes" followed by, "From the river to the sea, Palestine will be free." More recently, in Israel, when I dared defend Breaking the Silence, a so-called patriot in the audience bellowed *boged* — "traitor!" — into a megaphone. Many of my well-meaning countrymen, trapped in the land-based narrative from which I had only recently escaped, come at me with *boged* whenever I deny our exclusive property rights to the Land of Israel.

Sari greeted me at the front door. It was an unusually pleasant day, sunny and cool. Dressed in his customary houndstooth jacket, he proposed we sit in the garden. I followed him through rooms with chandeliers, oil paintings, family heirlooms, and shelves crammed with books. A black-and-white photo of his parents, Anwar and Nuzha, hung over a sofa. Once we were outside, chirping birds competed with the sound of cars on the road behind the house. What is now a major traffic artery was, before 1967, a no-man's-land separating West from East Jerusalem.

"Sugar?" Sari asked. I declined, and he stirred spoonful after spoonful into his own coffee. Sari quit smoking a couple years back and "now I need the energy boost of something sweet," he explained before asking me how I've been.

"On a personal level, no complaints. If I'm not out in the orchards with Biba or swimming, I'm writing research papers on democracy and terrorism. It's only when people ask me about politics that I feel like quoting Hegel. You're the philosopher and I don't want to make a fool out of myself. But I often think back to the old Marxists on the kibbutz who liked to go on about Hegel's dialectic."

"Which aspect of the dialectic? It's a rather complicated beast, you know."

"The part where Hegel says things have to hit rock bottom before a change can occur." Sari nodded for me to continue. "The way I see it, we Israelis might need a few more years of right-wing rule, attacks on Gaza, and tightening the choke hold on civil society before we finally realize we are living in a dystopian society that is tyrannical for those under our boots, and toxic and self-defeating for all."

"Interesting," he said.

"And on that note, how are things in Palestine?" President Abbas was old and sick, and with Gaza heating up again, I was curious to hear Sari's thoughts.

"Hard to say." Sari, ever the philosopher, has a way of qualifying every statement, and then qualifying his qualifiers. He ran his fingers through his white hair before placing a set of worry beads, the same indigo-blue ones he rubs every time we meet, on his thigh.

His cell phone began to sound — the ringtone, Beethoven's Ninth — and he let it play a few notes before finally turning it off. "When it comes to our politics," he continued, "I must say in all honesty that our civil society is alive and well. On radio talk shows you hear people speaking their minds and really trying to solve problems. Our problem is with the people in power, and this has nothing to do with Israel. The higher up the pecking order you go, the worse things get. You really have to hold your nose up there." Like Jibril, Sari saw his first and only attempt at elected office end in defeat at the hands of a Hamas candidate.

My mind turned to the shootings of unarmed demonstrators in Gaza, and I asked Sari how people in the West Bank felt about the protests and the killings.

He leaned languidly back in his desk chair and placed his hand on his worry beads. "Abbas and company aren't interested in people who are siding with Hamas, even though Hamas isn't really driving the protests. The guy who started the movement doesn't even belong to Hamas." He sounded resigned; after all, he has spent most of his life trying to steer his people in the direction of sanity and truth-telling, and mostly failed.

"On the theme of Palestinian politics," he said while his eyes followed the erratic flight of a mosquito, "just the other day . . . no . . . it must have been yesterday. Yes, yesterday. Maybe the day before. In any event, an old friend dropped by. He's over sixty so the Israelis gave him a permit to enter into Israel from the West Bank. This friend told me about visiting Jaffa for the first time since Sharon built the wall. He sat at a beachside café and soaked in the sea breeze. He watched kids splashing the water. None of the people sitting on beach towels seemed to care who he was, whether he was Muslim or Christian or Jewish. They left him alone.

"'And that's the way life should be,' my friend said. 'We should live by the law of the sea: Regardless of nationality or passport, everyone should be allowed to relax on the beach.' I rather like the phrase *Law of the Sea*. That's how Palestinians feel these days, Ami. They want to dangle their feet in the water and be left alone."

I didn't want to break it to him that with the discovery of natural gas fields offshore, the sea is becoming a vital national asset. We're not going to let them dangle their feet in the water much longer.

Sari, his eyes trained back on me, reached over and refilled my coffee cup.

I asked him if he'd heard anything from Jibril. "For months now he doesn't answer my phone calls. I've been wanting to talk to him about his brother, the Hamas guy. Finally, after my twentieth attempt, he picked up and gave me some cryptic line about being my friend no matter what. Then he hung up. What's going on with him?"

"It's politics," Sari declared. "As everyone knows, except perhaps Abbas himself, our dear president isn't going to live forever, and people in Fatah are already jockeying for position. If you ask me, Jibril's got a good shot to come out on top. He's ambitious and clever. He's also courageous and has no lack of confidence." Sari paused to reach for an ornate silver tray piled high with an array of sweets. "Can I offer you some cake?"

I declined. What Sari was saying made sense. If Jibril was vying for the top spot, I thought, he wouldn't want to give his rivals ammo by parading around with a former Shabak director.

Eventually I posed a question I'd wanted to ask for years: "Tell me about your mother."

"My mother?" Sari arched an eyebrow.

"Yes. I've always wondered why she never signed our paper. I got my parents to sign — nearly everyone on the kibbutz did."

"Mother was an angry person."

"Because of 1948?"

"Partly. Look, you have to understand her background. She grew up in a villa with servants in Wadi Hunayn, just outside of Ramle. Her father, a Cambridge graduate and member of the Supreme Muslim Council, practically owned the town. He was the mayor and traced his roots to a Sufi mystic who settled there in the 1400s.

"And then in the 1930s the British arrested him for his role in the uprising against the Zionists, packed him off into exile, and burned down the family villa. Things only got worse for my mother. In 1948, while pregnant with me, my father got his leg shot off by one of your soldiers, and then Rabin turned up and forced her and her extended family to leave Israeli territory and march by foot across to the Jordanian lines. In 1967, after you conquered East Jerusalem, she was the first Palestinian woman arrested by your soldiers for staging a demonstration on Salah al-Din Street.

"By the way, until her dying days she refused to return to where the family villa had once been."

"Did she ever tell you why?"

"I suppose because there was no place to go back to. Wadi Hunayn was turned into Ness Ziona. From what I gather, the mosque my grandfather built was made into a synagogue called 'Israel's Redemption,' or something along those lines.

"After the occupation began in 1967, what made matters even worse for my mother was just how accommodating my father was, how he invited Israelis into his home to discuss politics. Moshe Dayan himself sat in our living room. Never once did she go into the salon to meet Father's Israeli guests. Are you sure you don't want a piece of cake?"

"Why not?" He slid a slice of lemon pound cake onto my plate. As I took a bite, my mind turned to trauma and its enduring effects. Dr. Sarraj's writings had taught me a great deal, as had the response of my friend Zvika Shahak to the murder of his daughter by terrorists at Dizengoff Center. Through some superhuman effort, Zvika had turned his grief into the motivation to help build an organization that brought together Jewish and Palestinian parents of children killed in our conflict.

"The more you suffer," I said to Sari, "the harder it is to empathize with your enemy." I assumed this would be the last word we would exchange about his mother, but I was wrong.

As usual, Sari, who had once written on the role of jokes in philosophy, surprised me by saying, "Lack of empathy was not my mother's problem. Mother needed the human touch to overcome the pain others had caused her."

"How so?"

"During our campaign, on one of my daily visits, I asked her: 'Suppose a rabbi, say in 1940, had approached Father and asked him: I've come to you because a terrible catastrophe is about to befall my people in Europe and we need refuge to where our forefathers came from. If a rabbi would have asked Father this, what would he have said?' 'What do you think?' she snapped at me angrily. 'Of course, he would have said yes.'"

"So," I said in response, "she would have agreed that we Jews could immigrate?"

"Not only that. Many times, I heard her admit she wanted a political solution with Israel. 'I'd be happy with the two states,' I remember her saying. Her issue wasn't with moving on from the past and living with Israelis. She didn't try to stop me when I volunteered on a kibbutz."

"If she was willing to accept two states," I asked, "why didn't she sign our paper?"

"What held her back was mistrust."

"Of what?"

"Of whom, you mean. Don't take this personally, Ami, but she never believed in the peaceful nature of you Israelis. She never believed you'd grant us a state, no matter what we did. We could throw flowers instead of stones, we could all march around like Mahatma Gandhi, we could turn into peaceful Finns, and you'd continue occupying us. With our paper, she thought I was fooling myself. She had a point, too."

"You mean to say that your mother, who on the outside seemed like such a hardliner, was really just waiting for us to come around and give her a good reason to trust us."

"Well said, Ami."

"I'm sorry I never got to know your mother," I said, pushing away the cake because I had suddenly lost my appetite. "She must have been a very clever lady. She understood Israelis a lot better than I did during our campaign."

Sari chuckled. "Are you saying she was clever for not trusting you Israelis?"

"It looks like it. For years, left-wing and right-wing governments alike built settlements in Judea and Samaria, despite a Palestinian willingness to accept Israel in a two-state settlement and despite a clear statement from most members of the security community that continuing the occupation would increase terror. If you back up and think about this, you realize the impetus for our expansion is coming from the majority of Israelis. I don't mean we are intentionally dishonest. Some of us are, of course, but that's not our problem. It's deeper than lies. You see, I always believed we fought the Palestinians because of security. Your mother must have figured out the truth about us long before I did." I paused to take a sip of coffee before continuing. "Have you ever heard of Chaim Gans?"

"The philosopher?"

"Yes, at Tel Aviv University. I came across one of his books a few years ago. When I read it, I finally understood the mistake we made when we decided to avoid history. Remember how we thought all we had to do was create a common picture of the future, and then everyone except rogue settlers and Hamas people would come on board? Gans's book — I'll give you a copy next time we meet — taught me that the way we understand our history is the barrier to a real compromise because it controls our actions and fears, and therefore our future."

For the first time since we met in London fifteen years earlier, I told Sari about the Zionism I was raised on: how it was for all of us on the kibbutz an unquestioned fact that we Jews lost our identity when the Romans drove us from the Land of Israel, and we only got it back when we returned, title in hand, to reclaim our stolen property. The same Israeli education system that brought the Maccabees back to life taught Moroccan Jews, whose roots go back twenty-five hundred years in the Atlas Mountains, to feel as victimized by the Inquisition or the Holocaust as we Ashkenazim.

Even a fleet of high-tech submarines can't cure our ingrained fear that disaster lurks around the corner.

"We'll never make peace," I concluded, "until we change the narrative about the past and admit to ourselves that the Palestinians have a right to their own country alongside Israel, and on land we claim as ours."

"And that's why my mother understood Israeli politics better than you?" Sari asked, fidgeting with the spoon.

I nodded.

Instead of responding, Sari pointed to the cake. "It's really tasty!"

Sari raised one hand like he was going to say something, then he looked down at his watch. He had to get to Ben-Gurion Airport to pick up his wife, Lucy, he said, and apologized for running out of time.

I was about to get up when he gestured for me to wait. "Can I ask you a question?" he said.

"Of course."

"Why are you writing your book?"

"Maybe for the same reasons you had when you wrote yours, just from the other side of no-man's-land." I explained how my life story parallels much of what has happened in Israel over the past seventy years. From my encounter with the stone-throwing boy in 1988 to reading Chaim Gans, I, like many other Israelis, recognized the injustice of our occupation while never questioning the nationalist history on which we'd been reared.

"If I can pull it off, I want to show Israelis and Jews outside Israel that we can choose a different past. The past that my parents chose brought about the establishment of the state, but today it stands in the way of the future they dreamed of, a democratic state for the Jewish people. We don't have to continue seeing ourselves as a nation of ghosts who only returned to life by reclaiming a land that has been inherently Jewish since the time of Joshua. We can, and I would argue we must, see Zionist history as a struggle for national self-determination."

"What you just said about my mother understanding the Israelis so well, would you include that in your book?"

"I think I'll have to."

"That'll create quite the fuss in Israel, I imagine."

"I want to publish the book first in English."

"Can I ask why?"

"Look, we both know that to understand anything, especially politics in our part of the world, we need as many people as possible openly debating issues. I see the opposite happening in Israel today. There's a narrowing of horizons. The conflict is too close to the bone for us: Each time one of us is killed, we all feel the pain, and we have neither the capacity nor the desire to understand the enemy. And for these reasons, most Israelis won't understand what I have to say. We're so trapped behind our own walls, we can't see what seems obvious to outsiders. Whenever I tell Israelis we need to reinvent the past, they think I've lost it."

Sari stood up and shook my hand. He really had to get going. "I'm looking forward to reading your book," he said as he walked me to the door. "Do you have a title?"

"I've been toying with *Friendly Fire*."

"As in gunfire coming from your own side?"

"That's the idea."

"I rather like it," he said. I was pleased to have the endorsement of someone with so much experience with friendly and unfriendly fire of his own.

On my way home I felt strangely optimistic about our fate in the Holy Land, even if at the present the prospect of most Israelis accepting an alternative past seems so unlikely. Talking with Sari reminded me that at least our Israeli revolution won't require barricades. We don't need to overthrow the government, roll out the guillotine, or topple a corrupt class system. We don't even need to change our ethical standards, because our problem isn't that we are especially cruel — we're not — or that we enjoy humiliating millions of people under our boots and trampling their rights — we don't. Our Declaration of Independence ingeniously captures in a few short lines Israel's connection to humanism: Israel will "ensure complete equality of social and political rights to all its inhabitants irrespective of religion, race or sex; it will guarantee freedom of religion, conscience, language, education and culture . . ."

What it'll take is for a leader to, at long last, tell us the truth.

I arrived home in the late-afternoon heat, so I cracked a cold Maccabee beer and watched the grandkids splash around in the pool. After taking a dip, I headed alone out of the moshav with the dogs. At a brisk pace, I passed a vineyard and continued into a valley with forests and olive orchards on either side. Biba calls this valley the Israeli version of paradise, the forests and vineyards teeming with wild boar, deer, and falcons swooping overhead. The tranquillity of the pastoral landscape was only interrupted by the crackle of bullets from an IDF live-fire zone off in the distance.

I did a loop and returned to the moshav. The dogs raced ahead past the old Arab farmhouse with trees growing through the roof. I imagined for a moment what the original Arab village must have been like in the early 1940s, buzzing with life. Yes, the Palestinians were dealt a terrible blow in 1948. Which for me makes it all the more astonishing that on Nakba Day 1998 the poet Mahmoud Darwish wrote a new past for the Palestinian people, for Arafat to read to the world. "We recognize the suffering of the Jewish people . . . We do not seek to be captives of history or victims of the past. The Palestinian people have launched a redemptive journey to the future. From the ashes of our sorrow and loss, we are resurrecting a nation celebrating life and hope."

Whoever composes our new past could tear a page from Darwish. Our new past would acknowledge the suffering of the Palestinians over the past seventy years, while simultaneously emphasizing our natural right to defend ourselves. Our past is not the story of Jews returning to the Land of Israel as property owners evicting the tenants. It is the story of Jews like my father who, responding to racism, anti-Semitism, and nativist nationalism in Europe, demanded self-determination as a means to protect their lives and culture. And why in Israel? They knew that even though they stopped observing the religious commandments, it was only in the Land of Israel, where the Jewish people was born, that they could establish a state and live according to their heritage and language.

With the ovens of Auschwitz behind us, and in the face of the Arabs' total rejection of any form of Zionism, we fought a just war in 1948. Chaim Gans likened our situation to a "person who is dying and knows there is medicine that can save his life. If the pharmacist does not sell him this medicine, he has the right to use violence to get it. And no court will blame him because this is for his survival."

And for decades we continued to fight with justice on our side. Haim Sturman, Dani Levi, Srulik, and many thousands of others died defending our right to exist as a state. According to this new version of the past, our greatest victories since independence were not the Six-Day War, nor Sharon's daring counterattack in 1973. They were the Palestinian Declaration of Independence of 1988, which tacitly acknowledged Israel's right to exist; the Rabin-Arafat handshake in the Rose Garden; the security cooperation between the Shabak and Arafat's men; the Darwish Nakba Day speech; and the Arab Peace Initiative. With another cold Maccabee in hand, I pictured a future prime minister reading a speech on Independence Day. In it, she tells the Israeli people that we will still need the IDF, special forces, and the Shabak because in the Middle East the threat of terrorism and violence from other states will continue into the future. But their work will be within the context of a government fully committed to the values of civil rights, minority rights, human rights, pluralism, transparency, a rules-based international order, and peace with our neighbors. Only such a government can send the message to our friends and enemies that ours is a just war, that fanatics, whether Muslim or Jewish, will not be allowed to destroy our hard-won democracy.

This prime minister will then declare that our war to preserve our security and independence is inseparable from our decision to end our apartheid regime in the Occupied Territories and Gaza and to allow the Palestinians to exercise national self-determination in Gaza and what we call Judea and Samaria, along the lines set out in the People's Voice.

Yes, that's what she'll say, I imagine. Inspired by the grandkids playing Marco Polo in the pool, I thought of the perfect ending for her historic address. This imaginary leader of mine won't have Yehuda Amichai to write it because he died twenty years ago. What she can do is to conclude by quoting the same poem Amichai read aloud in Oslo when Rabin and Arafat received the Nobel Prize for Peace:

God has pity on kindergarten children,
He pities school children — less.
But adults he pities not at all.

He abandons them,
And sometimes they have to crawl on all fours
In the scorching sand
To reach the dressing station,
Streaming with blood.

But perhaps
He will have pity on those who love truly
And take care of them
And shade them
Like a tree over the sleeper on the public bench.

Perhaps even we will spend on them
Our last pennies of kindness
Inherited from mother,

So that their own happiness will protect us
Now and on other days.

NOTES

1. The organizer of the discussion was Professor Mary Kaldor from the London School of Economics, an expert on cosmopolitan democracy.

2. Moshe Dayan later described the deadly cat-and-mouse game this way: "We would send a tractor to plow some area where it wasn't possible to do anything, in the demilitarized area, and knew in advance that the Syrians would start to shoot. If they didn't shoot, we would tell the tractor to advance farther, until in the end the Syrians would get annoyed and shoot. And then we would use artillery and later the air force also, and that's how it was."

3. *Illustrated Dictionary of the Muslim World* (New York: Marshall Cavendish 2011), 46.

4. Shachiv Shinan.

5. Other luminaries in the cemetery include Ber Borochov, who used dialectical materialism to justify socialist Zionism; and Berl Katznelson, the intellectual of the labor movement and classic proponent of Syrkin's secular religion of Zionism as the liberation of our people and our land. His nephew, named after him, was in my class.

6. The monument jolted my memory back to the tragic event my father organized for the tenth anniversary of the parachute mission in 1954.

Abba's idea was for the four surviving parachutists from the Palmach operation to jump from the plane in a reenactment of their fateful mission. Thousands of people — one newspaper described the gathering as "nearly the whole local aristocracy" — turned up for the event, and the prime minister brought a convoy of senior government officials. Busloads arrived from the archipelago of kibbutzim. Ideological rivals — there were those who considered Ben-Gurion a traitor for disbanding the Palmach, our revolutionary strike force, following the establishment of the state — came together to honor the martyrs. Minutes after we sang the Hatikvah, our national anthem, a two-seater Piper plane carrying the parachutists crashed into the crowd, killing everyone on board and a dozen people on the ground.

7. Ben-Zion Dinur, the official Labor Party historian and the minister of education when I was a boy, summed up the prevailing narrative perfectly: "The Jews were never in the condition of a nation without a land, of a nation lacking a homeland. Even during their period of exile, they were always a robbed and dispossessed nation whose land was plundered and stolen and never ceased to plead and complain about its dispossession and to demand the return of the plundered property."

8. Our Passover Haggadah celebrated the way Jews, inflamed by the vision of freedom and the vitality of youth, liberated our land: "And we shall cross the stormy seas until we reach you and cling to you. In our blood and toil we shall redeem you until you are entirely ours."

9. Srulik, sadly, left our kibbutz in the early 1950s because of a squabble pitting his parents and their ideological fellows, Moscow-true communists, against the majority, which included my family, who supported Ben-Gurion's pro-Western line. Anti-Stalinists like Abba shrugged when some of the communists broke out in a chorus of "The "Internationale" or "The Song of the Hammer," or when they prayed to "Our Father Stalin Who Art in Moscow." This mutual toleration of the two camps ended after the Soviet Union cut diplomatic ties with Israel in 1954, and back in Russia the government launched a wave of anti-Zionist show trials, vilifying Israel as a bastion of imperialism. In some kibbutzim this rivalry exploded into fistfights.

10. An operation against military installations at the outpost south of the port in Adabiya.

11. The leaders of the settlement movement were able to exploit an internal struggle in the Labor Party between those who believed in "open borders" (Dayan and Peres) and those who believed in a clear political border (Rabin and Alon). The labor movement invented the "proprietary narrative," and its attitude toward the settlements was therefore ambivalent.

12. Six died in total: three from the Shayetet and three from Unit 269 (Sayeret Matkal), who arrived in boats in the second wave.

13. This attitude was best captured in the Arab League's Khartoum conference following the 1967 war. The conference came out with the "The Three Nos": No peace with Israel, no recognition of Israel, no negotiations with Israel.

14. Rafi Milo was my instructor in a commando course. He left the Flotilla unit. But since most of our fighters were wounded during Green Island, Milo returned to command the operation. Major Shlomo Eshel also returned to service before the operation.

15. *Shapira* is referring here to the seven laws that, according to some Jewish teaching, even non-Jews are supposed to follow: Establish a legal system and refrain from murder, blasphemy, idolatry, adultery, theft, and eating the flesh of living animals.

16. I read Tuchman in a class at the Kennedy School taught by Professor Herbert Kelman, a Jewish American and an expert on social and psychological perspectives on the resolution of international conflicts.

17. Gil was the director general of the Foreign Ministry under Shimon Peres.

18. *The New York Times* picked up the story. The title of the article was "Shhh! That's a (Not Very) Secret." https://www.nytimes.com/1996/01/14/weekinreview/the-world-shhh-that-s-a-not-very-secret.html.

19. Quoted in chapter 1 of Michael Karpin and Ina Friedman's *Murder in the Name of God: The Plot to Kill Yitzhak Rabin* (see http://movies2.nytimes.com/books/first/k/karpin-murder.html).

20. Dror Moreh, *The Gatekeepers: Inside Israel's Internal Security Agency* (New York: Skyhorse, 2015), 41.

21. In a region of the world charmed, or cursed, with producing strange and colorful birds, Yossi stood out. In 1986 he was forced out of the Shin Bet

because of his role in whitewashing the execution of two Palestinian bus hijackers by Shabak agents. Another of his reputed misdeeds was to torture a false confession out of a Muslim officer in the Israeli army for passing information to the PLO. See Lawrence Joffe, "Yossi Ginossar: Israel's Secret Envoy to the Palestinians in the Search for Middle East Peace," *Guardian*, January 16, 2004.

22. David Remnick, "The Democracy Game: Hamas Comes to Power in Palestine," *New Yorker*, February 2006.

23. At the end of the Six-Day War, Matti was a twenty-year-old conscript in the armored corps in Gaza. Our victories, he told me, "swathed" him in a feeling of "transcendence and accomplishment." Like so many others, Matti assumed "our troubles were over, and henceforth security and peace would prevail." Bursts of gunfire coming from local Palestinians, however, interrupted this mood of rapture. "I understood that one period in the history of the Israeli-Arab conflict had ended, but another — no less unsettling and demanding — had begun."

24. General Ephraim Sneh. Yossi Melman, "Hamas: When a Former Client Becomes an Implacable Enemy," *Los Angeles Times*, December 20, 1992.

25. His name was Mosab Hassan Yousef. In Mosab's case, for hours he sat strapped into a chair bolted to the concrete floor, hooded and shivering in a room as cold as a walk-in freezer, his body contorted into the so-called Banana, a painful, humiliating, exhausting position. Mosab went on to become an important asset for us inside Hamas. His experiences are described in his book *Son of Hamas: A Gripping Account of Terror, Betrayal, Political Intrigue, and Unthinkable Choices*.

26. Hagai Meirom is a former Israeli politician who served as a member of the Knesset for the Alignment (Labor) Party and the Centre Party between 1988 and 1999.

27. Jodi Rudoren and Jeremy Ashkenas, "Netanyahu and the Settlements," *New York Times*, August 18, 2015.

28. James Ciment, *World Terrorism: An Encyclopedia of Political Violence* (London and New York: Routledge, 2011), 809.

29. The murdered archaeologist was Dr. Albert Glock.

30. Having studied the notion of *din rodef*, the "law of the pursuer," in order to understand the theology brandished by the extremist settlement fringe, to my surprise I read in Maimonides that *din rodef* sounds like something out of Immanuel Kant. Killing the pursuer is only permissible if there is no other option — a situation in which you can't stop him or can't otherwise incapacitate him, and if you don't act, innocent people will die.

31. See Ronan Bergmann, *Rise and Kill First: The Secret History of Israel's Targeted Assassinations*, p. 476 ff Kindle edition

32. In 1997, Netanyahu ordered the Mossad to assassinate the Hamas political leader Khaled Mashal in Jordan. The botched attempt led to the release of the Hamas founder and spiritual leader Sheikh Yassin, weakening Arafat.

33. He served as chief of the General Staff until 1995, when Rabin appointed him Minister of Internal Affairs.

34. Address by Foreign Minister Ehud Barak to the Annual Plenary Session of the National Jewish Community Relations Advisory Council on February 11, 1996.

35. Deborah Sontag, "Peace. Period," *New York Times*, December 19, 1999.

36. On Fridays, I rarely left the office before hearing Matti's translation of the Mufti of Jerusalem's weekly sermon. I feared he would incite a religious war. The Jews and Christians were causing even bigger headaches. Informants helped us round up a particularly violent messianic Jewish gang from Yitzhar with plans to kill Muslims on the Temple Mount during Friday prayers; a different group schemed to toss the heads of pigs into Al Aqsa Mosque. We averted another cataclysm when the FBI gave us information on two Christian fanatics, members of a messianic cult, who planned to go to Al Aqsa, denounce Muslims as hell-bound unbelievers, and announce the Second Coming of Christ. It was effectively a suicide pact — they expected irate worshippers to beat them to death. Fortunately, we stopped them at the airport.

37. Dana Golan, the outgoing director regularly labeled a traitor by members of the Knesset, is a friend of ours, and the man replacing her, Avner Gvaryahu, had already become an object of loathing among right-wing social media.

38. The IDF military brass didn't even discuss the Shin Bet assessment, made in the first hours of what would come to be called the Second Intifada, that Arafat had nothing to do with it.

39. Many people in the army never believed the sides would come to terms and were bracing for a confrontation. "I'm creating all the necessary conditions so that I can apply force," said one of the IDF's top strategists two months before Camp David. "I thrust [Palestinians] into a kind of corner where they have no choice but to do what I expect them to do, and then I react with the force I've been preparing." Quoted in Moreh, *Gatekeepers*.

40. During my four years as director, we took out ten ticking bombs. The decision to kill someone was never made lightly. Playing God in this way led me to rethink the ethics behind preemptive killing.

Ultimately, I concluded that killing is only permissible if there is no other option — a situation in which you can't stop him or can't otherwise incapacitate him, and not acting will leave innocent people to die. Translated into the war on terror, I decided that to kill a terrorist preemptively required fulfilling specific criteria, one of which is that the person is a "ticking bomb." Lethal violence is permissible only against someone posing an imminent danger to innocent lives, or in our case a terrorist who is literally about to plant a bomb on a bus or in the trunk of a car. If there is no other option, taking out a terrorist is legitimate because the life of an Israeli citizen takes precedence over the life of the person trying to kill him.

41. Ephraim Sneh.

42. Matt Rees, "The Work of Assassins," *Time* magazine, January 7, 2001.

43. In Matti's words, the assassination drove Arafat's supporters, pragmatists who had once supported Oslo, "mad."

44. Moreh, *Gatekeepers*, 305.

45. Another important supporter was Maya Liquornik.

46. Ari Shavit, "Lydda, 1948: A City, a Massacre, and the Middle East Today," *New Yorker*, October 14, 2013.

47. A journalist would later ask us about this, picking up on our body language. "People who know Sari," I said, "know that he keeps his feelings to himself."

48. The program was run by Daoud Kuttab, an adjunct professor of journalism at Princeton.

49. Sari's crime was collaborating with Saddam Hussein, who had donated some money to Al Quds University. In the eyes of my government that constituted a high crime.

50. Kibbutz Hazorea.

51. And he had very smart people who agreed with his approach: In those days Ehud Barak, with the help of the historian Benny Morris, wrote in the august *New York Review of Books* that the world should "treat Arafat and his ilk in the Palestinian camp as the vicious, untrustworthy, unacceptable reprobates and recidivists that they are."

52. We quoted opinion polls by Shikaki's PCPSR on the Palestinian side and his Israeli counterpart Shai Feldman consistently showing that 70 percent of Palestinians and Israelis wanted a two-state solution.

53. Aviv Lavie, "The Peoples' Choice," *Ha'aretz*, July 11, 2003.

54. "Wolfowitz Backs Peace Petition," Jewish Telegraphic Agency, November 3, 2003. In the US we presented a stark message to the Washington Institute's Special Policy Forum: "Israel must withdraw from the territories. It must do so not because of social, economic, or international values, but rather because the consequence of not withdrawing will be a failure to maintain its vision of a safe, democratic haven for the Jewish people . . . If Israel creates a situation similar to that seen in apartheid-era South Africa, there will be neither a Palestinian state nor a safe home for the Jewish people. Although Israel does have the right to defend itself, the way in which it is building the wall will harm the prospects for a favorable future."

55. To fight the wall, Sari assembled a nonviolent force of three hundred ex-militants and supporters of our People's Voice / Hashd campaign. In the end the government changed the route of the concrete barrier after US national security adviser Condoleezza Rice chimed in.

56. See "The Spooks Speak," *Forward*, November 21, 2003.

57. Gideon Alon, "Lieberman Blasted for Suggesting Drowning Palestinian Prisoners," *Haaretz*, July 8, 2003.

58. A third factor was the letter signed by twenty-seven reserve pilots in the Israeli air force stating their refusal to fly missions that could endanger Palestinian civilians.

59. Confronted with dissent from within his own Likud Party, Sharon attempted to bring over the naysayers by revealing the deeper political logic behind the disengagement before the Knesset was scheduled to vote on the plan in October after the Jewish High Holidays. Addressing his Likud faction, the prime minister pointed to the People's Voice as a factor in his decision to remove the Jewish settlements in the Gaza Strip.

60. Arafat even instructed Fayyad, his finance minister, to support Sari's operation with ten thousand dollars a month. Even more significant was that Arafat stood by while Sari accessed Fatah's sociopolitical infrastructure in every village, city, camp, and university to marshal support.

61. A top Hamas leader in Gaza said about the disengagement that "the painful and qualitative blows which the Palestinian resistance dealt to the Jews and their soldiers over the past four-and-a-half years led to the decision to withdraw from the Gaza Strip. The suicide attacks . . . have taken their tolls on the Jews." In an essay I wrote: "I am in favor of leaving Gaza but opposing the way we are going about it. A unilateral withdrawal without creating a political horizon will be interpreted as capitulation."

62. In June, two months before the final evacuation, Biba and I took Rabin's daughter Dalia to meet Pinchas Wallerstein and his friend Avi Gisser, the chief rabbi of Ofra. We weren't military, political, or security functionaries issuing warnings or threats; we were fellow citizens, and fellow Jews, talking about matters that went to the core of our identities. Decisions of national importance, such as uprooting settlements, we all agreed should be subject to a national referendum; using people as pawns only leads to at least one party feeling betrayed.

63. Lawyers claimed that Al-Shami had been tortured by the Shabak: put in a freezing cell, handcuffed, shackled to a chair for hours, and "stretched."

64. Our walls against the Palestinian population centers might save hundreds of Israeli lives from suicide bombers, I said at the time. But world opinion would never accept our actions as legitimate because of the low-budget film *Five Broken Cameras*, which depicted the Separation Wall cutting off villagers in the West Bank village of Bil'in from their agricultural land. "I film to heal," says the amateur Palestinian filmmaker in the film. "I know they [the IDF] may knock at my door at any moment. But I'll just keep filming. It helps me confront life. And survive."

65. The *Haaretz* journalist Gideon Levy described a "feeling of nausea and of deep disgust welling up";" his fellow journalist Chemi Shalev likened watching the film to a "waterboarding of the soul."

66. An organization I helped found, Blue White Future, failed to get much traction. Some friends of mine asked me to join a group of retired IDF generals and top Shabak and Mossad leaders they called Commanders for Israel's Security. Never had so many experts, with nine thousand years of security experience among us, come together to deliver a damning assessment of the status quo and an impassioned call for the two-state solution as the only guarantor for Israel's survival as the democratic home of the Jewish people. This would be like a who's who among retired five-star US Army generals, along

with former heads of the CIA and FBI, warning that the US faced disaster if the government continued its old policy.

67. Chaim quotes Ben-Zion Dinur, the brains behind the education I got on the kibbutz: "For the past two millennia, we were always a robbed and dispossessed nation whose land was plundered and stolen, and we never ceased to plead and complain about its dispossession and to demand the return of the plundered property."

68. The sequel to Chaim's *A Political Theory for the Jewish People* is titled *A Just Zionism*.

ACKNOWLEDGMENTS

I first want to thank Biba, my life partner. From working with me on early drafts to giving me criticism and advice, she was as important to this book as any other person. I would like to thank: Chip Fleischer, our publisher and editor, who has from the start resolutely believed in this book. I also want to thank Rebecca Radding for her expert edits and superb sense for crafting a story. Finally, my friend Orni Petruschka is both an important character in this book and someone who helped me refine its overarching message.

Anthony David would like to thank his friend Anouar Majid, a Moroccan American scholar and novelist who taught him how to write creatively about politics.

ADMIRAL (RET.) AMI AYALON is a former Flotilla 13 (Israel's navy SEALs) commando, commander of the navy, director of the Shin Bet security agency, cabinet minister, Knesset member and a recipient of the Medal of Valor, Israel's highest military decoration. With Sari Nusseibeh, he established the People's Voice peace initiative in 2002. He is a member of Commanders for Israel's Security, chairman of the Executive Committee of the Haifa Research Center for Maritime & Strategy and chairman of AKIM Israel (the National Association for children and adults with Intellectual Disabilities). He organized and was featured in the Academy Award-nominated documentary, *The Gatekeepers*.

ANTHONY DAVID, historian and biographer, teaches creative writing at the University of New England's campus in Tangier, Morocco.

DENNIS ROSS, American diplomat and author, has served as the Director of Policy Planning in the State Department under President George H. W. Bush, the special Middle East coordinator under President Bill Clinton, a former special assistant to President Barack Obama and as a special adviser for to the former Secretary of State Hillary Clinton. He is The Washington Institute's William Davidson Distinguished Fellow.

ALSO AVAILABLE FROM T2P TRUTH TO POWER BOOKS

SUNLIGHT EDITIONS

T2P BOOKS // TRUTHFUL NARRATIVES = BETTER UNDERSTANDING

"Margaret Kimberley gives us an intellectual gem of prophetic fire about all the US presidents and their deep roots in the vicious legacy of white supremacy and predatory capitalism. Such truths seem more than most Americans can bear, though we ignore her words at our own peril!"
—CORNEL WEST, AUTHOR OF *RACE MATTERS*

PREJUDENTIAL

BLACK AMERICA AND THE PRESIDENTS

MARGARET KIMBERLEY

T2P BOOKS // TRUTHFUL NARRATIVES = BETTER UNDERSTANDING

"This moving and sprightly book is filled with backstories from America's struggle for religious freedom that I'll bet you have never heard before . . . a brilliant scholar's telling insights on the right way for church, state, and society to interact."
—E.J. DIONNE JR., AUTHOR OF *CODE RED* AND *WHY THE RIGHT WENT WRONG*

SOLEMN REVERENCE

THE SEPARATION OF CHURCH AND STATE IN AMERICAN LIFE

RANDALL BALMER

T2P BOOKS // TRUTHFUL NARRATIVES = BETTER UNDERSTANDING

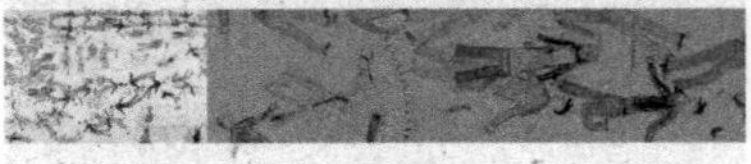

"Sjursen exposes the dominant historical narrative as at best myth, and at times a lie . . . He brings out from the shadows those who struggled, often at the cost of their own lives, for equality and justice. Their stories, so often ignored or trivialized, give us examples of who we should emulate and who we must become."
—CHRIS HEDGES, AUTHOR OF *EMPIRE OF ILLUSION* AND *AMERICA: THE FAREWELL TOUR*

A TRUE HISTORY OF THE UNITED STATES

Indigenous Genocide, Racialized Slavery, Hyper-Capitalism, Militarist Imperialism, and Other Overlooked Aspects of American Exceptionalism

DANIEL A. SJURSEN

T2P BOOKS // TRUTHFUL NARRATIVES = BETTER UNDERSTANDING

"[A] nuanced, open-minded, de-politicized discussion of our post-#MeToo world."
—*REFINERY29*

HAD IT COMING

Rape Culture Meets #MeToo: Now What?

ROBYN DOOLITTLE

ALSO AVAILABLE FROM T2P TRUTH TO POWER BOOKS

DOCUMENTARY NARRATIVES

T2P BOOKS // TRUTHFUL NARRATIVES = BETTER UNDERSTANDING
"Investigative journalism at its relentless and compassionate best." — KIRKUS REVIEWS
"Methamphetamine was a huge part of this case . . . A horrible murder driven by drugs." —PROSECUTOR CAL RERUCHA
"A gripping read." — PEOPLE MAGAZINE
THE BOOK OF MATT
THE REAL STORY OF THE MURDER OF MATTHEW SHEPARD
STEPHEN JIMENEZ
NEW INTRODUCTION BY
ANDREW SULLIVAN

T2P BOOKS // TRUTHFUL NARRATIVES = BETTER UNDERSTANDING
"During the height of the McCarthy era, thousands of government workers were driven from their jobs or barred from ever getting one because they were gay. To discover that . . . one of the authors of the notorious 1953 Executive Order that declared 'sexual perversion' a threat to national security, was himself a closeted gay man is astonishing . . . This is a book that deserves a wide audience."
— MICHAEL ISIKOFF, CO-AUTHOR OF RUSSIAN ROULETTE
IKE'S MYSTERY MAN
THE SECRET LIVES OF ROBERT CUTLER
The Cold War, The Lavender Scare, and the Untold Story of Eisenhower's First National Security Advisor
PETER SHINKLE
FOREWORD BY
CHARLES KAISER

T2P BOOKS // TRUTHFUL NARRATIVES = BETTER UNDERSTANDING
"A book that is both a history and a sports classic." — DETROIT FREE PRESS
"One of the most compelling sports biographies [ever]. A must-read." — (starred review) BOOKLIST
HARD DRIVING
THE WENDELL SCOTT STORY
The American Odyssey of NASCAR's First Black Driver
BRIAN DONOVAN
FOREWORD BY
JOE POSNANSKI

ALSO AVAILABLE FROM TRUTH TO POWER BOOKS

EYEWITNESS MEMOIRS

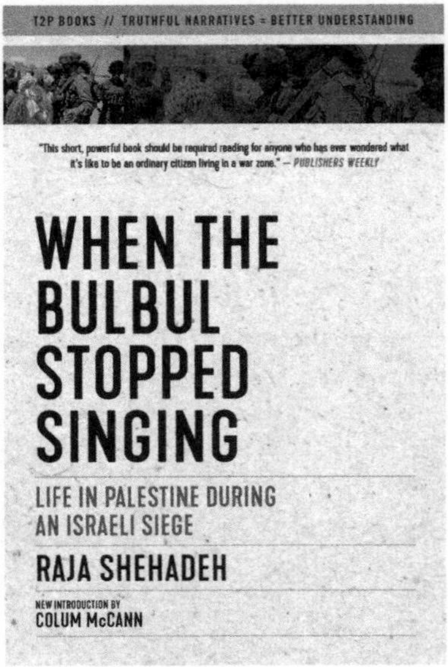